LINCOLN TAKES COMMAND

LINCOLN

TAKES

COMMAND

BY

JOHN SHIPLEY TILLEY

Distributed by: DIXIE DEPOT
POB 1448, DAWSONVILLE, GA 30534
FREE CATALOG AVAILABLE
www.dixiegeneral.com
E-Mail: folks@dixie-depot.com

To

WILHELMINA LANIER TILLEY

FOREWORD

By Avery Craven

The question of responsibility for commencing actual hostilities in 1861 is an important one. On the answer depends, to a degree, a sound understanding of the causes of civil war itself. Not that it makes so much difference as to who fired the first shot. That, after all, is a minor matter. But a clear understanding of the final steps to war should reveal most clearly the character of the forces which had long been at work to bring North and South into open warfare. Under strain and stress fundamental attitudes become clearer; under excitement real motives may be revealed.

If, as some writers now believe, Lincoln sought to bring matters to a head so that the people would face quickly and squarely the issues and settle them once and for all, then we have a clue which might make clear much that had gone before. If, on the other hand, Southerners were the aggressors, then little can be said for the notion of a South always on the defensive. And if neither of these hypotheses is borne out by events and the evidence seems to indicate "a blundering into war," then we may assume much of the same sort of thing in the days gone by.

Some Southerners speculated on the matter even at the time and tried to explain Lincoln's procedure in dealing with the South. "If reunion was his object," one of them wrote in May, 1861, "he showed want of common sense in adopting the course he did. If the restora-

tion of the Union was his object, which I believe was
his object,—then he is a fool. If his purpose was to drive
off all the Slave states, in order to make war on them
and annihilate Slavery, then he is a Devil and in the
latter supposition I could fight with a hearty good will."
That was the Southern point of view. But it was not
the one generally accepted. From that day until our own,
writers of history have been inclined to accept the Northern explanation, produced as part of the usual effort to
throw all responsibility upon the enemy, that Lincoln
merely met his constitutional obligations in a magnanimous way and impatient Southerners were responsible for
all the unfortunate things which happened. Victory enabled the victor to write the orthodox version of history
and "patriotism" gave that version unfailing support.
Few, in the years since 1865, have arisen to question its
soundness.

Mr. Tilley has gone back to the sources, and his investigations have brought a new point of view. He has
searched the records diligently. His legal training has
led him to weigh and sift with unusual care the evidence
found. His findings are, therefore, worthy of serious consideration. There may still be some room for honest difference of opinion, but the day for patriotic acceptance
of inherited historical ideas is gone. Americans all can
view the War Between the States as a national calamity.
They can allow the Northerner and the Southerner alike
to bear the responsibility as new investigations seem to
place it. The open-minded reader will find in Mr. Tilley's
work much that will both surprise and enlighten him.

The University of Chicago
January, 1940

ACKNOWLEDGMENTS

The generosity with which distinguished experts have reached out a helping hand has greatly impressed me. Grateful acknowledgment of encouragement, criticism, and suggestion is made to Dr. Avery Craven, professor of American history, University of Chicago; and Dr. Garland Greever, professor of English language and literature, University of Southern California.

My acknowledgment and thanks for permission to quote copyright material are due: The Macmillan Company (James F. Rhodes' *History of the United States*, Ida M. Tarbell's *Life of Abraham Lincoln*, Edward Channing's *Students' History of the United States*, Charles A. and Mary R. Beard's *History of the United States*) ; Charles Scribner's Sons (James Truslow Adams and Charles G. Vannest's *Record of America*, J. G. Nicolay's *The Outbreak of Rebellion*) ; Houghton Mifflin Company (*Diary of Gideon Welles*, Henry G. Connor's *John A. Campbell*, John T. Morse's *Abraham Lincoln*, A. B. Hart's *Salmon P. Chase*, Thornton K. Lothrop's *William H. Seward*) ; Harper and Brothers (Robert McElroy's *Jefferson Davis*, Harold U. Faulkner and Tyler Kepner's *America, Its History and People*, and Alfred Roman's *Military Operations of General Beauregard*) ; D. Appleton-Century Company (J. G. Nicolay and John Hay's *Abraham Lincoln*, and *Battles and Leaders of the Civil War*, edited by R. U. Johnson and C. C. Buel) ; American Book Company (Fremont P. Wirth's *Development of America*) ; Allyn and Bacon (J. H. Latané's *History of the Ameri-*

can People) ; Row, Peterson & Company (E. C. Barker, William E. Dodd, and H. S. Commager's *Our Nation's Development*) ; and Ginn and Company (David S. Muzzey's *History of the American People* and David H. Montgomery's *Leading Facts of American History*).

JOHN S. TILLEY

June, 1940

CONTENTS

III

THE SOUTH'S DESIRE FOR PEACEFUL SEPARATION

THE BACKGROUND

Almost from the founding of the Republic, partisanship has kept tireless vigil over the preservation of proper equilibrium between the sections. With North and South holding practically equal power there was, even at the time of the ratification of the Constitution, a dread of the coming influence of the Southwest. Upon the purchase of Louisiana in 1803, New England leaders were ready to sound the first note of secession. In a letter to Senator Pickering, of Massachusetts, George Cabot explained their threat of withdrawal: "The influence of our part of the Union must be diminished by the acquisition of more weight at the other extremity." With the idea of guaranteeing the balance, the nation pursued a policy of admitting new states in pairs, one with Northern, the other with Southern leanings: thus Indiana (1816) came in with Mississippi (1817); Illinois (1818) with Alabama (1819); Maine (1820) with Missouri (1821).

By 1840 there was observable a substantial shifting of influence. The population of the North was increasing rapidly, and to the South this carried its own warning. The North already had a substantial majority in the National Congress. With the hope of securing additional representation, the South proceeded to launch a campaign for the admission of Texas. This move aroused such opposition as again to imperil the Union; John Quincy Adams and twelve other members of Congress protested, declaring that the annexation of Texas would mean dissolution of the Union. Publication of census figures of 1850 was the handwriting on the wall for those who realized with dismay the disturbance of the equipoise of sectional influence. Up to this time, despite the disparity in numbers, the political genius of the Southerners had enabled them more than to hold their own. Now their hold was slipping. It so happened that their votes had blocked ambitious schemes of Eastern industrialists, among others one to construct at public expense transcontinental railways between North and West, which would open up vast granaries in competition with the agricultural Southern region.

If Southern ascendency in the national councils could be unhorsed, if the balance of power could be gained once and for all, there would be an end of the opposition which had frustrated Northern dreams of commercial expansion. Waging a desperate political battle, the industrialists were in a mood to welcome reinforcement from whatever quarter. It came from a strange source. There entered the lists a small but desperately sincere, fanatically minded, highly vocal group known as Abolitionists, latter-day crusaders obsessed with hatred of slavery, abhorrence of slaveowners. Making common cause with the newly born Republican party, they did their part in battering down the walls of Southern supremacy. The spearhead of their attack was agitation for the liberation and enfranchisement of several million slaves, many of them only a generation removed from voodooism and savagery. They must have known the story of the French colony on the neighboring island of Santo Domingo, where, only a few decades before, four hundred thousand blacks had celebrated their emancipation by the massacre of by far the greater part of the forty thousand white population. As to the consequences of their program for the Southern states, the Abolitionists appeared more than indifferent.

With the election of Abraham Lincoln in the fall of 1860, the final blow fell. The returns rocked the South like an earthquake. Following a campaign which had shunted aside national issues, in an election shot through and through with sectional animosity, the Southerners had felt the sting of defeat. Most disheartening of all, Lincoln had received only 1,866,452 popular votes out of a total of 4,690,193.[1] All eighteen states in his column lay north of Mason and Dixon's line.[2] Fifteen of the thirty-three states gave him no electoral votes. In ten states not a ballot bore his name.[3] The planter class reeled under the blow. It was under no illusion as to what all this meant. Its era of influence was of the past, its political sun was going into total eclipse. The Southerners knew only too well that, if they submitted to bitterly partisan rule, the future held in store for them economic, political, and social bankruptcy. So far as they could see, there was only one way out. Thirteen years before, a congressman from the West had risen in the house to blaze the trail with this announcement: "Any people, anywhere, being inclined and having the power, have the right to rise up and shake off the existing government, and form a new one that suits them better. This is a most valuable, a most sacred right, a right which we hope and believe is to liberate the world." [4]

The speaker was Abraham Lincoln. Strongly committed

[1] Woodrow Wilson, *Division and Reunion, 1829-1889* (New York and London, 1912), p. 207.

[2] A. H. Stephens, *A Comprehensive and Popular History of the United States* (Richmond, 1882), p. 559.

[3] Ida M. Tarbell, *The Life of Abraham Lincoln* (4 vols. New York, 1917), I, 386.

[4] Goldwin Smith, *The United States: an Outline of Political History, 1492-1871* (New York and London, 1893), p. 248.

to the theory of state sovereignty, naturally concurring in the Lincoln view, the Southerners set about to chart their course. They would leave the Union, the Union to the upbuilding of which their fathers had contributed such conspicuous leadership, but now a Union which, as they saw it, was about to crush them. To their thinking, there was no alternative. In the near future, secession was an accomplished fact.

In the meantime, the extremists of both sections, Abolitionists and radical Republicans in the North, secession irreconcilables in the South, were whipping up a storm of passion. Calmer heads there were who pleaded with the rival factions that efforts to avert a catastrophe should not stop short of exhausting all possibilities of negotiation. Looking backward after three quarters of a century upon the horrors of a war involving the expenditure of billions of dollars and the sacrifice of hundreds of thousands of the choicest youth of the country, there rises to view the well-nigh incredible revelation that militant minorities on both sides forced a conflict which the majority of the citizenship regarded as unspeakable and unnecessary. Proof of this assumes overwhelming proportions. After a critical analysis of the 1860 election returns, Appleton's *American Annual Cyclopædia* of 1861, published in New York City the following year, gave this summary:

> "Meantime the people began to move in every Northern, Middle, and the upper tier of the Southern States, in favor of the settlement of the difficulties. It was an indisputable fact, at this time, that the vote cast for Mr. Douglas, numbering 1,365,976, and that cast for Mr. Bell, numbering 590,631, and the vote for Mr. Breckinridge in the free States, numbering 284,422, making a total of 2,241,029,

was unanimously in favor of a peaceful and reasonable settlement of all difficulties with any of the
Southern States. The vote for Lincoln was 1,857,610,
of which at least one-fourth would have approved
of such a peaceable settlement. . . . Of the vote given
to Mr. Breckinridge in the slaveholding States,
numbering 563,531, more than one-fourth of it desired a peaceful settlement upon such terms as would
have been satisfactory to the friends of conciliation
and compromise in the Northern States. Thus, the
voice of the people of the country at this time was
overwhelmingly in favor of conciliation, forbear-
ance, and compromise." [5]

Within less than two months after Lincoln's election,
the venerable Senator Crittenden arose to present to the
senate of the United States his plan for safeguarding
the future of the nation. Known as the Crittenden Compromise, it proposed a constitutional amendment. This
was to make, among others, three provisions: the estab-
lishment of the line of latitude 36° 30′ as a boundary,
north of which slavery should be prohibited, south of
which it should be permitted; government compensation
of owners of rescued fugitive slaves; the denial of any
power on the part of congress to hinder transportation
of slaves between slaveholding localities, or to abolish
slavery in the District of Columbia without compensation.
The senate at once appointed the Committee of Thirteen,
charged to harmonize, if possible, differences between
slaveholding and nonslaveholding states. In January,
1861, Crittenden urged the submission of his plan to a
vote of the people. Immediately Senator Douglas, of
Illinois, threw the weight of his influence to the proposal
with the appealing argument:

[5] Appleton's *American Annual Cyclopædia and Register of Important Events,* for the years 1861-1865 (W. T. Tenney, ed. New York,
1862-1866), 1861, p. 700.

"Are we prepared in our hearts for war with our own brethren and kindred? I confess I am not . . . I prefer compromise to war. I prefer concession to a dissolution of the Union. . . . Why not allow the people to pass upon these questions? If the people reject them, theirs will be the responsibility and no harm will have been done by the reference." [6]

Again, in December, 1860, Senator Douglas said in the senate,

"I am ready to act with any party, with any individual of any party, who will come to the question with an eye single to the preservation of the country and the Union. I trust we may lay aside all party grievances, party feuds, partisan jealousies, and look to our country and not to our party, in the consequences of our action." [7]

The reaction from the North and the West was instant and reassuring. In a speech in the senate, Senator Joseph Lane, of Oregon, voiced the view that acceptance of the Crittenden measure would "delay the movements which are now going on, that are to result ultimately in the entire dissolution of the Union." [8] On March 3, 1861, Senator George E. Pugh, of Ohio, said in the senate,

"The Crittenden proposition has been indorsed by the almost unanimous vote of the legislature of Kentucky. It has been indorsed by the legislature of the noble old commonwealth of Virginia. It has been petitioned for by a larger number of electors of the United States than any proposition that was ever before congress. I believe in my heart, today, that it would carry an overwhelming majority of the peo-

[6] James F. Rhodes, *A History of the United States Told by Contemporaries* (New York, 1893-1919), III, 255.
[7] Appleton's *American Annual Cyclopædia*, 1861, p. 168.
[8] *Ibid.*, p. 177.

ple of my state; ay, sir, and of nearly every other state in the Union." [9]

Governor Seymour, of New York, in his message to the legislature, gave the proposal his indorsement:

"Let New York set an example in this respect; let her oppose no barrier, but let her representatives in congress give ready support to any just and honorable settlement." [10]

Exhibiting "the most extraordinary earnestness for the preservation of peace," a large assemblage of Bostonians in Faneuil Hall passed a resolution of approval of the Crittenden measure.[11] In the central states there sprang up a vigorous sentiment "for the immediate adoption of measures for the salvation of the Union and the adjustment of all questions of difference between the contending sections." [12]

Widespread among the people of the North was the conviction that Abolitionism was about to push the nation over the brink of a precipice. In numerous localities, citizens proceeded to make life uncomfortable for anti-slavery agitators,[13] in instances resorting to violence to harass or even break up their meetings. Decidedly disappointing to the radical element was the pacific position taken by such journals as the Albany *Evening Journal*, the New York *Tribune*, the New York *World*, the New York *Times*, and the New York *Herald*.[14] The attitude

[9] *Ibid.*, p. 224.
[10] *Ibid.*, p. 519.
[11] *Ibid.*, p. 453.
[12] *Ibid.*, p. 478.
[13] Ralph R. Fahrney, *Horace Greeley and the Tribune in the Civil War* (Cedar Rapids, Ia., 1936), p. 41.
[14] William E. Dodd, *Jefferson Davis* in "American Crisis Biographies" (Philadelphia, 1907), p. 195; Fahrney, *Horace Greeley and the Tribune*, p. 430.

of outstanding patriots indicates the favor with which the North looked upon the effort to avert a break. Edward Everett contributed his support. Thurlow Weed,[15] James S. Thayer of New York,[16] Seward, soon to be Lincoln's secretary of state,[17] and President Buchanan [18] evinced a desire to coöperate in the interest of conciliation. Douglas and Crittenden went so far as to telegraph Union stalwarts in the South of their hope that the rights of that section would be protected within the Union.[19] A large element of the Breckenridge and Bell faction were fearful of the prospect of armed strife.[20] Northern Democrats hoped to hold the Southern states in the Union.[21] Later, Greeley was to express the opinion that submission of the Crittenden proposal to a vote of the nation would have resulted in its adoption "by an overwhelming majority." [22]

August Belmont, of New York, wrote Crittenden that he had yet to meet the first conservative, Union-loving man who did not approve of the senator's proposition. In this letter he expressed the fear that the welfare of the country was in jeopardy as the result of the activities of "a handful of puritanical fanatics and selfish politicians." Shortly afterward, he informed Herschel V. Johnson, a former governor of Georgia and an open anti-secessionist, that the governors of seven Republican states

[15] *The Autobiography of Horace Greeley; or Recollections of a Busy Life* (New York, 1872), p. 396.

[16] Clark E. Carr, *Stephen A. Douglas, his Life, Public Services, Speeches, and Patriotism* (Chicago, 1909), pp. 119, 120.

[17] Wilson, *Division and Reunion*, p. 214.

[18] Moorfield Storey, *Charles Sumner*, in the "American Statesmen Series" (Boston and New York, 1900), p. 190.

[19] Allen Johnson, *Stephen A. Douglas: a Study in American Politics* (New York, 1908), p. 448.

[20] Fahrney, *Horace Greeley and the Tribune*, p. 41.

[21] *Ibid.*, pp. 57, 59.

[22] Greeley, *Autobiography*, p. 397.

had resolved to sponsor conciliatory legislation.[23] Patriotic Republicans were even endeavoring to influence Lincoln to include in his cabinet some representative Southern men.

Meanwhile, the voice of the people was making itself heard. Great numbers of petitions, carrying staggering totals of signatures, began to appear in Washington.[24] These urged adoption of some form of compromise.[25] Crittenden presented one from Massachusetts signed by twenty-two thousand citizens.[26] One from Philadelphia pledged the support of two thousand avowed Lincoln adherents.[27] A "monster petition" from New York expressed the interest of forty thousand friends of Crittenden's theory.[28] Another from New York with "an immense number of signatures, without distinction of party," bore the "names of leading capitalists of the country, as well as of the state." [29]

The legislature of New Jersey informed the state's representation in Washington of its desire for the success of the Crittenden movement. In a message recommending a convention to undertake adjustment of sectional differences, Governor Olden of New Jersey had said: "We cannot believe it possible that such a convention would fail to agree on terms acceptable to a majority in all sections of the country." [30] On January 19, 1861, giving approval to Crittenden's theory, the general assembly

[23] Rhodes, *History of the United States*, III, 252.
[24] Stephens, *A Comprehensive and Popular History of the United States*, p. 560.
[25] Appleton's *American Annual Cyclopædia*, 1861, p. 179.
[26] Storey, *Charles Sumner*, p. 192.
[27] Rhodes, *History of the United States*, III, 262, 263.
[28] Appleton's *American Annual Cyclopædia*, 1861, p. 521.
[29] *Ibid.*, pp. 519, 520.
[30] *Ibid.*, p. 515.

of Virginia adopted a resolution urging a convention for the purpose of settling "the present unhappy controversies in the spirit in which the constitution was originally formed." [31] From the New York and Ohio State Democratic conventions came strong endorsement. [32] The border states were not without their extremists but, as events proved, their people as a whole were not favorable to the plan of secession. Obviously the Crittenden suggestion would have fared well at their hands. Speaking of the endorsements, Senator Crittenden said in the senate:

"What is the number of petitions forwarded? I suppose if I should say that we have received petitions from not less than a quarter of a million, I should be within bounds. In addition to this, societies everywhere have been petitioning in the name of their whole body. State legislatures have memorialized, and, in fact, petitioned congress in the name of the people of their states. I do not know how many." [33]

Powerful as was the sentiment favoring reasonable adjustment, it was far from unanimous. As a matter of course, the Abolitionist saw only one side. The die-hard element in Republican ranks stood ready to incur any risk rather than yield an inch which might be construed as a concession to slaveholders. Ohio's Senator Wade observed that half a million people to whom he had argued the Republican theory of slavery had agreed with him; he gave notice that, as their commissioned representative, he would stand his ground to the end. [34] In December, 1860, he declared in the senate:

[31] *Ibid.*, p. 178.
[32] Rhodes, *History of the United States*, III, 263.
[33] Appleton's *American Annual Cyclopædia*, 1861, p. 223.
[34] Carr, *Stephen A. Douglas*, p. 111.

"Sir, I know not what others may do; but I tell you that, with the verdict of the people given in favor of the platform on which our candidates have been elected, so far as I am concerned, I would suffer anything to come before I would compromise that away." [35]

In December, 1860, Seward himself commented that the Republican party was no more inclined to yield than were the secessionists of South Carolina. Lincoln "stood like a rock" against compromise.[36] He not only held fast to the principles to which he owed his election, but succeeded in influencing Seward and Thurlow Weed to recede from their positions.[37] Even so, Republicans and Abolitionists constituted only a minority of the electorate. It was recognition of this fact, so clearly demonstrated by the election figures, which had encouraged in the advocates of the compromise program a willingness to submit it to popular decision.

What of the South, itself? Senator Douglas said in the senate on March 3, 1861, in his answer to Senator Pugh, of Ohio: "I can confirm the senator's declaration that Senator Jefferson Davis himself, when on the Committee of Thirteen, was ready at all times to compromise on the Crittenden proposition." [38] Far from a secession enthusiast, Davis regretted what appeared to him to be the necessity of the South's withdrawal from the Union.[39] Clement C. Clay, of Alabama, an intimate of Davis in the United States senate, wrote of him:

[35] Appleton's *American Annual Cyclopædia,* 1861, p. 172.

[36] Charles A. and Mary R. Beard, *History of the United States* (New York, 1932), p. 392.

[37] Dodd, *Jefferson Davis,* p. 196.

[38] Appleton's *American Annual Cyclopædia,* 1861, p. 224. See also Frank H. Alfriend, *Life of Jefferson Davis* (Cincinnati and Philadelphia, 1868), p. 217.

[39] Dodd, *Jefferson Davis,* pp. 207, 214.

"Mr. Davis did not take an active part in planning or hastening secession. I think he only regretfully consented to it as a political necessity for the preservation of popular and state rights . . . I know that some leading men, and even Mississippians, thought him too moderate and backward, and found fault with him for not taking a leading part in secession." [40]

At the suggestion of Governor J. J. Pettus, of Mississippi, the senators and representatives of the state held a conference at Jackson in the fall of 1860. Of their discussion of the proper attitude of their state on the issue of secession, Congressman O. R. Singleton wrote:

"The debate lasted many hours, and Mr. Davis, with perhaps one other gentleman in that conference, opposed immediate and separate state action, declaring himself opposed to secession as long as the hope of a peaceable remedy remained. He did not believe we ought to precipitate the issue. . . . After the conference was ended, several of its members were dissatisfied with the course of Mr. Davis, believing that he was entirely opposed to secession, and was seeking to delay action on the part of Mississippi, with the hope that it might be entirely averted." [41]

Varina Howell Davis quotes her husband as saying: "If they will give me time, all is not lost; violence on one side and extreme measures of wrong on the other now, will dissolve the Union." She adds, "And by telegrams and letters to every Southern State he endeavored to postpone their action." [42]

[40] Jefferson Davis, *The Rise and Fall of the Confederate Government* (2 vols. New York, 1881), I, 207.

[41] *Ibid.*

[42] Varina Howell Davis, *Jefferson Davis* (2 vols. New York, 1890), II, 3. See also Alfriend, *Life of Jefferson Davis*, p. 223.

In the Georgia convention, a delegate made the motion to secede. Herschel V. Johnson offered a substitute; namely, that the convention should invite the commonwealths of Florida, South Carolina, Alabama, and Mississippi, along with ten other states which had not seceded,[43] to send representatives to a meeting in Atlanta, there to consider ways and means of arriving at a solution of their common problem. Designating the Personal Liberty acts as the core of the trouble, the substitute implied that, upon their repeal, the states would carefully reconsider the issues. Advocating adoption of the substitute, Alexander H. Stephens, who was to become vice-president of the Confederate Government, clearly stated his position:

> "It is well known that my judgment is against Secession for existing causes. I have not lost hope of securing our rights in the Union and under the Constitution. . . . I have ever believed, and do now believe, that it is to the interest of all the States to be and remain united under the Constitution of the United States, with a faithful performance by each of all its Constitutional obligations. . . . I do further feel confident, if Georgia would now stand firm, and unite with the Border States . . . in an effort to obtain redress of these grievances on the part of some of their Northern Confederates, that complete success would attend their efforts. . . . In this opinion I may be mistaken, but I feel almost as confident of it as I do of my existence." [44]

The vote on the substitute was 133 for, 164 against.[45] Along with Davis and other Southern senators, R. M. T.

[43] A. H. Stephens, *A Constitutional View of the Late War between the States* (2 vols. Philadelphia and Chicago, 1868-1870), II, 302.
[44] *Ibid.*, pp. 305-306.
[45] *Ibid.*, p. 315.

Hunter of Virginia, and Robert Toombs of Georgia, later of the Confederate cabinet, were openly favorable to conciliation.[46] Senator Douglas stated on the floor of the senate that Toombs was friendly to the Crittenden measure.[47] Robert E. Lee, later to be proffered command of the Union armies, wrote his son: "I can anticipate no greater calamity for the country than the dissolution of the Union. . . . I am willing to sacrifice everything but honor for its preservation. I hope therefore, that all constitutional measures will be exhausted before there is a resort to force." [48] Stonewall Jackson was not an advocate of secession. "It is better," he said, "for the South to fight for her rights in the Union than out of it." [49] Judah P. Benjamin, also later to sit in the Confederate cabinet, bestirred himself to effect a lasting reconciliation.[50]

Governor Jackson, of Missouri, was "in favor of remaining in the Union as long as there was any hope of maintaining the guarantees of the constitution." [51] In Texas, Governor Sam Houston declared in his message to the legislature that he "favored delay as long as possible in holding state conventions," that "he himself was opposed to calling one, and believed that the Union could be preserved." [52] In one of the last appeals made in the senate, Senator Benjamin H. Hill, of Georgia, said:

> "Despite the attitude of South Carolina herself, I believe she is approachable with reason and words of

[46] *Idem, A . . . History of the United States,* p. 560.

[47] Appleton's *American Annual Cyclopædia,* 1861, p. 224.

[48] Henry A. White, *Robert E. Lee and the Southern Confederacy* (New York, 1897), p. 98.

[49] G. F. R. Henderson, *Stonewall Jackson and the American Civil War* (2 vols. New York, 1898), I, 119.

[50] Allen Johnson, *Stephen A. Douglas,* p. 453.

[51] Appleton's *American Annual Cyclopædia,* 1861, p. 477.

[52] *Ibid.,* p. 688.

kindness, and that she will listen to the voice of conciliation if it comes in so gentle a form as could be
tendered by gentlemen on the other side of the
house . . . I ask you to present to her, far gone as
you may consider her, the olive branch. Tender it
gracefully; you can afford to do it, as guardians
of this great and powerful government. South Carolina may be, and in my judgment she is, extreme in
her precipitancy. I have regretted it; I have remon-
strated against it, and I have implored the people
of my own state, notwithstanding her example, to
delay their action." [53]

The Southern leaders were expressing the sentiment
of an impressive element of their people. Their views confirm the statement of Woodrow Wilson that there was
powerful opposition to secession in the South.[54] The very
vote in the elections for delegates to the secession conventions is eloquent testimony of the prevalence of a
feeling to which any effort for peaceable adjustment
would have strongly appealed. In these elections, the
voter had his choice between a ballot for immediate secession and one voicing his preference for delay. In the
Georgia contest, 50,243 electors voted for withdrawal,
39,123 for delay.[55] In Louisiana, the vote was even more
balanced, 20,448 favoring prompt action, 17,296 pre-
ferring delay.[56]

With only slight encouragement there might easily
have developed a formidable movement against any course
of desperation. Strangely enough, some of the state conventions were conservative to a marked degree.[57] A

[53] *Ibid.*, p. 212.
[54] Wilson, *Division and Reunion*, p. 215.
[55] Pleasant A. Stovall, *Robert Toombs, Statesman, Speaker, Soldier, Sage* (New York, c. 1892), p. 209.
[56] Rhodes, *History of the United States*, III, 273.
[57] Dodd, *Jefferson Davis*, p. 215.

"strong Union sentiment" appeared in the Alabama convention, and a refusal to submit the secession ordinance to popular vote brought on a critical situation.[58] Of the general convention held in Montgomery, Alexander H. Stephens remarked that it was the ablest and most conservative body with which he had ever been associated.[59] On January 28, 1861, the Richmond *Whig* expressed confidence that the Crittenden Compromise plan would receive the approval of an unprecedented majority of the voters both North and South.[60] As long before as November, 1860, even under the excitement incident to the national election, there had appeared in the Savannah (Georgia) *Republican* an article which not only strongly urged a national convention but ventured optimism as to the result of the deliberations:

> "Such a body, composed of the wise and prudent men of the country, we feel sure, could agree upon a plan that would protect all interests, quiet all heartburnings, give peace to the nation, and place us once more on the highway of a glorious career.
> "We would have it assemble the 22d of February —the birthday of Washington—and in Independence Hall in Philadelphia, with the hope that the men selected as saviors of the country in 1860, may catch some of the patriotic fire that animated the breasts of the noble founders of the Republic." [61]

Despite the considered judgment of as able a historian as Rhodes that the Crittenden proposal would have received a great majority of the votes of the American people, the senate saw fit to kill the measure. Even with

58 Appleton's *American Annual Cyclopædia,* 1861, pp. 9, 10.
59 Dodd, *Jefferson Davis,* pp. 216, 217.
60 Rhodes, *History of the United States,* III, 263.
61 Copied in the Greenville (Alabama) *Southern Messenger,* November 21, 1860.

such a setback, Virginia was unwilling to admit defeat. Its general assembly sent out a call to every state of the Union. The announced object was that in a convention to be held February fourth in the city of Washington, they should undertake once again "to adjust the present unhappy controversies." Concurrently with the issuance of the invitation, the state let it be known that its own people would accept conciliation. It placed at the head of the Virginia delegation John Tyler, former president of the United States.[62] When the chairman called the convention to order, delegates were present from twenty-one commonwealths. In the opening address, ex-President Tyler said:

> "Gentlemen, the eyes of the whole country are turned to this assembly in expectation and hope . . . I trust that you may prove yourselves worthy of the great occasion. . . . Your patriotism will surmount the difficulties, however great, if you accomplish one triumph in advance, and that is a triumph over party. And what is one's party when compared to the task of rescuing one's country from danger? Do that, and one long, loud shout of joy and gladness will resound throughout the land." [63]

Knowing full well that in all likelihood this was the final peace move, the members seriously debated the issues. The result was a recommendation that congress should submit a constitutional amendment, with its chief item the regulation of slavery in the territories. In a vote taken by states, the resolution had a majority of only one state vote. This foredoomed it to death. When Crit-

[62] Stephens, *A Comprehensive and Popular History of the United States*, p. 589.
[63] Appleton's *American Annual Cyclopædia*, 1861, p. 564.

tenden presented it to the senate, only seven members voted aye.

This seemed the end, but even yet there was a glimmer of hope. The radicals had opposed and apparently blocked the compromise proposals, but two arresting facts assumed importance—the American people still contemplated with horror the growing threat of war; and, even if all attempts at conciliation failed, the Southern leaders had reason to believe that, as matters stood in Washington, all was not hostile. The Republican party was in the minority in both house and senate. Even in the event they could impose their will upon the majority and force their measures through, any oppressive legislation would have another hurdle to take. There was the Supreme Court of the United States, with the last word. Just three years before, that tribunal had handed down the Dred Scott decision which had not only infuriated Republicans and Abolitionists but now stood as a formidable legal precedent. More than this, the personnel of this court of ultimate authority consisted of three Democrats from the free states, four Democrats from the slave states, and one Republican. There was little prospect of hostile action from that quarter.

All in all, here was the perfect setting for a scene which, successfully staged, would have immortalized the cast. Desperate as was the situation, the door was not yet completely closed. That there remained the faint possibility of finding a way out constituted a clarion call to patriotism. The call was for a man of giant calibre, a leader of super-statesmanlike proportions, a patriot with character to subordinate personal ambition to the common good, hardihood even to defy political devotees if such a course gave promise of saving the nation. Further-

more, the need was for a leader so strategically placed as
instantly to command a national hearing.

There was one man and only one to play the dramatic
role. His star was in its ascendant. Only lately the voice
of the people had accorded him leadership. He was the
possessor of a unique personality which equipped him
powerfully to appeal to the lowest as well as to the highest stratum of the populace. The political idol of Republicans and Abolitionists, he was about to be cast in an
incomparably greater part, that of guardian of the welfare of all the people of all the United States. What if
this man had raised his hand in a gesture of friendliness
toward his fellow citizens of the Southern states, had
openly sent to Jefferson Davis some such message as this:
"Upon you and me fate has imposed a most solemn responsibility. We of the North and you of the South must
be broad-minded enough to iron out our differences,
whatever the cost. We will make concessions; we shall
expect the South to meet us half way. Upon every patriot
the crisis imposes the obligation to keep reason enthroned
in our national life. As one soon to become executive
head of the nation, and so charged to serve all sections
impartially, I call upon you to join with me in arranging
a conference to be participated in by every state. It is
my earnest request that each delegate shall come with one
and only one instruction, and that this shall be, 'There
is to be no war.' "

Such a call, from such a source, could hardly have
failed to weld into one harmonious whole the various
influences which had made known their undying opposition to war. It would have made a strong appeal to the
people of the South. If this man could have so risen
above sectionalism as to throw the great weight of his
position to the cause of peace, their impulse might have

been irresistible to demonstrate that they were capable of equal magnanimity and patriotism. Many thought then, and many think now, that even the remotest possibility of healing existing wounds was sufficient to justify heroic measures to quiet the warmongers, at least long enough to provide the opportunity for a last endeavor to restore sanity and good will. That such measures were not taken is one of the tragedies of our national history.

Thus war came. The procedure which brought it about, the steps which led to the indispensable "incident" of Sumter must ever be of great interest to the student of the period.

Four years later the guns were silent, the conflict over. Laying aside the sword with which they had led their armies to victory, the conquerors took up the pen to write the story for coming generations. The flush of success is not conducive to judicial bearing and it is perhaps only natural that their narratives should lack the merit of impartiality. The God-with-us delusion, war's almost unfailing mental reaction, laid its impress upon the story. Running true to ancient form, the late combatants set out to convince the world that they were altogether in the right, their adversaries wholly in the wrong. As usual, they ended by hypnotizing themselves into an assumption of their own freedom from fault. In this instance, as always, time and time alone can readjust the balances, restore capacity to see sanely and whole, make possible dispassionate review.

It is a far cry back to the booming of the guns of 1861. Happily, with the slipping by of decade after decade, animosities have cooled. Writers from all sections are extolling the courage of both armies and, more and more, there is recognition of worthy motives on the part of each faction. This is as it should be. What the years have accomplished is commendable but, even yet, this has fallen short of the reëstablishment of sincerely cordial relations. Such an achievement involves going beyond mere sentimental acquiescence in letting bygones be bygones. If there is an unfeigned desire to restore confidence, it is necessary to face facts with frankness, to locate responsibility where responsibility belongs. During the long interval since the war of the sixties, the undisputed facts of that eventful period should have become generally known. That this is not the case is remarkable. It would be difficult to conceive of a more striking historical hiatus than the omission, from presumably authoritative accounts, of material facts and circumstances which immediately preceded and proximately caused the clash of arms at Charleston. These many years the South has stood before the bar under indictment for recklessly firing on the flag. Yet there is reason to question the justice of this widely accepted belief. A mass of evidence seems to point in a different direction. It may be the time is ripe for a reëxamination of this material and the acceptance of a more sound and just understanding.

As illustrative of accounts of the events just preceding the Confederate assault on Sumter, two excerpts from school texts will suffice. The first appears in a history which many have regarded as carrying great weight:

"To hold Fort Sumter in the face of the gathering opposition to the federal government was plainly impossible. The administration, however, determined to supply the garrison *with provisions,* and notified the governor of South Carolina of its intention. On April 12 the Southern guns opened on the fort, which surrendered April 14. Not a man had been injured, but the little garrison had been *overcome by hunger and hardships.* Great was the rejoicing at Charleston; at last the flag of the United States had been

'humbled before the glorious little state of South
Carolina,' said the governor of that state.
    "The next day, April 15, 1861, President Lincoln
issued a proclamation calling for seventy-five thousand volunteers." [64]

A hungry little garrison, determination on the part of
the government to send provisions, notification to the
governor of South Carolina, then the firing on the flag.
There are, on the other hand, original sources which
appear to challenge the accuracy, even the fairness, of
the quoted narrative. From reliable witnesses there is
testimony that at the very moment Governor Pickens
received notice of the intention to "supply the garrison
with provisions," a formidable naval squadron, carrying
stores, ammunition, and troops, was headed for Charleston. Trustworthy information is available that, at the
same time, the head of the department of state in Washington was repeatedly assuring a Confederate peace commission that Fort Sumter was to be evacuated.
    Another school history, one from which multitudes
have gained what they accepted as accurate information,
says that Anderson sent to the president an urgent request for "provisions"; that his command of eighty-five
men faced seven thousand Confederates; that Lincoln set
about to send the needed supplies; that, "as soon as
Jefferson Davis heard of it," he gave orders which
brought on the attack on Sumter.[65] There is no intimation of any other issue, no suggestion, for example, of
reluctance on the part of the Confederates to fire on the

[64] Edward Channing, *A Students' History of the United States* (New
York, 1902), p. 510. Italics supplied.
[65] David H. Montgomery, *Leading Facts of American History* (Boston, 1891), p. 281.

fort, no disclosure of what the supplies were, no reference
to the unique method of conveying them to Charleston.[66]

The material for a revaluation has long been at hand
in the *Official Records* of the Union and Confederate
armies and navies. This monumental publication brings
to view the war-period reports, orders, telegrams, and
letters of army and navy officers, as well as of officials of
the civil governments. Available in printed form since
the year 1880, their value has not, it appears, impressed
many who have undertaken to present the issues of the
epoch which they cover. Hidden away in remote corners
of libraries, the sheer bulk of these records has guaranteed immunity from the curiosity of the average reader.
The large number and forbidding size of the volumes,
packed with ill-assorted, cumbersomely arranged, dry-as-
dust routine communiques, have repelled all except the
research student fortified with time, energy, and patience.
The serious investigator who digs his way through these
tomes unearths a mine of historical data; from the sayings
and writings of those who took part in the events, astonishing truths shine forth. Inescapable is the inference
that ignoring of relevant testimony has brought distortion of the picture.

Supplementing the official records are first-hand accounts by eyewitnesses of various scenes of the great
crisis. One of these is the *Diary* of Gideon Welles, secretary of the navy in Lincoln's cabinet. Intimately associated with Lincoln, occupying the vantage ground of
membership in the official family, he was one of fewer
than a dozen men who enjoyed the privilege of observing
the innermost workings of the administration. He wrote
what he saw, what he heard, and precisely what he thought
of what he had seen and heard, to say nothing of what

[66] For other accounts of the incident see Appendix I.

he thought of those whom he had watched and to whom he had listened. Another similarly situated onlooker, also a member of the cabinet and the writer of a diary, was Edward Bates. A third was Samuel W. Crawford who, during the crucial days at Fort Sumter, was assistant surgeon of the garrison and a member of the staff of its commander, Major Robert Anderson. Dr. Crawford not only observed closely developments within the fort, but seized the opportunity to visit and know the people of Charleston, to attend the meetings of the secession convention, to appraise the methods, motives, and character of the delegates in charge of the South Carolina side of the crisis. Later, leaving the medical branch of the service, he attained the rank of major general in the regular army. In addition, with his *Genesis of the Civil War*, he enriched literature with a brilliantly written, notably impartial record of the occurrences of the period.

The scope of this study is to be limited to a consideration of the facts and circumstances immediately preceding the secession of South Carolina and leading to the outbreak at Sumter.

Peace advocates had learned they were battling the fates; extremist propaganda had spread a prairie fire of feeling which had got beyond control. The breaking point came when the controversy reached an impasse over the presence of Union garrisons in forts located in the South. In particular, Florida and South Carolina viewed Federal occupation of fortifications at Pensacola and Charleston as an assertion within their boundaries of the authority of a government whose control they had repudiated. They protested vigorously, but their protests were unavailing. The Washington government denied their right to secede, contended they were still territory of the United States, rejected as unthinkable the suggestion of withdrawal of the garrisons, inasmuch as such action might be construed as tantamount to voluntary surrender of sovereignty. To Union officials, therefore, retention in their respective posts of the Charleston and Pensacola commands was more than a precautionary measure; it was a symbol of continued Federal control. Here was an issue which defied adjustment. The storm of discussion continued to rage and passion steadily rose until Fort Pickens and Fort Sumter developed into danger spots.

Conditions became intolerable. Presently, under the conviction that nothing short of heroic treatment would save the situation, Washington acted. Assembling ships of war with troops and supplies, the government reinforced Fort Pickens. Upon the arrival off Charleston of a similar expedition with orders to relieve the Sumter garrison, the Confederates proceeded to bombard the fortress. Thus it came about that the early activities of one of the most serious conflicts of modern times centered largely around these two fortifications.

I. FORT PICKENS

On as many as three separate stages—Pensacola, Charleston, and Washington—the actors presented the drama which is the subject of this story. As each incident is taken up, the narrative will turn back to the period which supplied its opening scenes.

Chapter I

RIVAL CLAIMANTS FOR CONTROL

THE FEDERALS OCCUPY THE STRONGEST FORT

When, in 1845, Florida gained statehood in the American Union, her people doubtless believed they were entering an era of peace and quiet. Their dream ended just sixteen years later when the throes of a mighty secession movement gripped the great Republic. It was not long until a condition of intense irritation revealed that sectional misunderstanding had reached an acute stage. The situation was one in which a chance spark might easily set off a conflagration. In characteristic soldier parlance General Scott summed it up: "We are now in such a state that a dog fight might cause the gutters of the capital to run with blood." [1] One of the main sources of dissatisfaction was the presence of Federal garrisons in Southern forts. Many in the North shared with their fellow citizens of the South the fear that, sooner or later, the Federal government's insistence upon retention of these forts would provoke an outbreak. In both sections opinion was far from being all one way. In all parts of the country onlookers held their breath when, on the floor of the United States senate, Stephen A. Douglas electrified that body with the plain-spoken observation that the government could not justify the holding of Southern forts "unless

[1] *Battles and Leaders of the Civil War; being for the most part contributions by Union and Confederate officers. Based upon "The Century War Series"* (Eds., Robert Underwood Johnson and Clarence Clough Buel. 4 vols. New York, 1887-1888), I, 13. Hereafter cited as *B. & L.*

we intend to reduce those States, themselves, into subjection." [2]

Even as the senator spoke, Fort Barrancas in the harbor of Pensacola was flying the flag of the United States. Pending efforts to adjust the differences and thereby preserve the peace, the Floridians were urging the withdrawal of the garrison. To all appearances Washington was as yet without a definite policy; the administration had drifted into an eddy of indecision. In the meantime, forces from Florida, Georgia, Alabama, and Mississippi were moving into the vicinity. Control of the fortifications commanding the entrance to Pensacola harbor was a matter of concern to all the states bordering on the Gulf of Mexico. In particular, they considered it important that, for the time at least, the state of Florida should be in possession of Fort Pickens, which they regarded as "an almost impregnable stronghold." [3] The garrison at Barrancas was a company of artillerymen under command of Lieutenant Adam J. Slemmer. In location and strength Barrancas was inferior to its neighboring work, Fort Pickens. Slemmer sensed that there was serious trouble in the offing. He knew that, inasmuch as Fort Pickens, properly manned, would dominate the harbor, its seizure by opposing forces would render his own position practically hopeless.[4]

Presently there came startling news. State troops were taking over United States property at various points. Rumor had it that next on the list was seizure of the Pensacola navy yard and forts. In Slemmer's judgment,

[2] Stephens, *A Constitutional View of the Late War Between the States,* II, 351-352.

[3] General Clement A. Evans (ed.), *Confederate Military History* (12 vols. Atlanta, 1899), XI, 13, 14.

[4] Don Carlos Seitz, *Braxton Bragg, General of the Confederacy* (Columbia, S. C., 1924), p. 23.

the time had come for action. Consequently, on January tenth, the day on which Florida seceded from the Union, Slemmer called to his aid boats from the United States steamer *Wyandotte* and the store ship *Supply* and transferred his garrison into Fort Pickens.[5]

That same day, Slemmer notified Adjutant General Cooper that he had acted "under special instructions received the preceding day from the general-in-chief." [6] His more detailed report of several weeks later disclosed that the instructions from Washington had directed him to confer with the Union commander of the navy yard regarding what would be required to forestall seizure of the Pensacola forts. This he had done: "I called on Commodore Armstrong. . . . He had received orders to co-operate with me. We decided that with our limited means of defense we could hold but one fort, and that should be Fort Pickens, as it commanded completely the harbor and the forts, and also the navy yard." [7] It was a strategic move, a bold stroke. Slemmer, Armstrong, and the general in chief at Washington were aware that the movement involved defiance of the sentiment prevailing in Florida, that their course was one which almost inevitably would incite reprisals.

The strength of Fort Pickens was impressive. Two hundred and one seacoast and garrison cannon were available.[8] Among these were ten four-inch columbiads, four ten-inch mortars, fifty eight-inch and flanking howitzers. Other items included some five thousand projectiles, three

[5] *B. & L.*, I, 27, 28; John Thomas Scharf, *History of the Confederate States Navy from its Organization to the Surrender of its last Vessel* (New York, 1887), p. 599.

[6] *The War of the Rebellion: A Compilation of the Official Records of the Union and Confederate Armies* (130 vols. Washington, 1880-1901), Ser. 1, Vol. I, p. 334. Hereafter cited as *O. R. A.*

[7] *Ibid.*, pp. 334, 335.

[8] Evans, *Confederate Military History*, XI, 21.

thousand loose shot, five hundred twenty-four-pounder stands canister shot, twelve thousand pounds of powder. Once established there, Slemmer had reason to congratulate himself that the Southerners would think twice before throwing themselves against such a formidable barrier. It was immediately obvious that he had acted none too soon, for within two days the Floridians were masters of the navy yard, and, shortly afterward, of Barrancas.[9]

FLORIDA REQUESTS THE SURRENDER OF FORT PICKENS

While at the time of Lieutenant Slemmer's shift of his command the cause of secession was making notable headway, the seceding states had not as yet found themselves. The Confederate government had not come into being and, in consequence of the lack of a central directing agency, disorganization was prevalent. As individual units, nevertheless, the several commonwealths were striving as best they could to marshal their respective resources for the protection of their interests. Where confronted by fortifications garrisoned by Union troops, they were naturally alert to any change which might work to their disadvantage. Even so, there was no desire for, nor as yet any expectation of, hostilities. Stephen R. Mallory, United States senator from Florida, telegraphed the commander of the Florida forces advising against a collision, insisting that Fort Pickens was "not worth a drop of blood." [10]

Lieutenant Slemmer had occupied his new post only two days when a sentry announced the presence of three visitors, one civilian and two officers. In the name of the governor of the state they made a respectful demand

9 Scharf, *History of the Confederate States Navy,* pp. 600, 601.
10 Evans, *Confederate Military History,* XI, 14, 15.

for the surrender of the fort. Replying that he was in his position by authority of the president of the United States and that he acknowledged no right in the governor to suggest his handing over of United States property, Slemmer took occasion to add the comment, "a governor is nobody here." [11] Ignoring the slur, the representatives of the state took their departure. Three days passed. Then arrived Colonel William H. Chase, commander of the Florida troops, accompanied by Captain Farrand, lately of the United States navy. Their conference with Lieutenants Slemmer and Gilman the last-named officer describes in an account which relates that the visitors brought a prepared document, but that both Chase and Farrand were so overcome by emotion that they handed the paper to Gilman for him to read aloud.[12]

Dated January fifteenth and signed by Colonel Chase, the communication gave notice that its writer held instructions to take possession of the harbor forts, a duty he earnestly desired he might perform without conflict. On behalf of the governor, it made formal request for the surrender of the work. It contained a stipulation that the state would hold it subject to such agreement as might be "entered into between commissioners of the State of Florida and the Federal government at Washington." Following a reminder that after all they were "brethren of the same race," the document further clarified the proposal: "If the Union now broken should be reconstructed Fort Pickens . . . passes peacefully under Federal authority. If a Southern Confederacy separates itself from the Union would it not be worse than folly to attempt the maintenance of Fort Pickens or any other fortified place within its limits?" The concluding words

[11] *B. & L.*, I, 29; Evans, *Confederate Military History*, XI, 22.
[12] *B. & L.*, I, 30, 31.

carried a tone almost of entreaty: "Listen to me, then, I beg of you, and act with me in preventing the shedding the blood of your brethren. Surrender the fort. You and your command may reoccupy the barracks . . . at Barrancas on your simple parole to remain there quietly until ordered away, or to resume the command of the harbor should an adjustment of present difficulties in the Union be arrived at. . . . I beg of you to receive this communication in the same spirit in which it is offered." [13]

Chase's appreciation of the far-reaching possibilities of the situation inspired the brotherliness of the appeal. It occurred to him that, possibly, Slemmer was proceeding on his own initiative, unmindful of the offense the course would give; if so, a friendly reminder of the likelihood of danger, even bloodshed, might effect a dissipation of the looming crisis. With power to act, Chase was willing to compromise. If only Slemmer would quiet excitement by returning to Barrancas, all would be well. Not only would such action involve no real sacrifice of Federal interests but it would be a voluntary, patriotic contribution to an adjustment of differences. The colonel was aware that, in such a cause, willingness of the concededly superior force to adopt a conciliatory attitude could hardly fail to impress the discriminating element of the opposition. The day following, Slemmer sent his reply:

". . . we have decided, after consultation with the Government officers in the harbor, that it is our duty to hold our position until such a force is brought against us as to render it impossible to defend it, or until the political condition of the country is such as to induce us to surrender the public property in

[13] *O. R. A.,* Ser. 1, Vol. I, pp. 337-338.

our keeping to such authorities as may be delegated
legally to receive it.

"We deprecate as much as you or any individual
can the present condition of affairs, or the shedding
of the blood of our brethren. In regard to this matter, however, we must consider you the aggressors,
and if blood is shed that you are responsible there-
for." [14]

For the first time, the lieutenant was experiencing the
thrill of the imminence of armed conflict. His reaction
was natural. He represented the power of the United
States government. He was in command, he was strictly
within his rights, and an opponent had challenged his
action. Into his reply there crept a belligerence strangely
at variance with the kindliness of Chase. Translated into
common parlance, his message said, "Irritation or no
irritation, we are here in Fort Pickens; bloodshed or no
bloodshed, we intend to remain; and what, pray, are
you going to do about it?" The condition becomes the
more striking in view of the fact that Slemmer was thirty-
three years of age, while Chase was sixty-three. The
colonel was a native of Massachusetts, a graduate of the
United States Military Academy, and had attained his
rank of major when his opponent was eleven years old.
With a distinguished record as an army engineer, it so
happened he had been in charge of the defenses at Pensacola in 1854.

Apparently Slemmer did not reckon with another contingency; namely, that his brashness might produce an
unexpected boomerang. Inside the fortress there was no
appeal from his decisions, but on the mainland the forces
of Florida were in control, and on that mainland was
the post office upon which he and his command depended.

[14] *Ibid.*, p. 338.

Inasmuch as it was in the power of the Florida commander to shut him off completely from channels of communication with his friends and his government, he discovered he was about to accomplish his own isolation. To his discomfiture, eight days later he came face to face with the alternative of being without his mail or of asking a favor of the officer to whom he had addressed his aggressive letter of January sixteenth. Swallowing his pride, he mailed to Colonel Chase a note phrased with studied courtesy. Would the colonel permit one of the officers from Pickens to procure letters and papers belonging to the garrison and which, unaccountably enough, the Warrington postmaster was withholding? "I therefore," he wrote, "make this request of you as commander-in-chief of the forces, and from a knowledge of your personal character." [15]

The response was even more noteworthy. Slemmer had not misjudged the character of Chase, the veteran with patience born of experience. That his impulsiveness had aroused no spirit of resentment, he learned when, two days later, he read:

"I have this moment received your communication of the 24th instant. I have been absent at Montgomery, which will account for the delay. I will immediately inquire at the post office about your mail matter, and attend to your request. I would also inform you that you may be supplied with fresh provisions daily if you desire. I will communicate with you again.

"In haste, respectfully, your obedient servant,

W. H. CHASE
Colonel, Commanding" [16]

[15] *Ibid.*, p. 339.   [16] *Ibid.*, p. 340.

The tension eased, the atmosphere of friendly regard restored, that same day Slemmer wrote Chase that he had directed a second lieutenant to proceed to the navy yard for a conference relative to supplies of fresh provisions and the mail facilities of the Pickens command. And, again, on the same day came Chase's answer: "I send over your mail. The mail will be delivered to you in future without delay." [17]

The Florida commander was fully cognizant that occupation of Fort Pickens by Federal forces was an unfriendly move, one affording ample provocation to strike back. In addition, there was the combativeness of the younger man's answer to as sincere an appeal as he was capable of writing. Determined to preserve cordial relations as long as possible, the elder soldier was exerting every effort to quiet the swelling tide of animosity.[18] His generosity saved the immediate situation, but something occurred later to stir irritation in other quarters. In a letter of February twenty-first, a newspaper correspondent commented: "There has been too much dallying and courtesying to Lieutenant Slemmer and his men—make them in future keep their places, for you need expect no return for your kindness." [19]

REINFORCEMENT ORDERED

The thoughtful among Florida's people understood the gravity of their situation now that she was no longer one of the union of states. The venturesome step involved sentiment, but sentiment could not shut out the cold facts. There were practical considerations such as loss of prestige of association with a great nation and deprivation

17 *Ibid.*   18 Seitz, *Braxton Bragg*, p. 26.
19 *Southern Messenger* (Greenville, Ala.), March 6, 1861.

of protection afforded by the armed forces of the Federal government. With a length of shore line unapproached by that of any other state, without the semblance of a navy, an attack from the sea would find the state helplessly vulnerable. Over against such considerations was the pressure of strong conviction that the discomfort and apprehension occasioned by sectional antagonisms justified the rash gamble of secession. A feeling approximating hopelessness was necessary to develop provocation for so desperate a decision. The most that they could hope for now was that no opposition to their withdrawal would materialize, but it was becoming increasingly evident that the government did not intend to allow them to go out in peace. Not only had their suggestion of the removal of Federal troops from their territory accomplished nothing but, at Pensacola, without notice of any sort, the Union commander had moved his garrison into a far stronger position. Was this the answer to their overtures for a continuation of friendliness? Did this mean that Washington had already made up its mind, that what they were witnessing were mere preliminaries to a message which the guns of Pickens would deliver?

Slemmer's declination to follow the course proposed by the Florida commander had cut deeply but, thanks to Chase's levelheadedness, there was no reprisal. The troops had yielded to counsel that for the present, at any rate, even a successful storming of the fort would not be worth what it would cost. Even so, there was no escaping realization that inside its own domain the state's sovereignty was being flouted. In consequence, nerves were on edge; nevertheless, they would defer resort to arms. Even yet, there was the possibility that Northern appreciation of the reasonableness of their proposal for neighborly separation would be the reward of patience. Their hopes were fruitless. With serene unconcern, the Washington government proceeded to the one move which would most aggravate ill-feeling; namely, a plan for reinforcement of the fort. By direction of Winfield Scott, general in chief of the army and, as it happened, a native of Virginia, there went out on January twenty-first from the department of war an order to Captain Israel Vogdes. It instructed that officer to embark with his company of artillery on "the sloop-of-war Brooklyn to re-enforce Fort Pickens, of which you will become the commander as well as of other forts and barracks which it may be in your power to occupy and defend with the co-operation of any naval commander or commanders at hand." The following words leave no question of Scott's realization that he was flirting with fate: "It is probable that the Brooklyn may be obliged to land you outside the harbor, but it is hoped not so far from Fort Pickens as to be beyond the protection of its guns if the debarkation should be opposed." [20]

Two days later, the department undertook to arrange for supplies, arms, and ammunition for Vogdes' command. Notice went to headquarters at Fort Monroe to provide supplies for three months which, the paper commented, would require all space on the warship subject to allotment for the carriage of provisions. Fifteen thousand rounds of musket-ball cartridges, four mountain howitzers, two twelve-pound field howitzers, with not exceeding one hundred rounds of ammunition for each gun, were items of the requisition. The instructions continued, "Sealed orders received from the General-in-Chief have been furnished Captain Vogdes, to be opened when at sea." [21] The captain, of course, knew the main objective

[20] *O. R. A.*, Ser. 1, Vol. I, p. 352.   [21] *Ibid.*, p. 353.

of his mission, but the final secret orders meant nothing
less than that certain of his instructions were to be unknown even to him, until the *Brooklyn* was completely out
of touch with land, and there was consequently no possibility of a leakage of information.

Not so successfully guarded after all, within five days
after Scott signed the order, the press was blazoning the
scheme. A dispatch appearing in a Montgomery newspaper announced the identity of the warship, disclosed the
mission on which its captain was engaged, and told of the
reaction which the news produced:

"Pensacola, Fla., Jan. 26.

"The volunteers are making every preparation for
storming Fort Pickens. It is known that the steamer
Brooklyn is on her way to this place with reinforcements." [22]

The *Brooklyn* was carrying supplies, ammunition,
muskets, artillery, and troops to strengthen the garrison
at Pickens; and, barring merciful intervention of some
well-balanced agency, her captain was piloting a nation
into war.

[22] Montgomery *Weekly Post,* January 29, 1861.

Chapter II

THE ARMISTICE

Spreading like wildfire, news that a United States man-of-war was heading for Pensacola created something akin to consternation among those who saw in this latest maneuver a threat which promised violent repercussions. Nor were such apprehensions without foundation. Should the landing of reinforcements necessitate, in Slemmer's judgment, his use of the guns of Fort Pickens, there would almost certainly follow retaliation in the nature of an attempt to capture the fortress, all of which was leading to one result and one alone; the stupidity of the entire proceeding was building up a crisis, an emergency which called urgently for a strong man, a commanding personality with a kindly heart and a clear brain.

It was the height of good fortune that in Stephen R. Mallory the desperately needed firm hand was immediately available. He was of good Connecticut ancestry, admitted to the bar in 1840 and eleven years later a member of the United States senate. His fame as a leader of ability and integrity had gone far beyond the limits of his state. Later, as secretary of the navy in the Confederate cabinet, he was to handle with masterful ability his department's affairs. A close student of naval construction, he was to have a part in inspiring the experiment of the *Merrimac*. Largely through his initiative the Confederacy was "to anticipate modern invention in deadly torpedoes and submarines to such extent that it terrorized the Federal navy." [1] Sensing that this was no time for further Federal interference and, moreover, genuinely alarmed, Senator Mallory went at once into action. On January 28, 1861, through influential friends in Washington, he took up by telegraph with President Buchanan the appalling and apparently unconsidered consequences likely to follow an effort to throw reinforcements into Fort Pickens. He forcefully presented the issue:

> "We hear the Brooklyn is coming with re-enforcements for Fort Pickens. No attack on its garrison is contemplated, but, on the contrary, we desire to keep the peace, and if the present status be preserved we guarantee that no attack will be made upon it, but if re-enforcements be attempted, resistance and a bloody conflict seem inevitable. Should the Government thus attempt to augment its force—when no possible call for it exists; when we are preserving a peaceful policy—an assault may be made upon the fort at a moment's warning. Our whole force—1,700 strong—will regard it as a hostile act. Impress this upon the President, and urge that the inevitable consequence of re-enforcement under present circumstances is instant war, as peace will be preserved if no re-enforcements be attempted. If the President wants an assurance of all I say from Colonel Chase, commanding the forces, I will transmit it at once. I am determined to stave off war if possible.
> "Answer promptly." [2]

Hideous possibilities latent in the witless blundering of those responsible for the sending of the *Brooklyn* justified, Mallory thought, any means effective to prevent an explosion. Up to the time of this newest development,

[1] *Dictionary of American Biography* (Allen Johnson, ed. 20 vols. New York, 1928-1936), XII, 224.

[2] *O. R. A.,* Ser. 1, Vol. I, p. 354. See also Evans, *Confederate Military History,* XI, 22, 23.

he and his associates had determinedly checked the spirit
of retaliation aroused by Slemmer's transfer of his command. They had bridged that gulf. Even so, smoldering
resentment was about to flare up again now that news of
an approaching reinforcement was in the air. It was of
no use to waste time with war and navy departments.
These agencies, he realized, were necessarily coöperating
in the project; the officers on the warship and the troops
on board were, of course, acting under orders. For all
that, there was an official whose authority exceeded that
of heads of departments. With rare confidence in himself
and in his people, Senator Mallory demonstrated courage
and statesmanship by going straight to President Buchanan with the assurance that the threatening storm
would blow over if only the government would press no
further the unfriendly attitude at Pensacola. He informed
the chief executive that, while for the moment the recently
ominous situation was well in hand, the landing of the
company from the *Brooklyn* would once and for all disrupt amicable relations. The spirit of the message shines
forth in the words, "I am determined to stave off war if
possible." [3]

Governor Moore, of Alabama, had occasion to refer to
the result of Mallory's intervention. The convention in
Montgomery had requested the governor's opinion as to
the advisability of recalling the Alabama troops which
were at the moment in Pensacola. He opened his response
by quoting a telegram which had come to Colonel Chase
from Southern Senators Mallory, Yulee, Slidell, Benjamin, Iverson, Fitzpatrick, Wigfall, Hemphill, Clay, and
Davis; it voiced their vigorous protest against any assault on Fort Pickens in view of the fact that bloodshed
might be fatal to the cause. It meant something that ten

[3] *O. R. A.*, Ser. 1, Vol. I, p. 354.

of the South's foremost representatives in Washington, including one by the name of Davis, had united in such a telegram.[4] To this juncture, at any rate, they were speaking the language of peace. The governor also told the convention of a conference held by Southern Senators Mallory, Slidell, and Fitzpatrick with the secretary of the navy and President Buchanan. If, as some have charged, the Southern group in the capital were adroitly playing a game of deception, Mallory, Slidell, and Fitzpatrick must have given a masterful exhibition. At any rate they convinced the president and the secretary of their sincerity. These Federal officials assured the senators that no excuse would be given "for the shedding of blood . . . and that they deemed it of great importance that no attack should be made by South Carolina upon Fort Sumter, or by the troops of the seceding States upon Fort Pickens, in the present aspect of affairs." [5]

From Governor Moore's message it appears that the senators had told him something else; namely, that the current view in Washington was that Republican leaders wanted war, intended to have war, but preferred to shoulder Buchanan's administration with responsibility for conflict. The outstanding revelation of their conference was that the president did not want war, did not intend to have war, and was willing wholeheartedly to join in an effort to save the nation from the threatened tidal wave of disaster. The governor then came to the point immediately at issue:

"It was further stated by Mr. Mallory that a special messenger had been sent by the Secretary of the Navy to the officer in command at Fort Pickens, directing that officer to prevent the ships which had

4 Seitz, *Braxton Bragg,* p. 27.
5 *O. R. A.,* Ser. 1, Vol. I, pp. 445, 446.

been ordered to Pensacola from entering the bay. The officer sent was Captain Barron, of Virginia, in company with Mr. Mallory . . .

"Notwithstanding it now appears from the authority above given that no attack is to be made upon the forts at Pensacola now in possession of our forces at that point, I deem it inexpedient that all the troops should be withdrawn." [6]

NEGOTIATIONS FOR AN ARMISTICE

Captain Barron, the officer mentioned by Senator Mallory, made his report on January twenty-ninth. Upon his arrival at Pensacola, he wrote, it gratified him to discover that the attitude of the Floridians toward the Pickens garrison was one of courtesy and kindliness; the command received its mail without delay and experienced no difficulty in securing fresh provisions from neighboring territory. He learned, though, of a definite determination to prevent any reinforcement of the fort. If the government had made plans to land additional troops, he thought the course of wisdom, at least for the present, would be to lay them aside. The sane procedure, it occurred to him, would be to have the *Brooklyn* "lay off and on the harbor" in readiness to throw in the reinforcements should occasion arise to require such action. In his judgment, this course would "stave off all pretense for a collision."

His specific mission he reported as happily successful. His arrival with orders to warn vessels not to enter the harbor apparently had given great satisfaction and comfort. The fifteen-hundred-odd troops in the district were, according to his information, anxious to make an assault, but were being restrained by the firm hand of Colonel

[6] *Ibid.*

Chase. Nevertheless, he confirmed what Senator Mallory had said; the landing of reinforcements would likely arouse such antagonism as to make it impossible for even Colonel Chase to curb their impatience.[7]

A memorandum prepared by Senator Mallory mentions further details of Barron's visit. On his arrival, his first move was to secure an interview with Colonel Chase and Mallory. Introducing himself as a messenger from Secretary of the Navy Toucey, he made known that he was the bearer of written orders for momentarily expected naval vessels, the *Macedonian*, the *Sabine*, and the *St. Louis*. These orders gave positive directions for the ships to remain outside the harbor. In addition, he had verbal instructions authorizing him to intercept and prevent the entrance of any other Federal warship which might approach Pensacola. Upon the officers of the several ships he was to impress the desire of the navy department that they should carefully refrain from any action which might cause trouble.[8]

Learning the purpose of Captain Barron's visit, Colonel Chase readily authorized him to call on Lieutenant Slemmer in Fort Pickens and to go out to the United States vessels upon their arrival; more than this, he detailed Captain Randolph to arrange necessary transportation.[9] Thus, again, accredited representatives of the opposing factions held a conference. For Florida there appeared a United States senator and the commander of the military forces of the state; for the United States, a naval captain carrying credentials from the secretary of the navy. Singularly enough, Captain Barron, a Virginian,

---

[7] *Official Records of the Union and Confederate Navies in the War of the Rebellion* (31 vols. Washington, 1894-1927), Ser. 1, Vol. IV, p. 71. Hereafter cited as *O. R. N.*

[8] *Ibid.*, p. 212.   [9] *Ibid.*, pp. 212-213.

represented the Federal end of the negotiations, while Colonel Chase, a native of Massachusetts, represented that of Florida.

His telegram of the twenty-eighth, bringing to Buchanan's notice the danger incident to reinforcement, Mallory had addressed to his intermediaries, Senator Slidell, Senator Hunter, and Governor Bigler. Their reply of the next day had informed him that instructions from the secretaries of war and the navy would indicate the favor with which the president had received his message.[10] The senator, it will be recalled, had suggested that, in addition to his own pledge, Colonel Chase would give similar assurance, should President Buchanan care for it. Although no such intimation was forthcoming, Mallory preferred that Chase should place himself on record. He therefore sent the commander this note:

> "These gentlemen you will perceive send me the instructions of the Navy and War Department, as the President's answer to my telegram. Knowing that you did not design to attack Fort Pickens under existing circumstances, I assured these gentlemen that no attack would be made unless reenforcements were attempted, in which case I could not feel assured that the troops here would not attack. Permit me to suggest that if you shall act upon this dispatch and give the assurance as indicated therein, you can have this dispatch delivered to Lieutenant Slemmer and the officers named, by Captain Barron, whose mission is of a peaceful character." [11]

The day following the date of Governor Moore's message to the convention, a Montgomery weekly carried this dispatch from Washington: "The President has countermanded the order for the Brooklyn to enter Pensacola harbor. He has sent an order to be delivered when the

[10] *Ibid.*, p. 213.   [11] *Ibid.*

Brooklyn heaves in sight, thus avoiding a collision. This news is reliable." [12]

Reliable or not, this was good news. At last the ironing out of the misunderstanding appeared certain. Secretary of the Navy Toucey's prompt action in sending Captain Barron to Pensacola with a stop order for Federal warships meant a reopening of the road to peace. Mallory's intervention was the mainspring of it all. Rarely does a man face responsibility for grappling with an emergency of such direful potentialities. Rarely is there found in one individual such a combination of sagacity to perceive what is about to happen, intelligence to know what to do, and boldness to do it. All in all, it was a superb performance; rising splendidly to the occasion, walking single-handed into the critical situation, Senator Mallory had succeeded in averting disaster. Now the peace bird fluttered again into view, and hopes were high.

Meanwhile, in the mind of the populace a hope lingered that even yet there was a possibility of the relinquishment of Fort Pickens. The Montgomery *Weekly Post* of January 29, 1861, copied an article from the Florida *Tribune*: "To the westward of Fort Pickens, under the guns of that fort, is anchored the U. S. steam gunboat, Wyandotte; for what purpose is not known, but it is supposed she is there to render any assistance possible to Lieutenant Slemmer—if he should choose to leave, she will take him off."

In Captain Barron's possession was the order to Federal army and navy commanders on the Pensacola station. The document was clear and explicit:

[12] Montgomery *Weekly Post,* February 6, 1861.

"WASHINGTON, *January 29, 1861*

"In consequence of the assurances received from Mr. Mallory in a telegram of yesterday to Messrs. Slidell, Hunter, and Bigler (with a request that it should be laid before the President) that Fort Pickens would not be assaulted, and an offer of such an assurance to the same effect from Colonel Chase for the purpose of avoiding a hostile collision, upon receiving satisfactory assurances from Mr. Mallory and Colonel Chase that Fort Pickens will not be attacked you are instructed not to land the company on board the *Brooklyn* unless said fort shall be attacked or preparations shall be made for its attack. The provisions necessary for the supply of the fort you will land. The *Brooklyn* and other vessels of war on the station will remain, and you will exercise the utmost vigilance and be prepared at a moment's notice to land the company at Fort Pickens, and you and they will instantly repel any attack on the fort. . . .

"J. Holt
Secretary of War
I. Toucey
Secretary of the Navy

"James Glynn, Commanding the *Macedonian;* Captain W. S. Walker, Commanding the *Brooklyn,* and other Naval Officers in Command, and Lieutenant Adam J. Slemmer, First Regiment Artillery, U. S. Army, Commanding Fort Pickens, Pensacola, Fla." [13]

Instantly this instrument arrests attention. It possesses the unique dignity of a document executed by both the secretary of war and the secretary of the navy of the United States. Nor is this all. Nicolay, Lincoln's private secretary, tells of President Buchanan's assertion that this

[13] *O. R. N.,* Ser. 1, Vol. IV, p. 74. See also John George Nicolay and John Hay, *Abraham Lincoln, a History* (10 vols. New York, 1890), III, 168. Hereafter cited as *Lincoln.*

order received the approval not only of every member of his cabinet but of General Scott as well.[14] Stanton's statement that he, Judge Black, and General Dix opposed its issuance, and Scott's disavowal of knowledge of it, leave unimpaired authoritative information that, with the concurrence of a majority of the cabinet, President Buchanan gave it his sanction, and the secretaries of war and the navy signed it.

The document carries a distinct proposal of an armistice conditioned only upon reception of proper pledges from Mallory and Chase. In the event such assurances were forthcoming, it gave positive directions: the Union officers were not to land the troops on the warship save in case of an attack or preparations for attack on Fort Pickens. The circumstance that Secretaries Holt and Toucey sent the paper in care of Captain Barron and addressed it to Captains Glynn, Walker, "other Naval Officers in command," and Lieutenant Slemmer heightens its impressiveness. Its scope swept the field of Federal army and navy officialdom at Pensacola. The willingness with which the Floridians gave the requested assurances is indicated by the circumstance that, only four days after the secretary of the navy signed the order, Captain Barron wrote this reply:

"NAVY YARD, WARRINGTON, FLA.,

February 2, 1861

"SIR: Herewith I have the honor to send you a copy of the letters from Colonel Chase, commanding the forces in this district, and the Hon. S. R. Mallory. I have delivered a copy to Lieutenant Slemmer, commanding Fort Pickens, and shall deliver the origi-

14 *Ibid.*, pp. 168, 169.

nals of these and the telegram from the honorables the Secretaries of War and Navy Departments to the senior naval officer that may arrive here. Neither of the vessels for whom I have dispatches has yet arrived. I understand that some of the forces which have assembled here from other States will in a short time return to their homes, in consequence of the armistice established by these papers. I am inclined to believe that my mission here has been productive of much comfort and has prevented a collision of arms. Colonel Chase and Captain Randolph have extended to me every facility for executing my orders, and are uniformly courteous and kind . . .

". . . I think the vessels expected off this harbor may be looked for in the course of three or four days." [15]

Colonel Chase's letter, a copy of which Captain Barron enclosed, thus confirmed Mallory's assurance:

"SIR: I enclose herewith a note, relating to a dispatch sent to him from Washington, from the Hon. S. R. Mallory.

"This dispatch I also enclose, it having been delivered to me by Mr. Mallory for that purpose. These documents speak for themselves, and I would request that you communicate them to the officers, or any one of them, to whom the telegram is addressed, and also my assurances that, on condition the companies on board the U.S.S. *Brooklyn* . . . shall not be landed, Fort Pickens shall not be attacked and the preparations for an attack shall be discontinued.

"Communications by special messenger between the army and naval officers on the Pensacola station and the U. S. Government, to and from, shall not be obstructed in any way." [16]

Barron also made a part of his report the text of the pledge from Senator Mallory:

[15] *O. R. N.,* Ser. 1, Vol. IV, pp. 76-77.
[16] *Ibid.,* p. 77.

"Being assured myself that no attack will be made
upon Fort Pickens unless an attempt to reenforce
the garrison shall first be made, I give this assurance
to the officers named in the dispatch to which Colonel
Chase refers, together with the further assurance of
the discontinuance of Colonel Chase's preparations
for such attack, and of the unrestricted communication to which he also refers." [17]

Even Nicolay, who denounced Mallory as one of what
he called the senatorial cabal,[18] concedes that the formal
orders were the outgrowth of an understanding between
the senator and Buchanan.[19] It is unaccountable that
General Crawford, usually as magnanimous as Nicolay was
severe, could bring himself to refer to the agreement as a
"quasi-truce," unless, in a momentary lapse from his
customary accuracy, he came under the influence of a
similar characterization on the part of Lincoln, which
will appear later.[20]

Captain Barron justifiably took pleasure in the success which rewarded his handling of the critical problem.
Calling attention to his understanding that some of the
Southern states would withdraw their troops, he set out
the reason for their action in words of momentous significance: "In consequence of the armistice established by
these papers." [21]

An armistice is a formal agreement which opposing
forces enter into for the purpose of suspending hostile
relations either for a stipulated, or for an indefinite, period. Here was a truce of the most binding character, the
stronger because of its simplicity. Captain Barron was

[17] *Ibid.*
[18] *Lincoln*, III, 167.
[19] *The Outbreak of Rebellion* (New York, 1882), p. 38.
[20] *The Genesis of the Civil War* (New York, 1887), p. 402.
[21] *O. R. N.*, Ser. 1, Vol. IV, p. 77.

right. The papers did constitute an armistice and the
terms were transparent and explicit. There was no am-
biguity for the most technical legalist to pounce upon;
in the parlance of the courthouse, it was airtight.[22] Not
only this, it was more than a formal obligation. In the
truest sense, it was a gentlemen's agreement executed by
honorable men whose several high positions in their respective sections attested their entire responsibility. The
violation of the terms of such an armistice, the purpose of
which was to allay irritation in a period in which the spec-
ter of war loomed, is unthinkable.

A report made by Slemmer to Secretary of War Holt
shows the painstaking care with which Colonel Chase was
observing the truce and his willingness to make all concessions to the end there should be no possible misunderstanding. In his communication Slemmer enclosed a copy
of a note which he had sent Chase in which he had said:
"I observe that you are erecting and arming a battery
west of the light-house. I deem it my duty to protest
against its further continuance, and also of all batteries
which may bear on Fort Pickens." [23] He added that he
had received the following satisfactory reply from Colonel
Chase:

> "I have this moment received your letter of the
> 11th instant. I am determined to make good the as-
> surances that I have given, that no attack shall be
> made on Fort Pickens, and to discontinue all prep-
> arations for one, as stated in my letter to Capt. S.
> Barron, dated January 29. I do not consider the
> erection of batteries on this side as aiming at an at-
> tack on Fort Pickens; but, desiring to avoid all ac-
> tual or implied preparations for an attack, I will

[22] Scharf, *History of the Confederate States Navy*, pp. 604, 605.
[23] *O. R. A.,* Ser. 1, Vol. I, p. 359.

give orders for the discontinuance of the erection of
the battery." [24]

It mattered not to Chase whether Slemmer's objection was captious or sincere; that he had made the complaint was enough. There was no counter demand for
cessation of the strengthening of the fort, no imputation
of caviling in the forwarding of the protest. The spirit
of the Florida commander was clear: reasonable or unreasonable, his opponent's letter carried the implication that
he was not living up to his agreement; he, therefore, immediately answered that he would give orders which would
eliminate the ground of the criticism.

THE *Brooklyn* ARRIVES

Under the reinforcement orders of January twenty-
first, Captain Vogdes was to take his command to Pensacola, land the company, and assume charge of Fort
Pickens.[25] The *Brooklyn* dropped anchor outside the harbor February sixth and, on the day following, Vogdes reported his arrival to Adjutant General Thomas, detailing the reasons for his failure to execute the department's
instructions:

> "I met orders here which prevent the landing of
> my company or the reenforcement of the garrison
> . . . at present . . .
> "The seceders have a considerable force in and
> about Pensacola; what number I am unable to say
> positively, but they are estimated at about 1,700
> men. They are disorderly, and very unwilling to be
> controlled. Their leaders, from what I can learn, I
> believe are sincere in their intention to observe the
> armistice, but their ability to control the men under

[24] *Ibid.*
[25] Crawford, *The Genesis of the Civil War*, p. 401.

their command is very doubtful. They are engaged in erecting batteries, are making sand bags, &c. They have plenty of means of transporting their troops to Santa Rosa Island, and can attack the fort on all sides at once. . . .

"Should the armistice be broken, my company, all the marines, and as many soldiers as may raise the garrison to four hundred men should be immediately landed. All of the advantages of the present armistice are entirely on the side of the seceders. I would therefore urge on the Department the necessity of immediately re-enforcing the garrison . . .

"P.S.—I must not be understood as recommending any violation of the existing armistice, but the collection of an amount of troops on the station as may be necessary for the defense should anything occur to rupture the present armistice." [26]

The writer quoted as referring to the agreement as a "quasi-truce," and the distinguished personage later to adopt the phrasing "quasi-armistice" apparently were not familiar with Vogdes' report. Its repeated references leave no doubt that the armistice profoundly impressed him. With orders in his pocket to proceed with the reinforcement, he found awaiting him on his arrival orders countermanding the earlier instructions and directing the *Brooklyn* to remain outside the harbor. This means that the captain of the *Brooklyn* had received the January twenty-ninth communication from the secretaries of war and the navy. Not only did Captain Vogdes at once discover the existence of the agreement, but, from the Federal officers on the station, he heard estimates of the character of their opponents which led him to express the belief that he could trust them to respect its terms. Nevertheless, he outlined a course which in his judgment Wash-

[26] *O. R. A.*, Ser. 1, Vol. I, pp. 357, 358.

ington should follow should any occurrence terminate the truce.

Captain Vogdes was a soldier, a West Pointer, and no academy-trained officer could be ignorant of the import of an armistice. After writing his letter, there stole into his mind the fear that his superiors in the department might misinterpret his meaning, might read into his message a significance he did not intend, and so might even question his code of honor. He, therefore, added a postscript; his note was not to be construed as recommending any violation of the armistice.

In his letter of February second to Mr. Toucey, it will be recalled, Captain Barron stated that the originals of the documents constituting the armistice would be turned over by him to the "senior naval officer that may arrive here." In a few days this officer, Captain H. A. Adams, reached Pensacola on the *Sabine*. On February nineteenth he wrote Mr. Toucey. After reporting the condition of the ships of the squadron, the *Sabine*, the *St. Louis*, the *Brooklyn*, and the *Wyandotte*, and discussing the method by which an attack might be successfully made on the fort, he said: "Should the existing pacific arrangements come to an end the people on shore will have the advantage of knowing it long before we can. There seems to be no agreement that notice shall be given of its termination by either party." [27]

A careful reading of the documents in question will disclose the correctness of Captain Adams' construction. There was no limitation as to time, no trick phrasing, no adroitly worded escape clause. The agreement was simple, sincere, direct: the United States government was not to reinforce unless the Floridians should attack, or prepare to attack, the fort; the Southerners were not only not to

[27] *O. R. N.*, Ser. 1, Vol. IV, p. 85.

assault the garrison but were to discontinue preparations for hostilities, unless the Federals should attempt reinforcement.

That was all.

CHAPTER III

"THE ENGAGEMENT MADE BY
MR. MALLORY AND COLONEL CHASE
WITH THE UNITED STATES GOVERNMENT"

LINCOLN BECOMES PRESIDENT

On March 4, 1861, Abraham Lincoln took office as president of the United States.

Whatever the estimate of the man, whether the large or the small end of the telescope be focused on him, all must agree that the path ahead was anything but smooth. The situation was loaded, and he knew it. The political barometer was registering a steadily increasing partisan pressure. Swirling gusts of hate were warning of the oncoming hurricane.

Talk of an "irrepressible conflict" was in the air. Seward was discovering his "higher law." Radicals were characterizing the constitution as "a covenant with death and an agreement with hell." The Northern war governors were breathing out threatenings and slaughter. Montgomery Blair was demanding drastic action to break the secession movement. Secretary Chase was talking openly of unsheathing the sword and was saying, "We do not wish this, we deplore it because of the ruin, confiscation of property, and of the servile insurrections, too horrible to contemplate, which would follow." [1] Only a year or two before, Gerrit Smith had written: "Is it entirely clear

---

[1] Albert B. Hart, *Salmon Portland Chase,* in the "American Statesmen Series" (Boston and New York, 1899), p. 264.

32

that these slave insurrections will be put down promptly and before they have spread far? Remember that the railroads and the telegraphs can be rendered useless in an hour. Remember too, that many who would be glad to face the insurgents would be busy in transporting their wives and daughters to places where they would be safe from the worst fate which husbands and fathers can imagine for their wives and daughters." [2] A matter of recent history was John Brown's raid in which he carried to Harpers Ferry arms for thirteen hundred men, with specially made weapons for slaves.[3] On the day of Brown's execution, many Northern churches tolled their bells and held services glorifying the raider as a saint. Wendell Phillips and William Lloyd Garrison acclaimed him a martyr. So extreme was the feeling that Emerson compared to the cross of Jesus of Nazareth the gallows on which Brown died.[4] In consequence, Lincoln realized that radicalism was rapidly getting out of hand; John Brown's body was in the grave, but his soul was on the march.

Not all the trouble was originating with the radicals. Many others in the North, chafing under what they regarded as political domination by the South, were ready to welcome conflict as the instrumentality by which they could put an end to it. The balance of power was the prize for which both sections were contending and sectional animosity was at white heat. Whether Lincoln was the incarnate ideal of the war faction or the victim of a tide he was powerless to stem, whether the obligation was his to crush the South and preserve the Union or to make a supreme effort to placate the secessionists, to silence the

[2] James F. Rhodes, *History of the United States,* II, 400.
[3] *Ibid.*
[4] William Edward Dodd, *Expansion and Conflict* (Boston, New York, Chicago, 1915), p. 259.

warmongers, to reënthrone reason in both sections, and so to save the nation from the terrors of war, the fact remains that he was the one man with power to act.

Almost immediately after the inauguration, strange things began to happen.

Silent as to the nature of the new administration's conferences between March fourth and March twelfth on the subject of Fort Pickens, the official record divulges on the latter date a peremptory order, one which cracked like the report of a rifle:

"HEADQUARTERS OF THE ARMY
Washington, March 12, 1861

"SIR: At the first favorable moment you will land with your company, reinforce Fort Pickens, and hold the same till further orders.

"Report frequently, if opportunities present themselves, on the condition of the fort and the circumstances around you.

"I write by command of Lieutenant-General Scott. . . .

"E. D. TOWNSEND
"Assistant Adjutant-General

"CAPTAIN I. VOGDES
"First Artillery, U. S. A., on board Sloop of War Brooklyn.
"Off Fort Pickens, Pensacola, Fla." [5]

So General Scott was reviving the reinforcement project. But there was more to it than this. The paper bore the signature of Townsend and recited that he wrote it by command of Scott, but this time the commanding general was not assuming sole responsibility. As a matter of fact, he was acting under pressure. Fully determined greatly to strengthen the garrison at Fort Pickens, Lin-

[5] *O. R. N.*, Ser. 1, Vol. IV, p. 90. See also Evans, *Confederate Military History*, XI, 23.

coln had become impatient upon his discovery that the war department apparently was either indifferent to, or unaware of, his desire for prompt reinforcement. When on March eleventh nothing had occurred, he took matters into his own hands. A messenger from the executive office delivered that day to General Scott a paper which speedily put an end to procrastination. It was an order from Lincoln. The next day the warship *Mohawk* steamed out for Pensacola, her captain carrying the order to Vogdes.[6]

It will appear presently that this order, charged with dynamite, did not reach Captain Vogdes until March thirty-first. In the meantime the Southerners were largely in the dark as to what was going on in Washington. That, however, something in the changed situation had proved a source of uneasiness is learned from a terse note of March thirteenth addressed to the commander of Fort Pickens: "The bearer of this communication, Captain R. C. Wood, Army of Confederate States, waits upon you in my behalf, with the purpose of obtaining information necessary to enable me to understand our relative positions. He will communicate to you my views, and receive such reply as you may be pleased to make." The note bore the signature "Braxton Bragg, *Brigadier-General, Commanding.*"[7]

The contents of the message indicated a new development. As a result of material progress in organization on the part of the lately created Confederate government, the soldiers at Pensacola were no longer the forces of Florida, but troops of the army of the Confederate States. Moreover, there was another hand at the helm; General Bragg had replaced Colonel Chase. The incoming com-

[6] Nicolay and Hay, *Lincoln,* III, 393-394, 409; Ida M. Tarbell, *The Life of Abraham Lincoln,* III, 16. See p. 48, *infra.*

[7] *O. R. N.,* Ser. 1, Vol. IV, p. 92.

mander was also a West Pointer, with a unique record. Entering the academy at the age of sixteen, he had found his youth no handicap, for at graduation he ranked fifth in a class of fifty, a circumstance which presaged his future brilliant career. By one of fate's whims, among his classmates was one Israel Vogdes, none other than the Captain Vogdes of the reinforcement detail.[8] Still in command at Pickens, Lieutenant Slemmer knew of no change in Washington policy. He had his orders from the secretaries of war and the navy, and they were still in effect. Somewhat mystified by the message from the Confederate general, he answered the same day: "I have the honor to send you a copy of the agreement entered into between Colonel Chase, Senator Mallory, and the War and Navy Departments, with such other communications as may enable you to understand our relative positions. Please let me know as soon as convenient whether you will consider the agreement binding on your part or not."[9]

This means that, as information necessary to bring about mutual understanding, Slemmer simply forwarded a copy of the armistice documents. Inasmuch as the transaction occurred prior to Bragg's assumption of command, the lieutenant naturally wished to know what Bragg's attitude would be. The answer came the same day, announcing the Confederate officer's intention "to conform strictly to the spirit of the agreement entered into by Colonel Chase."[10] Bragg was a cultivated man with appreciation of the niceties of language, a fact which lends added impressiveness to his expressed purpose to adhere rigidly to "the spirit" of the understanding. This interchange of notes between the United States commander of the fort and the Confederate general resulted in writing

8 Seitz, *Braxton Bragg*, pp. 1, 2.
9 *O. R. N.*, Ser. 1, Vol. IV, p. 92.   10 *Ibid.*, p. 93.

into the record a further ratification of the armistice.[11]
Two days later, in an acknowledgment of receipt of
Bragg's letter, Slemmer brought another Federal officer
into the picture: "I placed yesterday your communication
of the 13th instant before the commander of the squadron
off the harbor. This will account for the delay in announcing to you that the assurances given are perfectly satisfactory." [12]

This meant nothing less than that, in an official conference between the Union officer in charge of the fort
and the commander of the Federal squadron, Bragg's
pledge had brought from Captain Adams still another
ratification. Even so, while he had Slemmer's statement
as to Adams' acquiescence in the arrangement, as yet no
personal word from Adams had come to Bragg. Unfamiliar with the situation, the Confederate general was feeling his way cautiously. Neither his first message nor the
reply of Captain Adams is available, but that the naval
officer's response was satisfactory is shown by a note of
March fifteenth from Bragg to Adams:

> "I have the pleasure to acknowledge the receipt of
> your communication of yesterday's date, and with a
> view of producing a perfect understanding between
> us beg leave to call your attention particularly to the
> last paragraph of my letter to Lieutenant Slem-
> mer . . .
> "I sincerely trust that the reports you receive of
> the probability of an amicable settlement of present
> difficulties may prove well founded." [13]

News which he was sure would interest General Bragg
had come to Captain Adams and he had taken pleasure

[11] Seitz, *Braxton Bragg*, p. 32.
[12] *O. R. A.*, Ser. 1, Vol. I, pp. 362-363.
[13] *O. R. N.*, Ser. 1, Vol. IV, p. 95.

in writing that he was not without reason to believe there
was a likelihood of troubled relations being smoothed out.
He would have omitted reference to such a cheering prospect had he known that, two days before the date of his
letter, Assistant Adjutant General Townsend, writing by
command of General Scott, a command inspired by President Lincoln, had sent to Vogdes the order to go ahead
with the reinforcement. On March eighteenth, just four
days after writing Bragg, and still in ignorance of the
order to Vogdes, Captain Adams reported to his chief,
Secretary of the Navy Gideon Welles:

> "The officers and men . . . are kept in readiness
> to land at the shortest notice; but I have received the
> assurance of General Bragg . . . that he will re-
> spect *the engagement made by Mr. Mallory and
> Colonel Chase with the U. S. Government,* and will
> make 'no disposition for the attack of Fort Pickens.'
> This engagement, as you are aware, *binds us not to
> reenforce* Fort Pickens unless it is attacked or threat-
> ened." [14]

The secretary of the navy of the new administration knew that the warships *Brooklyn, Sabine,* and probably others were even at the moment off Pensacola, and
that the *Brooklyn* was carrying reinforcements. He was
aware that Vogdes had not landed his company and must
have inferred that there was some reason for the failure
to execute the order. There appears no explanation why
he should not have known of the armistice to which his
predecessor in office was one of the contracting parties.
At any rate, Captain Adams was of the opinion that
Welles knew of it, for he wrote, "This engagement, as you
are aware, binds us." Whether or not the secretary knew
of it before, upon reading Adams' report he was the re-

14 *Ibid.,* p. 98. Italics supplied.

cipient of definite, authoritative information of the armistice, its terms, its binding obligation; he learned further that the Confederates were respecting it, and, most important of all, that the covenant was made by Mr. Mallory and Colonel Chase "with the United States government."

ALL QUIET AT PENSACOLA

The record is clear that on March eighteenth the armistice agreement was working to the full satisfaction of both factions at Pensacola. There were floating rumors of brewing trouble but, among other offsets to these, the Montgomery *Weekly Post* carried a Washington dispatch written March twentieth: "There is not a shadow of truth in the statement, widely published here and elsewhere today, to the effect that Fort Pickens is to be reinforced. We have the highest and best authority for contradicting this rumor." [15]

This was reassuring and it seemed that the dispatch was not without foundation for, on March thirtieth, Lieutenant Slemmer wrote the assistant adjutant general: "I have the honor to report that matters have not assumed a hostile attitude. Everything appears quiet. Troops are being quietly concentrated and preparations made for an immediate movement should the present amicable agreement be interrupted." [16]

There was no prospect of such interruption. With honorable men in command on both sides, Confederates and Federals were facing each other with confidence that all was well. A "perfect understanding" existed; the assurances relative to the armistice were "perfectly satisfactory"; the opposing factions were "conforming strictly to the spirit" of the agreement; the "amicable agreement"

[15] Issue of March 27, 1861.　　[16] *O. R. A.,* Ser. 1, Vol. I, p. 365.

was substituting friendliness for suspicion; there could be no clash unless one side or the other violated its pledged word.

Everything appeared quiet.

A NEW ADMINISTRATION AND A NEW ATTITUDE

As late as March thirtieth neither the Federal nor the Confederate commander at Pensacola had learned of the order to Captain Vogdes, nor did either dream that on April first there was to go out from the new administration to Colonel Harvey Brown the following instruction:

> "SIR: You have been designated to take command of an expedition to reenforce and hold Fort Pickens, in the harbor of Pensacola. You will proceed with the least possible delay to that place, and you will assume command of all the land forces of the United States within the limits of the State of Florida. . . . The engineer company of sappers and miners . . . Company M, Second Artillery . . . Company C, Third Infantry . . . will embark with you on the first steamer. Other troops and full supplies will be sent after you as soon as possible . . .
>
> "The object and destination of this expedition will be communicated to no one to whom it is not already known. The naval officers in the Gulf will be instructed to cooperate with you, and to afford every facility in their power for the accomplishment of the object of the expedition, which is the security of Fort Pickens against all attacks, foreign and domestic. Should a shot be fired at you, you will defend yourself and your expedition at whatever hazard, and, if needful for such defense, inflict upon the assailants all the damage in your power within the range of your guns . . .
>
> ". . . Captain Barry's battery will follow as soon as a vessel can be fitted for its transportation. Two or three foot companies will embark at the same time

with the battery. All the companies will be filled up
to the maximum standard . . .

". . . The naval officers in the Gulf will be instructed to cooperate with you. . . . You will fully
communicate with them for this end, and will exhibit
to them the authority of the President herewith." [17]

The document carried the signature of the commanding general of the army, Winfield Scott. That alone would
appear to render it sufficiently authoritative but, obviously, someone did not think so; accompanying it was a
most unusual memorandum, one the like of which neither
Colonel Brown nor General Scott had ever before seen:

"EXECUTIVE MANSION, *Washington*
April 1, 1861

"All officers of the Army and Navy to whom this
order may be exhibited will aid by every means in
their power the expedition under the command of
Colonel Harvey Brown, supplying him with men and
material, and cooperating with him as he may desire.
"ABRAHAM LINCOLN" [18]

The *Brooklyn* with Vogdes and his command on board,
the *Sabine* with Captain Adams, to say nothing of the
St. Louis and the *Wyandotte*, were already at Pensacola.
This was not enough. Another expedition, one to reinforce
the reinforcing squadron, was to move. No delay was to
be tolerated. And, again, haste was causing confusion.
Still in command of Fort Pickens, Lieutenant Slemmer
would have had disquieting thoughts had he known that
just outside the harbor on the *Brooklyn* Captain Vogdes
was waiting impatiently with the Lincoln-inspired order
to reinforce Fort Pickens, of which post the paper said
further, "you will become the commander as well as of
other forts and barracks which it may be in your power

17 *O. R. N.*, Ser. 1, Vol. IV, pp. 107-108.   18 *Ibid.*, p. 108.

to occupy and defend." Vogdes, in turn, would have experienced similar annoyance had someone whispered that Colonel Brown was on his way with instructions, also concurred in by Lincoln, one detail of which set out that he was to "assume command of all the land forces of the United States within the limits of the state of Florida."

The Lincoln memorandum made ample provision for any assistance the expedition might require: "All officers of the army and navy . . . will aid." Colonel Brown could not have asked more; it placed squarely behind him the entire fighting force of the United States government. Any regiment or division of the land forces, any man-of-war or squadron flying the flag, was to be subject to his call. More than this, the president was exerting the utmost vigilance to throw about his mission a veil of secrecy. The colonel himself was charged to bridle his tongue: "The object and destination of this expedition will be communicated to no one to whom it is not already known." So far as is revealed, this meant that only the general who signed the order, the officer to whom he addressed it, and the president were to know its objective. It meant also that it was altogether remarkable that such rigid restraint of speech should be imposed upon the officer for whom no less a personage than the president was providing such unheard-of support. That same day Lincoln issued another instruction:

"EXECUTIVE MANSION, *April 1, 1861*
"Lieutenant D. D. Porter will take command of the steamer *Powhatan*, or any other United States steamer ready for sea which he may deem most fit for the service to which he has been assigned by confidential instructions of this date.
"All officers are commanded to afford him all such facilities as he may deem necessary for getting to sea

as early as possible. He will select the officers who are
to accompany him.

"ABRAHAM LINCOLN

Recommended: "WM. H. SEWARD" [19]

On the same day Lieutenant Porter was the recipient of
personal instructions which also went out from the White
House over the signature of the president:

"EXECUTIVE MANSION, *April 1, 1861*
"SIR: You will proceed to New York, and with the
least possible delay assume command of any naval
steamer available. Proceed to Pensacola Harbor, and
at any cost or risk prevent any expedition from the
mainland reaching Fort Pickens or Santa Rosa.
"You will exhibit this order to any naval officer
at Pensacola if you deem it necessary after you have
established yourself within the harbor, and will request cooperation by the entrance of at least one
other vessel.
"This order, its object, and your destination will
be communicated to no person whatever until you
reach the harbor of Pensacola.

"ABRAHAM LINCOLN" [20]

This has an ominous ring. Lincoln was doing some concentrating on his own initiative. Could it be the situation
was too critical to take time to inquire at the navy department what men-of-war were then at the port of New
York? Of this procedure, this granting to a mere lieutenant blanket authority to take his choice of the navy's
warships, General Crawford was to write that it was "an
extraordinary course to pursue, justifiable only by the exigency and the high source that directed it." [21]

Even as he was writing his orders for Porter, the president must have known of the status at Pensacola. Surely

[19] *Ibid.,* p. 108.   [20] *Ibid.,* pp. 108, 109.
[21] *Genesis of the Civil War,* p. 411.

he was aware that, in addition to the formidable squadron
lying off the harbor and the artillery company of Vogdes
on board the *Brooklyn* ready to land at a moment's notice,
Colonel Brown was on the way with no fewer than seven
or eight companies, all filled to the maximum standard.
Nevertheless, Lieutenant Porter was to commandeer a
man-of-war and go with all speed to the scene. It was to
be his responsibility to keep the Southerners away from
Fort Pickens and off Santa Rosa Island. The instruction
charged him to do this "at any cost or risk," an expression inviting reflection inasmuch as the words were those
of the chief executive of the nation. The giving of the
order, its object, the destination of the vessel, the lieutenant was not to disclose even to his fellow officers; to "no
person whatever."

The tone of the order carries implication of a desperately critical emergency. It might be imagined that information had reached the White House that frenzied
Southerners in overwhelming masses were making ready
to massacre the Pickens garrison. Yet the fact is that no
hostilities of any sort had occurred; all Federal and Confederate officers on the post were enjoying tranquillity of
mind, secure in the consciousness of protection guaranteed
by the armistice. Only two days before, the Federal commander of the fort had summed up the status in the words,
"Everything appears quiet." That was a straightforward
statement of truth. Pickens was still intact. The flag of
the Union was flying to the breeze. No massacre was imminent. No army was marching. No one had suggested
an assault. There was no emergency. But Lincoln was not
through. On the same day, April first, there went forth,
again over his own signature, a message to Captain
Samuel Mercer commanding the exceptionally powerful
man-of-war *Powhatan*:

"Sɪʀ: Circumstances render it necessary to place in command of your ship, and for a special purpose, an officer who is duly informed and instructed in relation to the wishes of the Government, and you will therefore consider yourself detached; but in taking this step the Government does not intend in the least to reflect upon your efficiency or patriotism; on the contrary, have the fullest confidence in your ability to perform any duty required of you.

"Hoping soon to be able to give you a better command than the one you now enjoy, and trusting that you will have full confidence in the disposition of the Government toward you, I remain,
                                        "Aʙʀᴀʜᴀᴍ Lɪɴᴄᴏʟɴ" [22]

Samuel Mercer's ability and service record had won for him realization of the dream of every young naval officer, command of a warship. He was, of course, subject to the supervision of the department of the navy. Notice of any charge preferred against him, any criticism of his conduct, naturally would emanate from that source; yet now he held in his hand a communication, signed by the nation's president, summarily removing him from his ship, and assigning as the sole reason that "circumstances" rendered it necessary. The notice did not so much as disclose the name of the officer who was to supersede him; he learned only that his successor was to be one to whom Lincoln had confided his secret purposes.

The president's note was the more striking because of its disclaimer of any intention of disparagement, its acknowledgment of Mercer's efficiency and trustworthiness. All this presented an enigma without a solution; if neither his ability nor his patriotism was in question, if the government had the fullest confidence that he could perform any duty required of him, why should he be deprived of

[22] *O. R. N.*, Ser. 1, Vol. IV, p. 109.

his command? The intimation of possible future reward was scant consolation for one who was to pack his belongings and leave his ship without being able to suggest to his brother officers any plausible explanation of his hurried departure.

The same day, the fifth consecutive order over the president's signature went to the commander of the Brooklyn Navy Yard: "Fit out *Powhatan* to go to sea at the earliest possible moment under sealed orders. Orders by a confidential messenger go forward to-morrow. Abraham Lincoln." [23]

Again the imperious demand for haste; and again "sealed orders." The cloud of secrecy thickens. Not even the commander of the ship, the officer selected by Lincoln himself, was to learn the details of his mission until he was out on the high seas. The carefully guarded instructions a trusted agent would place in his hands; as far as possible, the president was keeping strictly to himself the secrets of his newest expedition.

And, again, on the same day, April first, Lincoln forwarded to the commandant of the New York Navy Yard his sixth consecutive, personally signed order: "You will fit out the *Powhatan* without delay. Lieutenant Porter will relieve Captain Mercer in command of her. She is bound on secret service, and you will under no circumstances communicate to the Navy Department the fact that she is fitting out. Abraham Lincoln." [24]

Already that day he had notified the Brooklyn Navy Yard to prepare the *Powhatan*. He was risking no chance of losing the services of this superior fighting machine. "She is bound on secret service." This was sufficiently mysterious, but the message carried another, a unique provision, one without precedent in the records of the

[23] *Ibid.*   [24] *Ibid.*

navy. What must have been the reaction of the official in charge of the navy yard, commanded by the president to condition a man-of-war for instant service, when further on in the document he read the stern admonition that under no circumstances was he to let the navy department know what he, a subordinate, was doing with one of the warships of the navy?

Even General Crawford, loyal Unionist that he was, found this difficult of explanation. The best he could make of it was that the president and the secretary of state had "no desire to slight either the War or Navy departments. They were yet in an unorganized condition," he continued, "and the Secretary of State did not even trust his own Department." So far, so good; apparently the general was making progress toward a plausible explanation; but he could not quite manage it. Giving it up as a bad job, he wrote, "But why the Secretary of the Navy, the chosen and trusted counsellor of the President should have been included in this determination, is not so clear." [25] Later Gideon Welles, the secretary in question, and, as it happened, less a master of disciplined restraint of expression than Crawford, also commented on the occurrence. He said that when confidential friends of the administration learned from letters of Lincoln and Seward that these officials were giving to Captain Meigs and Lieutenant Porter "unlimited authority over the military and naval service —confessedly without the knowledge of the Secretary of War or the Secretary of the Navy—they were alarmed for the safety and welfare of the Government. It betrayed weakness in the executive head." [26]

A reader of the order addressed to the commandant of the New York navy yard, if he regarded its writer as re-

[25] *Genesis of the Civil War,* pp. 419, 420.
[26] *Diary of Gideon Welles,* I, 38.

sponsible, would have no option other than to conclude
that there was impending some disaster of tragic proportions. Otherwise it would tax credulity to believe that, in
addition to all other reinforcements rushed to the scene,
Lincoln considered it imperative to send the *Powhatan* so
hurriedly on so carefully guarded a mission. In the same
connection, surely it would be only natural to inquire:
unless he believed that he was facing a crucial emergency,
what could have induced the president, dealing with a
matter which so vitally concerned the department of the
navy, expressly to exclude from his confidence the secretary of that department whom he had placed in his cabinet
less than one month before?

Something was going on in the wings. Lincoln was
no weakling. No passing rumor could stampede him. He
was able, shrewd, coolly practical. Could it be that some
interested group, possessed of influence not to be with-
stood, was resorting to powerful pressure? Or was the
chief executive the voice of a war faction which was ready
to welcome a break? Unless one or the other alternative
is the answer, the personal issuance of the six emergency
orders in one day is comparable to the conduct of one
.unning about town, turning in alarms which call out
every available unit of fire-fighting apparatus—when
there is no fire.

A CAPTAIN IGNORES A GENERAL'S ORDER

It was just eight days after Lincoln's inauguration
that the order went out to Captain Vogdes [26a] to seize
the first favorable opportunity to place his company in
Fort Pickens. For some undisclosed reason it was not
until nineteen days later that it reached him. He and his

26a See p. 35, *supra.*

troops were still on the *Brooklyn.* As commander of all Federal naval forces at Pensacola, it was the prerogative of Captain Adams to direct movements of naval vessels on the station. On April first, the day after Scott's order arrived, Vogdes sent Adams this note: "Herewith I send you a copy of an order received by me last night. You will see by it that I am directed to land my company at the earliest opportunity. I have therefore to request that you will place at my disposal such boats and other means as will enable me to carry into effect the enclosed order." [27]

Captain Adams was the officer whom Captain Barron had in mind when he said in a former report that he would deliver to the senior naval officer of the squadron the originals of the letters from Senator Mallory and Colonel Chase, and the telegram from the secretaries of the war and navy departments. This Barron had done. Therefore, the initial papers constituting the armistice were in Adams' possession. The pacific arrangements which they accomplished, he had mentioned in a letter to the secretary of the navy. The telegram signed by Secretaries Holt and Toucey had said very plainly that the Federal officers were not to land the troops "unless said fort shall be attacked or preparations shall be made for its attack.[28]

In so far as it concerned Adams, that order stood. Now, however, Vogdes, with instructions bearing the signature of Scott, was asking his coöperation in what, to his thinking, amounted to a deliberate violation of the armistice. What could all this mean? Surely someone had blundered. The same day, April first, he sent the Vogdes note and a copy of the Scott order to Secretary of the Navy Welles:

"Sir: I have the honor to inclose a copy of a letter addressed to me by Captain Vogdes, U. S. Army,

[27] *O. R. N.,* Ser. 1, Vol. IV, p. 110.   [28] *Ibid.,* p. 74.

who is here in command of some troops sent out in January last to reenforce the garrison of Fort Pickens. I have declined to land the men as Captain Vogdes requests, as it would be in direct violation of the orders from the Navy Department under which I am acting.

"The instructions from General Scott to Captain Vogdes are of old date (March 12) and may have been given without a full knowledge of the condition of affairs here. They would be no justification to me. Such a step is too important to be taken without the clearest orders from proper authority. It would most certainly be viewed as a hostile act, and would be resisted to the utmost. No one acquainted with the feelings of the military assembled under General Bragg can doubt that it would be considered not only a declaration but an act of war. It would be a serious thing to bring on by any precipitation a collision which may be entirely against the wishes of the Administration. At present both sides are faithfully observing the agreement entered into by the U. S. Government with Mr. Mallory and Colonel Chase. This agreement binds us not to reenforce Fort Pickens unless it should be attacked or threatened. It binds them not to attack it unless we should attempt to reenforce it. I saw General Bragg on the 30th ultimo, who reassured me the conditions on their part should not be violated. While I can not take on myself under such insufficient authority as General Scott's order the fearful responsibility of an act which seems to render civil war inevitable, I am ready at all times to carry out whatever orders I may receive from the honorable Secretary of the Navy.

"In conclusion, I beg you will please send me instructions as soon as possible, that I may be relieved from a painful embarrassment." [29]

So, despite his knowledge that the order exhibited to him by Vogdes bore the signature of the commanding

[29] *Ibid.*, pp. 109, 110.

general of the army of the United States, Captain Adams declined flatly to obey it.[30] His refusal to become a party to what he considered a repudiation of an explicit compact which he and all officers at Pensacola, Federal and Confederate alike, were in honor bound to respect, created consternation in Washington. Nicolay's reaction was that, while the incident was a source of mortification, the captain's unquestionable loyalty exonerated him from serious blame.[31] To what he called the January truce the same writer attributed responsibility for the entire affair.[32] Writing on the same subject, Secretary Welles observed that the naval officer was depending for justification upon the obligation of the armistice; in the discussion the secretary revealed his knowledge of the agreement, and of the connection with it of two members of the preceding cabinet, as well as of its terms. Neither he nor Nicolay intimated that, as of the date of Adams' reputed disobedience, the parties had terminated the armistice by agreement or otherwise.

Regardless of his personal convictions, his suspicion that government wires were crossed, Captain Adams was an officer of the navy, orders were orders, and he would, as a matter of course, execute such instructions as might be forthcoming from the only authoritative source, the department of the navy. That he believed, once it understood the true conditions, Washington would approve his course and revoke the order is shown by his concluding, apparently confident appeal for instructions which would free him from painful embarrassment. All of which means

[30] Channing, *A Students' History of the United States,* p. 484; Nicolay and Hay, *Lincoln,* IV, 7; Evans, *Confederate Military History,* XI, 23; Tarbell, *The Life of Abraham Lincoln,* III, 19.

[31] Nicolay and Hay, *Lincoln,* IV, 8.

[32] Nicolay, *The Outbreak of Rebellion,* p. 53.

that, in language as outspoken as he dared, a high-minded navy officer was saying in effect:

The United States government has agreed not to do the very act this order commands. We have given our word not to reinforce the fort under existing conditions and the obligation involves our personal honor. Even at General Scott's instance I am unwilling to repudiate this armistice agreement without the slightest provocation from the Southerners who have the right to expect us to keep the faith even as they are keeping it. All of us on this station, honored with the confidence and trust of our opponents, are suffering painful embarrassment. If you send word to land the troops, I will place them in the fort. However, the department should not issue such instructions without full appreciation of what to me appears the bad faith involved in such conduct. You, as the official to whom we look for guidance, must tell me what to do—must share responsibility.

Chapter IV

THE SCRAP-OF-PAPER DOCTRINE

WELLES ORDERS ADAMS TO COÖPERATE WITH VOGDES

Prior to appointment to a post which carried responsibility for directing operations of the United States navy, Gideon Welles' career was that of lawyer, newspaperman, and politician. In full keeping with this circumstance, he owed his place in the cabinet to a president who, in the words of one of his biographers, "probably enough had never seen an ocean-going ship." [1] The communication from Captain Adams placed squarely up to him assumption of responsibility. What had Gideon Welles to say in response to the earnest appeal, one based on such unanswerable reasons? The answer, marked "Confidential," went out on April sixth:

"SIR: Your dispatch of April 1 is received. The Department regrets that you did not comply with the request of Captain Vogdes to carry into effect the orders of General Scott sent out by the *Crusader* under the orders of the Department.

"You will immediately on the first favorable opportunity after receipt of this order afford every facility to Captain Vogdes by boats and other means to enable him to land the troops under his command, it being the wish and intention of the Navy Department to cooperate with the War Department in that object.

"I am, sir, respectfully, etc.,

"GIDEON WELLES." [2]

[1] *Diary of Gideon Welles,* I, xxi (Introduction written by John T. Morse, Jr.).   [2] *O. R. N.,* Ser. I, Vol. IV, pp. 110-111.

This was not only an absolute order to coöperate in the reinforcement project, but a thinly glossed official rebuke to an officer who shrank from a step which, as he saw it, involved disparagement of his word of honor, violation of an obligation of his government, rupture of peaceful relations, probable commencement of war. Such considerations, so potent as to give pause to a captain of the navy, apparently failed to impress the naval representative of the new administration. In Welles' answer there was no hint of excuse for riding roughshod over the agreement; it did not so much as mention the armistice. The secretary chose to invoke the scrap-of-paper doctrine. "The agreement entered into by the United States government"—what of it? The "painful embarrassment" of the squadron commander—he would not humor such squeamishness. To the captain's deliberate warning he gave no consideration. Crisp and curt, the answer said in effect: "You asked for orders. You have them now. Execute them."

There was one other person who would have learned the meaning of the words "painful embarrassment" had he foreseen that the future would bring two comments, observations singularly at variance. The first is from Lincoln's private secretary: "The exposed situation of Fort Pickens had become known to Lincoln, and one of his earliest official acts was to order its reinforcement from the fleet; *but of the conditions of the January truce he was not informed.*" [3] Holding in mind that Adams' memorable protest went to Welles, set out the details of the armistice which Nicolay called the January truce, stated that the United States government was a party to it, gave assurance of its faithful observance by both sides, warned that its violation would mean war, the

[3] Nicolay, *The Outbreak of Rebellion*, p. 51. Italics supplied.

ground is cleared for the second comment, one from the pen of Gideon Welles himself: "*I went immediately to the President with Captain Adams's communication,* and we both deemed it absolutely essential that a special messenger should be forthwith sent overland with orders to immediately land the troops." [4]

THE REPUDIATION OF THE ARMISTICE PACT

When Secretary Welles prepared his answer to the protest from Captain Adams, the administration program of secretiveness forbade its transmittal through the mails. According to the secretary's own account, there was in Washington such an atmosphere of uncertainty and suspicion as to cause him grave anxiety in selecting someone to whom he could entrust such an important paper.[5] He finally chose Lieutenant John L. Worden. Arriving at Pensacola after a hurried trip, Worden secured an interview with General Bragg, to whom he represented himself as the bearer of verbal messages of a pacific nature from the department of the navy to Captain Adams. His apparent sincerity so impressed the Confederate commander that he readily granted the lieutenant permission to visit the fleet. On April twelfth Worden delivered Welles' order to Adams; thereupon, in pursuance of the policy of urgent haste, that very night Captain Adams transferred Vogdes and his artillery company from the warship into Fort Pickens.[6]

After accomplishing the object of his mission, Worden lost no time getting ashore to begin the return journey to Washington. On the trip down there was no real rea-

[4] *Diary of Gideon Welles,* I, 29-30. Italics supplied.
[5] *Ibid.,* p. 30.
[6] Scharf, *History of the Confederate States Navy,* p. 606; Evans, *Confederate Military History,* XI, 23.

son to hurry; but there was excellent inspiration for
haste on the way back, and he knew it. Under pressure
of the imperative demand for speed, none of the participants had paused to reflect that they might very well
defer for a day or two the execution of the instruction
in order that Worden might pass safely beyond reach
of Confederate agencies. This lack of foresight resulted
in a troublesome complication. He had hardly begun his
return journey when Confederate Secretary of War
Walker telegraphed Bragg to intercept the dispatches
which Worden had in his possession. Bragg replied:

> "Barrancas, *April 12, 1861.*
> "Mr. Worden had communicated with fleet before
> your dispatch received. Alarm guns have just fired
> at Fort Pickens. I fear the news is received and it
> will be reenforced before morning. It can not be
> prevented. Mr. Worden got off in cars before I
> knew of his landing. Major Chambers is in the cars.
> He will watch Mr. Worden's movements. If you deem
> it advisable, Mr. Worden can be stopped in Mont-
> gomery." [7]

Just what it was the record does not reveal, but something had occurred to prompt an arrangement for an
unknown and unsuspected traveling companion for Worden. The landing of Vogdes' company so soon after his
call on Captain Adams struck Confederate leaders as
rather more than a coincidence.[8] Accordingly, Bragg
ordered Worden's arrest. Officers intercepted him in
Montgomery and took him into custody.[9] On the thirteenth Secretary Walker telegraphed General Bragg,

---

[7] *O. R. N.,* Ser. 1, Vol. IV, p. 135.
[8] *Diary of Gideon Welles,* I, 31.
[9] Evans, *Confederate Military History,* XI, 23.
[10] *O. R. N.,* Ser. 1, Vol. IV, p. 135.

asking what instructions Worden carried at the time of his arrest.[10] Bragg answered:

"PENSACOLA, *April 14, 1861*
"Lieutenant Worden assured me he had only a verbal message of pacific nature. The reenforcement of Pickens was preceded by signal guns from there. What caused it I can not ascertain. Worden's message may have had no connection with the move. He was in Pensacola when the move was made. Five thousand men here now and 2,000 more coming. Subsistence, forage, and transportation should be hurried. You can now spare the supplies from Sumter, which is ours." [11]

Later the same day additional information was at hand and Bragg telegraphed Secretary Walker:

"Captain Adams, commanding the fleet, writes on 13th, just received. Subsequently to the date of your last letter, as you are probably aware, reenforcements have been placed in Fort Pickens in obedience to orders from the U. S. Government. Lieutenant Worden must have given these orders in violation of his word. Captain Adams executed them in violation of our agreement." [12]

Thus the administration carried into action a thoroughly considered disregard of the armistice covenant. In view of the laudable purpose which inspired all parties concerned in the making of the compact, the prominence and official status of the United States representatives who pledged the faith of their government, the repeated ratification by Federal officers on the station, the moving appeal to Welles by naval commander Adams, it does not make pleasant reading.

Strong suspicion of Worden's complicity in the scheme

[11] *Ibid.*, p. 136. Beauregard had taken Sumter on April thirteenth. See Chaps. XII and XIII, *infra*.   [12] *Ibid.*, p. 135.

fell short of definite proof of guilt; accordingly, a few months later, the Confederates released him. Later he was to be the happy recipient of a signal honor; on February 4, 1863, the president of the United States nominated him to receive a captain's commission in the army.[13] In a report made September 20, 1865, to G. V. Fox, acting-secretary of the navy, Captain Worden reviewed his April, 1861, experience. Fox had instructed him to provide the department with a copy of the order under which he had proceeded to Pensacola in April, 1861 "as a bearer of dispatches." In his answer, Worden said:

". . . I never received a written order to proceed on that duty. Late in the evening of April 6 I was sent for by the Secretary of the Navy (Hon. Gideon Welles) and was verbally ordered by him to proceed with all possible speed to Pensacola with dispatches for Captain Adams. . . . I started early next morning . . . reaching Pensacola about midnight of April 10. On April 11 by the time I was enabled to reach the *Wyandotte*, then lying inside the harbor under Fort Pickens, the wind was blowing so hard that her commander declined to take me out to the squadron. The next day (April 12) I was taken out and delivered the dispatches about noon, or rather the substance of them, having destroyed the dispatches near Atlanta, Ga." [14]

It thus indubitably appears not only that Welles gave Worden written dispatches, but that the lieutenant carried them as far as Atlanta, at which point there dawned on him realization that it might be just as well that they should not be found on his person. His September, 1865,

---

[13] *A Compilation of the Messages and Papers of the Presidents, 1789-1897* (10 vols. Washington, 1896-99), VI, 151.
[14] *O. R. N.*, Ser. 1, Vol. IV, p. 111.

statement, made after all danger had passed, varies rather strikingly from the fiction in which he indulged in his April, 1861, declaration to Bragg; namely, that he had only a verbal message of a pacific nature. That Worden was expert in adaptation of his utterances to the exigency of whatever occasion presented itself, he further demonstrated by his statement from Montgomery on April 16, to the Confederate secretary of war, while he was under arrest:

"I left Washington City on the morning of April 7 with a communication from the Secretary of the Navy to Captain Adams, of the U. S. ship *Sabine*, and was informed by the Secretary that I would have no difficulty in making the communication to Captain Adams under the existing agreement. I arrived at Pensacola on the morning of the 11th instant, announced myself to Mr. LeBaron as an officer of the U. S. Navy, who sent an officer with me to General Bragg. I informed General Bragg that I had come from Washington, and desired to communicate with Captain Adams. . . . He wrote me a pass authorizing me to go to the *Sabine*, and upon handing it to me he asked if I had dispatches for Captain Adams. I replied that I had not written ones, but that I had a verbal communication to make to him from the Navy Department. I then asked him if I would be permitted to land on my return toward Washington. He replied that I would, provided Captain Adams or myself did nothing in violation of the agreement existing between them. I remarked that I knew nothing of the agreement he mentioned. . . .

". . . I made my communication to Captain Adams and stated to him what General Bragg had said in relation to the agreement between them. He nevertheless gave me a written order to return to Washington as 'special messenger,' which order you have. . . . I was told by Captain Adams that it was

not necessary for me to see General Bragg on my
return, and therefore I did not stop at his quarters.

"I make this statement, ready with the solemnity
of an oath to be confirmed. It is made not with regard to personal safety or of any consequences that
might result to me personally, but purely in defense
of my honor as an officer and a gentleman. . . ." [15]

So the secretary of the navy did know of the "existing
agreement." More than this, he was putting his knowledge to good account. In full keeping with the attitude
of the new administration relative to the situation at
Pensacola, Welles actually informed Worden that this
very understanding would remove all obstacles from his
path. Here is revealed a strange sense of honor. Deliberate advantage is taken of an agreement, described by
Captain Adams himself as entered into by the United
States government, to make it possible for a member of
the cabinet to arrange furtive delivery of a command for
its ruthless repudiation.

The orders entrusted to Worden were in writing,
marked "confidential." In spite of his official report to
the secretary of the navy that he destroyed the dispatches,
the message addressed to Captain Adams, signed by
Welles, shows up in the official records compiled and
published by the United States government.[16] Furthermore, upon his arrival in territory under Confederate
control, the Southern officers graciously received Worden
and extended him every courtesy.[17] Believing that he
was dealing with an officer and a gentleman, General
Bragg granted his request to go out to the *Sabine*. Gideon
Welles had judged aright; the armistice-pact solved all

[15] *Ibid.*, pp. 136-137.　　　　　　　[16] *Ibid.*, pp. 110-111.
[17] *Ibid.*, pp. 136-137.

difficulties which otherwise might have impeded his messenger.

In his statement to the Confederate secretary of war, Worden made two declarations which it is difficult to reconcile; the first, that, before he left Washington, Welles told him that he would experience no difficulty in reaching Adams "under the existing agreement." This must have suggested to him that there was in force between opposing factions at Pensacola some sort of understanding. Yet a few sentences later in the same paper, after mentioning Bragg's statement that he would not be denied permission to land on his return from the fleet, provided neither he nor Adams should do anything in violation of the "agreement existing" between them, Worden wrote that he thereupon remarked that he knew nothing of any such arrangement. Strangest of all, he saw fit to conclude his statement with an offer to make oath to its truthfulness. Proudly he affirmed his indifference to considerations of personal safety, insisting that he was writing in defense of his honor as an officer and a gentleman. Whatever the effect of this performance on his honor, it accomplished his purpose; it saved him from the inconvenience of being dealt with as a spy.

A fitting conclusion to the story of the reinforcement is provided in a letter of April thirtieth in which Captain Adams reviewed for a brother naval officer, Captain Du Pont, his predicament of a few weeks before. After his arrival at Pensacola, he wrote, orders had come "four times repeated, not to enter the harbor, but to remain off Fort Pickens ready to cooperate in its defense if it was attacked, and to act strictly on the defensive." He came to the matter of the reinforcement order:

"The *Brooklyn* brought an order from General Scott to Captain Vogdes to land his troops at Fort

Pickens. Vogdes applied to me for boats. I refused, stating that it would be in direct violation of the orders under which I was acting from the Navy Department, and I could receive none from General Scott. At this time a sort of armistice existed by which we were bound not to reenforce Fort Pickens unless it was assaulted or threatened, and the other side were not to assault it unless we undertook to reenforce it. This armistice was entered into by the Secretary of War and of the Navy on our side and Mr. Mallory and Colonel Chase on theirs, and my orders were based on it. I wrote, however, immediately to Mr. Welles; told him what I had done, but that though I could receive no orders from General Scott I was ready to carry out any he might choose to give. I sent this communication by an officer of the Army to Washington and received an immediate answer by Lieutenant Worden. That answer I received about 2 o'clock on the 12th instant. It was an order to land the troops, and by 12 o'clock that night it was done, without collision and without discovery, I think, till it was accomplished." [18]

The import is clear. Eighteen days after he carried out the administration's reinforcement scheme, Captain Adams was not retreating an inch from the position taken by him in his April first letter to Gideon Welles.

"THIS IS THE BEGINNING OF THE WAR"

The record has brought to light Secretary Welles' sharp criticism of Lincoln and Seward because of their granting unprecedented authority to an army captain and a navy lieutenant.[19] Lieutenant Porter, whom the president had seen fit secretly to place in command of the *Powhatan*, was one of the officers the secretary had in

18 *O. R. N.*, Ser. 1, Vol. IV, p. 125.
19 *Diary of Gideon Welles*, I, 38.

mind.[20] The second of the favored subordinates was Captain M. C. Meigs who introduces himself in a report of April sixth to Secretary Seward. Army captains are under supervision of, and answerable to, the secretary of war. Captain Meigs' overriding army routine by reporting to the secretary of state instead of to the secretary of war affords illustration of the secrecy in vogue, as well as of Seward's intermeddling in army and navy affairs. The contents of his letter justify the inference that, behind closed doors of executive mansion and state department, certain officials had held conferences, knowledge of which would have resulted in an epidemic of apoplexy among ranking officials of army and navy. His communication said:

> "By great exertions, within less than six days from the time the subject was broached in the office of the President, a war steamer sails from this port; and the Atlantic, built under contract to be at the service of the United States in case of war, will follow this afternoon with 500 troops. The Illinois will follow on Monday with the stores which the Atlantic could not hold.
> "While the mere throwing of a few men into Fort Pickens may seem a small operation, the opening of a campaign is a great one.
> "Unless this movement is followed up by the navy and supported by ample supplies . . . it will be a failure. This is the beginning of the war which every statesman and soldier has foreseen since the passage of the South Carolina ordinance of secession. You will find the Army and the Navy clogged at the head with men, excellent patriotic men, men who were soldiers and sailors forty years ago, but who now merely keep active men out of the places in which they could serve the country. . . .

[20] *O. R. N.*, Ser. 1, Vol. IV, p. 109.

". . . Let us be supported; we go to serve our country; and our country should not neglect us or leave us to be strangled in tape, however red." [21]

Rarely has a letter told as much in as few words. "The subject broached in the office of the President." What subject? Meigs gives the clew. Bearing the date of April sixth, his letter carries information that, "within six days" from the date of the discussion in the executive office, a war steamer was sailing. This fixes the time of the conference at about April first and it is more than a coincidence that this was the day on which Lincoln had issued his six personally signed emergency orders. One of these was for the fitting out of the *Powhatan*. Its urgency had inspired strenuous exertion to complete the work. Now the warship was on the way. Not officially classed a military or naval expert, Lincoln was giving a convincing exhibition of what a man can accomplish once he has made up his mind and charted his course. The document leaves no doubt that those in the executive-office conference understood what the consequences would be. At any rate, Meigs thought he knew: "This is the beginning of the war."

It was long afterward that the letter became accessible to others than the executive-office conferees. Its closing sentences throw wide the door to further appreciation of the intemperate outburst of the secretary of the navy. A captain, a military underling, was going over the heads of generals, admirals, secretaries of war and navy. He was confiding to Seward the observation that both army and navy were top-heavy with resplendently uniformed fossils, very nice old chaps to be sure, but ineffective these forty years, who, incidentally, were devoting their energies to holding back active men—captains, for example—

[21] *O. R. A.,* Ser. 1, Vol. I, p. 368

thereby depriving the country of the services of repressed genius. Had the letter appeared on the bulletin board of the department of war, what a tribal uprising Washington would have witnessed! The tom-toms would have sounded, the chiefs would have lighted the fires for the dance of death, and, with the conclusion of the ceremonies, there would have been one loose-tongued brave stripped of his feathers, and possibly around the council fire, lamentation for a voice that was stilled.

Four days later, at sea, Captain Meigs again favored Secretary Seward:

> "The dispatch and the secrecy with which this expedition has been fitted out will strike terror into the ranks of rebellion. All New York saw, all the United States knew, that the Atlantic was filling with stores and troops. But now this nameless vessel, her name painted out, speeds out of the track of commerce to an unknown destination. Mysterious, unseen, where will the powerful bolt fall? What thousands of men, spending the means of the Confederate States, vainly beat the air amid the swamps of the southern coast, and, filling the dank forts, curse secession and the mosquitoes!
>
> "Buy all the steamships, fill them with troops and stores, start them on such mysterious errands, and Mr. Memminger will need more loans and South Carolina herself will grow sick of rebellion.
>
> "God promised to send before his chosen people an advance-guard of hornets. Our constant allies are the more efficient mosquitoes and sand-flies. . . ." [22]

Meigs' talents transcended mere military limitations. He waxed dramatic, but flights of bombast in no wise obscured the significance of his utterance. It is to be regretted that he was not quite definite as to whether the

[22] *Ibid.*, p. 369.

Almighty provided also the latter-day chosen people's shock troops of mosquitoes and sandflies. Nevertheless, the captain may be forgiven much. Posterity is indebted to him for a distinct service. Definitely he located responsibility for one of the outstanding tragedies of all time: "The office of the President."

"WE OBEYED ORDERS"

At his first opportunity after placing Vogdes' company in the fort, on April fourteenth Captain Adams reported to Secretary Welles the details of the movement:

> ". . . immediately on receipt of your order by Lieutenant Worden, on the 12th instant, I prepared to reinforce Fort Pickens. It was successfully performed the same night by landing the troops under Captain Vogdes and the marines of the squadron under Lieutenant Cash. No opposition was made nor do I believe the movement was known on shore until it was accomplished. A strong party of officers and seamen were sent to assist in case of resistance. . . .
> "The whole expedition was under the charge of Commander C. H. Poor. . . . The *Brooklyn*, Captain Walker, and the *Wyandotte*, Lieutenant Commanding Mullany, were very skillfully managed. They carried the landing party to the designated point with accuracy, in spite of the darkness of the night, and not having the light-house to guide them, the light having been extinguished early in the evening." [23]

From a technical viewpoint, the operation was a pronounced success. Not only the troops under Vogdes, but all marines of the entire fleet were safely in the fort. No occasion had arisen to use the detachment of officers and seamen; they encountered no opposition for the simple

[23] *O. R. N.*, Ser. 1, Vol. IV, p. 115.

reason that the Confederates were lulled into relaxation of watchfulness by their implicit trust in the Federal officers who, since becoming parties to the armistice, had ratified it again and again. The *Brooklyn* of the fleet outside the harbor, and the *Wyandotte*, detailed for service inside as Slemmer's convenience might require, their respective crews had handled with such perfect technique as to call for special commendation. Navigation had proved the more difficult by reason of the time chosen for the operation—"the darkness of the night."

Leading participants in this somewhat hazardous, but, for them, happily triumphant, project were Captain Vogdes, Captain Walker, Lieutenant Slemmer, and Captain Adams.

Vogdes was the officer who two months before wrote the adjutant-general to construe his report only as urging the assembly of a sufficient force to meet the issue should anything happen to bring about rupture of the agreement. And no one knew better than Vogdes that nothing of the sort had occurred. Walker was one of the officers addressed by name in the order prohibiting reinforcement except in the event of an attack. To the captain's certain knowledge, no suggestion of attack had come. Slemmer also was one of the recipients of the stop order of the two cabinet members. It was he to whom the commanding Confederate general had pledged strict conformity to the spirit of the engagement. And the lieutenant was aware that neither Bragg nor any of his associated officers had veered an inch from this course. Adams was the very man to whom Barron had entrusted the originals of the armistice documents. Not only had he repeatedly insisted that reinforcement would violate the armistice, but he had gone on record that both sides were keeping the faith. In the light of this knowledge, he had refused point-blank to obey General Scott's command. When, at Welles' insistence, he executed the landing order, he well knew that the Southerners had carried out to the letter their obligation under the agreement.

The landing was successful, it is true, but there was another side to it; at best it constituted a rather questionable performance. Thoroughly conversant with the armistice, in the consummation of which indeed three of the four had personally participated, with full consciousness of the absence of provocation on the part of their opponents, these were the United States army and navy officers whom the lash of the new administration drove to a course which they knew involved deliberate deception. As they doubtless expected, the reinforcement brought from the Confederate commander an indignant protest. Vogdes wrote Captain Adams:

> "General Bragg has just sent me a verbal message by his adjutant-general, Colonel Wood, requesting to know why the armistice had been violated by reenforcing Fort Pickens. In reply I stated that I never had been a party to any armistice, but that in landing from the *Brooklyn* . . . I had acted under orders from the General Government. He then stated that he was directed by General Bragg to demand from the late commander, addressing himself to Lieutenant Slemmer, why it had been violated on his part. He answered that he obeyed the orders of his government. No further official communication passed between us." [24]

Nor did the Confederate general confine to Vogdes and Slemmer his embarrassing questioning. Captain Adams, it appears, had taken the trouble officially to notify Bragg of the movement. On the fourteenth, he read a stern rebuke:

[24] *Ibid.,* p. 117.

"Your communication of the 13th instant, announcing the reenforcement of Fort Pickens, was received by me this evening. How you could suppose I was aware of the fact, and that it was done 'by order of the U. S. Government,' I do not understand, when it was accomplished under cover of the darkness of night and in violation of a solemn compact. I only wish I could construe the orders of your Government as a justification of the act." [25]

Plainly, Bragg was angered. He had fought the Seminoles in Florida, participated in the military occupation of Texas, taken his turn on the firing line during the Mexican War, but his experience had provided no comparable ruse. Besides, he knew personally some of the Federal officers at Pensacola. He had sat in class with Vogdes at the military academy. All he had honored with his respect and trust. The closing words of his message to Adams made known the keenness of a soldier's resentment of the stratagem: "I only wish I could construe the orders of your Government as a justification of the act."

None of the three was in a mood to attempt reply. They had to carry out orders, but they recognized no obligation to undertake to explain to a distinguished West Pointer how the violation of an armistice, entered into by the United States government, could be justified by instructions from that government.

They had outwitted the Confederates, they had done the job, the reinforcements were in the fort, they had notified Washington, Walker was back on the *Brooklyn*, Adams on the *Sabine;* but in the still of the following night, as two captains paced the deck, looked up at the silent stars, and reflected upon the work of the day, they could not have failed to realize that the success was dearly bought.

[25] *Ibid.*

CHAPTER V

THE DESCENT TO TRICKERY

LIEUTENANT PORTER'S GREAT DISAPPOINTMENT

The hurried fitting out of the *Powhatan*, the mysterious detaching of Captain Mercer, the withholding of information from the navy department, the confidential messenger with the sealed orders from the president are, by this time, an old story.

General Crawford provides additional particulars of a painstaking program of craftiness. When all was in readiness for the *Powhatan* to put to sea, a stranger in the uniform of a naval lieutenant came aboard and straightway went below. His personal effects bore the identifying mark "American Minister, Vera Cruz," but, oddly, carried no trace of his name. When the ship hoisted anchor and steamed out into the channel, Captain Mercer was on the bridge. The newcomer, "unseen and unknown," was behind closed doors. Arriving opposite Staten Island, Mercer stopped the ship, beckoned to his ranking junior officer, walked with him down to the stateroom, and, after introducing Lieutenant Porter as the future commander, immediately left to go ashore. Remaining in his room, the new commander warned the junior officer not to divulge his presence until after they dropped the pilot.[1]

The record has shown that Captain M. C. Meigs, one of the subordinates whose exaltation above their superiors so aroused Secretary Welles, was not only making his

[1] *The Genesis of the Civil War,* pp. 413-414.

reports to the secretary of state, but gratuitously giving offense by volunteering his verdict that the incompetence of officers of highest rank was crippling the usefulness of both army and navy. In the matter of reporting, Navy Lieutenant D. D. Porter, the other officer whom Welles had in mind, was following a similar course. On April twenty-first he forwarded, not to the department of the navy, but to Seward, a note with the rather arresting suggestion that the secretary lay it before the president. He was writing to acquaint these dignitaries with the reasons for his still being outside the harbor of Pensacola. Noting that he had arrived only a few hours behind the *Atlantic*, he proceeded to make a record of some gripping information:

> "I had disguised the ship so that she deceived those who had known her, and after nearing our squadron, was standing in (unnoticed) when the steam gunboat *Wyandotte* . . . commenced making signals to me, which I did not answer, but stood on. The steamer then put herself in my way, and Captain Meigs, who was on board, hailed me and I stopped. In twenty minutes more I should have been inside or sunk." [2]

If solely on his own initiative he was adopting such a course, it was assuredly an ambitious performance on the part of a mere lieutenant, this sailing the high seas in a United States warship under disguise. Could those sealed orders brought by the confidential messenger from the president have included instructions so to camouflage the *Powhatan* as completely to conceal her identity? This, however, is not all the story. More than a year after Welles had placed Captain Adams in such an awkward dilemma, the incident was still a live topic of discussion in the navy. As if to fortify the position taken by his

[2] *O. R. N.*, Ser. 1, Vol. IV, pp. 122-123.

brother naval officer, Captain C. H. Poor wrote Captain
Adams:

> "I know that during the first period of your com-
> mand an armistice existed which required that noth-
> ing should be done by the ships that could be con-
> strued into a reenforcement of Fort Pickens, during
> which time the squadron enjoyed many advantages
> in procuring supplies from the port and navy yard.
> . . . In the meantime every preparation was made
> to land a force (night or day) in case the rebels
> should violate the armistice and make an attack.
> Men, marines, boats, and officers were detailed and
> kept in a constant state [of] readiness to embark.
> . . . Subsequently an order was received to reen-
> force. . . .
> ". . . I recollect that upon the approach of the
> *Powhatan* under English colors, with the purpose,
> as afterward ascertained, of entering the port, her
> destination was changed by the request of Colonel
> Meigs, who had seen the enemy's strength, the con-
> dition of affairs in the fort, and conferred with its
> commander." [3]

Captain Poor was commander of the *St. Louis*, one
of the warships lying off Pensacola harbor at the time
of the arrival of the orders signed by Secretaries Holt
and Toucey. His ship remained on the station and he
not only was a witness of what occurred, but was in
charge of the operation of landing the troops. His ready
disclosure that he shared the view of Captain Adams as
to the obligation of the armistice may be indicative of
the feeling in navy circles. His letter brings to light
another revelation; besides being effectively disguised, the
Powhatan was actually flying the flag of a friendly foreign power. It was common knowledge that British sympathy had greatly encouraged the Confederates. Had

[3] *Ibid.,* pp. 131-132.

someone figured it out that the English flag would command respect and, incidentally, disarm suspicion until the man-of-war should be in position inside the harbor? It was a dangerous mission on which the *Powhatan* was engaged and her entry into the port might easily have provoked a clash of arms. Such misuse of the British flag is not to be charged to personal stupidity. Porter was no fool. Within four years he was to become superintendent of the United States Military Academy. He knew precisely what he was about. Did those sealed orders intimate such resort to imposture? Could any naval officer have failed to realize that it involved likelihood of international complications? Would a mere lieutenant have dared to incur such risk without prior assurance that powerful influence would be available if things went wrong?

When Lincoln issued the *Powhatan* instructions, representatives of the Confederate government were in the capital where for weeks they had engaged in negotiations looking to a friendly separation. The armistice agreement had relaxed strained relations at Pensacola. With the stealthy landing of reinforcements on the twelfth of April, however, there had come a decided rise in feeling. On that very day, it so happened, news had come of what was going on at Charleston; there, the Federals had gone too far and they had heard from Beauregard's batteries. This had suggested similar procedure at Pensacola; why not give Slemmer a dose of what Anderson had tasted? The war witches were furiously stirring the hellbroth, but Bragg's masterful hand had succeeded in scattering the embers; nevertheless, the cauldron was still simmering, and fuel in abundance was not far to seek.

Straight into this tense situation, enveloped by a cloud of mystery and deception, the powerful *Powhatan* was steaming. Her commander held orders from Lincoln to prevent at any cost or risk an expedition from the mainland from reaching the fort. The threat of a critical emergency inspired immediate action on the part of the Federal officers on the station. In Captain Poor's words, "Her destination was changed by the request of Colonel Meigs"; [4] but the captain understated the occurrence. Not so well disguised after all, she was recognized by Colonel Brown and Captain Meigs. Instantly resolving that such recklessness should be curbed, and with the intention of boarding her to acquaint her commander with the hazard of his going in, Meigs signaled from the *Wyandotte*. Ignoring the signals from a sister ship of the navy, Porter headed for the harbor entrance with unslackened speed. This was simple madness, Meigs thought, and he risked a desperate measure; on his order the captain of the *Wyandotte* moved his ship directly across the course of the *Powhatan*, thereby presenting to Porter the alternative of stopping, or of ramming a Union ship. [5]

The moment had come when the glorified army captain was essaying to control the glorified navy lieutenant. True, Porter was acting directly under orders of the president, but Meigs likewise was rather confident of his position. Going on board, he handed Porter a communication, dated April seventeenth, which set forth that, for the purpose of avoiding a collision, he felt it his duty to request postponement of the *Powhatan's* entering. The note had more to say: "My connection with the expedition [and] my knowledge of the views and intentions of the President justify me in making this request with almost the force of an order from the President." [6]

---

[4] *O. R. N.*, Ser. 1, Vol. IV, p. 132.
[5] *Ibid.*, p. 123; Nicolay and Hay, *Lincoln*, IV, 16.
[6] *O. R. N.*, Ser. 1, Vol. IV, p. 123.

It thus appears that, five days after the reinforcement of Fort Pickens, officers of the Union forces were still writing one another of the necessity of preventing an outbreak. This means that even as late as April seventeenth the Confederates had not attacked the fort. How does this harmonize with the pretense that conditions demanded most urgent haste in going to the rescue of Slemmer and his garrison? Any inference that the Southerners had not acted because of their unpreparedness leaves meaningless Commander Poor's remark in the letter to Captain Adams that Colonel Meigs explained his desire for the *Powhatan* to remain outside by saying that he had "seen the enemy's strength." [7] The day following his receipt of the "request" from Meigs, Porter sent a note to Colonel Brown. Its opening sentence serves to emphasize the unprecedented nature of the incident: "In looking carefully over the orders of the President to me in relation to my entering the harbor I find them so imperative that they leave no margin for any contingency that may arise." [8]

What mattered it that conditions at Pensacola might have undergone a complete change since the date of his orders? Of what consequence was it that, in the judgment of the Federal officers in command at the port, his entering at that particular time would be calamitous? Who were they, anyway, to interfere with the president's plans? Nevertheless, the *Powhatan* remained outside. The matter had resolved itself into a simple issue, the common sense of the Union staff on the scene against ill-advised orders in the hands of Lieutenant Porter.

That he had ungraciously yielded to pressure, was still keen to carry out his instructions regardless of consequences, and resented the interference which had blocked

[7] *Ibid.,* p. 132.   [8] *Ibid.,* p. 123-124.

him is shown by a letter from Porter to Captain Adams in August, 1862. He wrote of his amazement upon his discovery of the authority reposed in Colonel Brown: "His orders from the President authorized him to call upon every naval officer for assistance and obedience to his orders." Mentioning the colonel's insistence that the fleet remain inactive until he should give the word, he acknowledged his irritation: "I know that the great disappointment of my life was not being permitted to enter the harbor . . . when my plans were so well laid and when I was certain of success." In his view, the unsoldierly irresolution of the commanding officer had deprived the navy of an opportunity: "The oft-expressed opinion of Colonel Brown that 'we must act on the defensive' prevented the Navy from showing that zeal it has since exhibited against stronger places than Pensacola." [9]

All of this supplies the key to the utter confusion which resulted from issuance of conflicting orders and secret manipulation of movements of naval vessels. According to Welles, in the absence of instructions from the navy department relative to either Porter or the *Powhatan*, Captain Adams was without obligation even to recognize the ship as part of his squadron. In the secretary's words, "While he could not disregard the strange instructions to which the Secretary of State had persuaded the President to affix his signature, there was nothing requiring his action as commander of the naval forces." [10] This seems to imply that the president might write all the orders he pleased, but the department of the navy would control the actions of naval officers.

Lieutenant Porter urged that his orders, emanating from the highest possible source, left no margin for any

9 *Ibid.*, p. 130.
10 *Diary of Gideon Welles*, I, 28.

contingency that might arise. Unfortunately, he did not foresee one possibility that not only might, but did, stalk forth to confound him; Colonel Brown likewise held orders from Lincoln, orders requiring "all officers of the army and navy" to aid "by every means in their power the expedition under the command of Colonel Brown." In the exercise of this near-blanket authority, the colonel stopped the *Powhatan*. More than a year afterward, Porter had not forgiven him.

"The great disappointment of my life." Who shall have heart to blame him? The Lincoln-Brown combination had rudely shattered a glorious dream—a dream that comes to every man—a dream of a moment when fame's spotlight will single him out, and an admiring world will pause to do him honor. History's page was waiting for his story—a story that was to end before the telling.

OPERA BOUFFE

Lincoln's order of April first for Porter to assume charge of the *Powhatan*, and another on the same day removing Mercer from command of the ship were, it turned out, preliminaries to another unique muddle. Matters might have worked out smoothly but for one hitch; under the reasonably pardonable delusion that his office required him to supervise, and empowered him to direct, movements of naval ships, Secretary of the Navy Welles issued on April fifth three orders, each stamped "confidential."

The first was for Captain Mercer, commanding the *Powhatan*. It stated that the warships *Powhatan*, *Pawnee*, *Pocahontas*, and *Harriet Lane* were to make up a squadron which, under Mercer's charge, was to proceed to Charleston, there to coöperate with an expedition arranged by the war department and headed by Captain G. V. Fox. The *Powhatan* was to "leave New York . . . in time to be off Charleston bar . . . on the morning of the 11th instant, there to await the arrival of the transport or transports with troops and stores."[11] The second was a telegram, giving instructions to Commander Foote, of the Brooklyn Navy Yard: "The Secretary of the Navy desires that all dispatch be made in preparing the *Powhatan* for sea. Recall officers by telegraph."[12] The third directed the commander of the Home Squadron at Norfolk to withdraw the *Powhatan*, the *Pawnee*, and the *Pocahontas* for "special service." [13]

The wires were sadly crossed.

As a matter of course, the secretary did not suspect that for some reason, undisclosed to official Washington, Lincoln was issuing sealed orders for naval vessels. Nor did he know that the president had relieved Captain Mercer of command of his ship. No information had come to him or to the department that, under orders from Lincoln, Porter was to take the *Powhatan* to Pensacola. General Crawford refers to the preparations for the expedition, "originating by the direct and personal authority of the President," as "unusual and contrary to official custom and departmental routine." [14] The general was putting it mildly; the contradictory instructions were playing havoc.

Some unforeseen complication arose. On the same day, April fifth, Welles wired Commander Foote a second message, "Delay the *Powhatan* for further instructions." [15]

11 *O. R. N.*, Ser. 1, Vol. IV, p. 235; Crawford, *The Genesis of the Civil War*, p. 406.
12 *O. R. N.*, Ser. 1, Vol. IV, p. 234.
13 *Ibid.*
14 *The Genesis of the Civil War*, p. 407.
15 *O. R. N.*, Ser. 1, Vol. IV, p. 237.

Here was more trouble and Lieutenant Porter gave vent to his impatience in a communication to Foote:

"I am with Captain Meigs and we are telegraphing to Mr. Seward. Meigs thinks Mr. Welles's telegram is bogus. Would he, think you, dare to countermand an order (written order) of the President? Meigs and myself (knowing all the circumstances) think it impossible. I shall stay over to-night to keep on telegraphing. So much depends on having no mistakes made in this matter. If you hear anything will you send me word? I will be at the yard at 6 o'clock in the morning." [16]

Porter and Meigs, singled out by Lincoln and Seward, were telegraphing, but not to the departments to which they owed obedience. As before, they were wiring the secretary of state. The real explanation, that Lincoln was not honoring Secretary Welles with his confidence, did not enter the lieutenant's mind. At the navy yard next morning Porter exhibited Lincoln's order to Commander Foote. Besides assigning Porter to the command of the *Powhatan*, it directed "all officers" to place at his disposal every facility for getting under way as soon as possible.[17] According to General Crawford, Foote was "very much astonished at a proceeding so unusual and so contrary to all naval and official precedent." The general adds that, while the commander's first inclination was to take the matter up by telegraph with the secretary of the navy, he abandoned this course after Porter impressed upon him "the *secrecy* of the orders, and their high source." [18]

The day following that on which he telegraphed Seward, Lieutenant Porter had his answer. The secretary

[16] *Ibid.,* p. 111-112.
[17] *Ibid.,* p. 108.
[18] *The Genesis of the Civil War,* p. 412.

of state, whose name had appeared with Lincoln's in the instruction of April first, wired a terse message, "Give the *Powhatan* up to Captain Mercer." [19] Seward soon made the discovery that someone else possessed the gift of conciseness of expression. A few hours later a telegram signed "D. D. Porter" said simply, "I received my orders from the President and shall proceed and execute them." [20] Open defiance from a subaltern of the navy must have appreciably jarred the second ranking official of the government of the United States.

Shortly after Lieutenant Porter put to sea, he heard from Commander Foote, but that the message was far from satisfactory his reply indicates:

> "The telegram you sent me afforded me no comfort; on the contrary, burdened me. Still the President says nothing and I must obey his orders; they are too explicit to be misunderstood. I got them from his own hand. He has not recalled them. . . . This is an unpleasant position to be in, but I will work out of it." [21]

As far as conditions would permit, Lincoln had pursued throughout a policy of taking no one into his confidence. From time to time he had transmitted orders by confidential messenger but that to which Porter refers he had entrusted to no one. What possible combination of circumstances could have brought it to pass that the president of the United States should, with his own hand, deliver his orders to a lieutenant of the navy?

Also after the sailing of the *Powhatan*, a telegram from Seward for Porter reached Commander Foote at the navy yard. Foote immediately telegraphed, this time not Seward, but Secretary Welles:

[19] *O. R. N.,* Ser. 1, Vol. IV, p. 112.   [20] *Ibid.*
[21] *Ibid.*

"The *Powhatan* sailed at 2:45 this afternoon, just before Mr. Seward's telegram reached me for Captain Porter. I have ordered a lieutenant to go after her in a steamer unless she is out of sight; she goes direct to sea; Captain Porter is aboard. I handed Captain Mercer your orders of yesterday . . . but Captains Meigs, Porter, and Mercer, after a consultation, concluded to have Porter go in *Powhatan*." [22]

Ever since the first experience with Porter on which, pointing to the exalted name signed to his order, the lieutenant had stopped him from inquiring of the secretary of the navy what it was all about, the irregularity of the procedure had troubled Commander Foote. With the appearance of the telegram from the secretary of state to a naval officer, he decided that it was high time the head of the navy department should know of this queer performance. A sidelight which attracts notice is his remark that a lieutenant was to go after the *Powhatan* "unless she is out of sight." He had no idea whether, on reaching the open sea, the ship would steam north, east, or south; "she goes direct to sea," his message said, and that told all he knew. He followed up his telegram with a letter to Secretary Welles, dated April sixth:

"Your orders of the 5th were received by Captain Mercer to-day. Captain Meigs, Lieutenant Porter, and Captain Mercer, after consultation, concluded that Lieutenant Porter should go out in the *Powhatan*, as the arrangements were vital to success; at least so I was informed, not being present at the consultation. . . . at 3 o'clock, when the *Powhatan* was out of sight, I received a dispatch directed to Lieutenant Porter from Mr. Seward, telling him to proceed without the *Powhatan*, as directed in the

dispatch to Captain Meigs. I have sent to New York
a lieutenant with orders to charter a steamer and
chase the *Powhatan,* unless there is no hope of over-
taking her." [23]

It was confusion confounded, but it was not lacking
in glamor. An officer on a hastily chartered steamer was
"chasing" the man-of-war with the object of delivering
to Porter the message from Seward. The commander of
the navy yard was giving away the secret that a conference of an army captain, a navy captain, and a navy
lieutenant had ended with a decision to disregard flatly
orders from the secretary of the navy and the secretary
of state.

In a report of April eighth to Welles, Captain Mercer
gave his version of the affair. His story was that while,
pursuant to the secretary's instruction, he was making
ready to assume command of the expedition, Porter and
Meigs showed up unexpectedly with an order which bore
the signature of the president. They represented to him
that the president would be displeased by any interference
with his plans. Confronted by contradictory orders, one
signed by Welles, the other by Lincoln, he was in a close
place. A choice had to be made, and he made it: "I regarded the order from the President of the United States
as imperative, and accordingly placed Lieutenant Porter
in command of the *Powhatan.*" [24]

At six o'clock on the afternoon of April sixth Foote
sent a note to Secretary Welles carrying both the good
news that Lieutenant Roe had overtaken the *Powhatan*
and the not-so-pleasing information as to what Lieutenant
Porter had said. He enclosed the report made by Roe:

[23] *Ibid.,* p. 238.
[24] Nicolay and Hay, *Lincoln,* IV, 5.

"The dispatch intrusted to me for Lieutenant Porter has been delivered into his hands. The *Powhatan* was below quarantine and under way for the Narrows when I reached her. Lieutenant Porter desired me to express his regrets to you that the dispatch came to his hands so late, and that it was too late to change his plans inasmuch as the *Atlantic* had already gone to sea." [25]

Welles had wired Commander Foote to delay the *Powhatan;* the ship had gone straightway to sea. Seward had wired Porter to give up the ship to Captain Mercer; Mercer had left and Porter had retained command. Porter sent his regrets.

All this rapid-fire correspondence and ticking of telegraph echoed in reverberations which shook official Washington. The record is doubtless the poorer by reason of its failure to preserve what unquestionably would have been a spicy contribution from Welles. While it does not reveal just what he did say, he must have given a rather impressive performance for, on May eleventh, he was the recipient of the following letter:

"Lieutenant D. D. Porter was placed in command of the steamer *Powhatan* and Captain Samuel Mercer was detached therefrom by my special order, and neither of them is responsible for any apparent or real irregularity on their part in connection with that vessel.

"Hereafter Captain Porter is relieved from that special service and placed under the direction of the Navy Department, from which he will receive instructions and to which he will report.

"ABRAHAM LINCOLN." [26]

COLONEL BROWN RESORTS TO CHICANERY

On the part of the Federal staff at Pensacola, the record has revealed an apparently sincere desire to steer

[25] *O. R. N.,* Ser. 1, Vol. IV, p. 239.   [26] *Ibid.,* p. 128.

clear of a collision. A few weeks after the date of the reinforcement, however, there developed a notable exception to this attitude. An event took place which unmasked in Colonel Brown, the new commander of Fort Pickens, something of the same spirit which characterized the Washington administration, one which promised, sooner or later, to throw wide the floodgates holding back a rapidly rising torrent of Southern exasperation. Among other measures incident to the defense of their position, the Confederates maintained a dry dock at Pensacola; slipping its moorings, it drifted into a position a mile or so distant from the fort. Discovering its presence, Colonel Brown on May twenty-second wrote General Bragg:

> "In my letter to you of the 17th ultimo I announced my intention of acting only on the defensive, unless assailed. Since then your so-called government has commenced an unholy, unjust, and parricidal war on our common country, and you personally have been almost constantly hostilely engaged in erecting batteries against this fort, and last night in anchoring a floating battery within range of and menacing my command. You will therefore be pleased to notice that I shall act on the offensive whenever the interests and honor of my country, in my opinion, require it." [27]

Bragg replied at once that, while Brown was at liberty to take the offensive at his pleasure, there was scant justification for his complaint relative to the erection of batteries inasmuch as he likewise was strengthening his own position. The general volunteered a word of advice to the colonel:

[27] *O. R. A.,* Ser. 1, Vol. I, p. 419.

"The merits of the controversy between our respective governments I choose not to discuss with you. Impartial history will decide that question for us; but I must insist on the propriety and necessity of your observing those courtesies of style and language which I have a right to expect from one holding your high position, in any future communication addressed to these headquarters." [28]

The rebuke fell on deaf ears. Replying the same day, carefully noting on his letter the exact hour of his writing, "2 p.m.," Colonel Brown wrote that, inasmuch as he was unable to learn the nature or object of the "vessel" threatening his fort, he must infer that Bragg designed some hostile act. He added a threat: "I have therefore to notify you that any effort to remove or to occupy her will be considered an act of hostility, which I shall resist with what means I possess, unless I shall receive a satisfactory explanation." [29]

Colonel Brown had discovered the "floating battery" the night before; by two o'clock of the following afternoon, it would seem, he had enjoyed ample opportunity to ascertain what the object was. Nevertheless, he went so far as to lay down his ultimatum. Great as was the provocation, the broad experience of Bragg here played him in good stead. He did not lose his head but, with the control of one who was willing to make large concessions in the interest of peace, answered that the imagined "vessel" was nothing more than a dry dock, unarmed and unmanned, which by accident had floated into the position in which Colonel Brown discovered it.[30]

Presumably, the fort's equipment included a field glass; besides, its commander was not so inexperienced as not to understand that Bragg would hardly have delayed until

[28] *Ibid.,* p. 420.   [29] *Ibid.*
[30] *Ibid.*

long after daybreak an intended surprise night attack. At the time of the colonel's last letter, although the dock had occupied its then position for eleven hours, including at least eight hours of broad daylight, nothing of a hostile nature had occurred. Nevertheless, Brown gave voice to what sounded like genuine alarm. Five days later, however, it developed that it was not fear which was influencing him. The truth came out when he reported the incident to the department of war. A brilliant idea had thrilled him with his first glimpse of the dock; here was his chance, one that, passed by, might not return. He wrote Assistant Adjutant General Townsend:

> "On Wednesday morning about 3 o'clock it was reported to me that the dry-dock was moving out. It had been for a long time rumored that she was being fitted out as a water battery, with heavy guns. She accordingly—a huge black monster—moved slowly toward Battery Lincoln until within less than a mile, when she stopped broadside to this fort. At daybreak she was seen in this position, but, no hostile demonstration from her or elsewhere being made, we remained quiet. *I thought it a good opportunity to free myself from a false position—that of being obliged to act only on the defensive.* I therefore wrote a note to General Bragg (E), and not receiving an answer, having taken the opinions of the older officers of my command, I wrote him a letter marked G. My messenger brought back answers to both, F and H, all of which I herewith inclose. The next morning we discovered that she had been sunk, and she so remains at this time, and is apparently unoccupied. . . . General Bragg says her present position is accidental, and I doubt not it is so. He probably intended to move the dock to Pensacola or some other place. . . ." [31]

[31] *Ibid.*, p. 417. Italics supplied.

CHAPTER VI

AN EXECUTIVE ACT AND A SENATE RESOLUTION

"IT WAS AN EXECUTIVE ACT"

In practically every order he issued in this period, Lincoln included some such phrase as "with all possible speed." The resultant demoralization brought unanticipated complications. For one thing, they were making history at such a rate that later there was to come to some among the leading participants the revelation that there was no record of authority for their acts; they understood fully that many of these operations had violated all regularity of procedure, not only opening a fruitful field for, but inviting, investigation, and, therefore, peculiarly needful of justification.

With the approach of the end of the conflict, there came again to the fore the author of the panegyric on "nameless vessels," "mysterious, unseen bolts," "advance guards of mosquitoes," "men beating the air amid Southern swamps." The former captain, who halted Porter and the *Powhatan* with the reminder that his request was almost the equivalent of an order from the president, was now, after a rather extraordinary record of promotion, Major General Meigs. His latest appearance was in a new role not so conducive to rhetorical flights. He was busily ransacking the files of the departments, searching for record evidence of the orders under which he and Porter had enjoyed their brief but glorious ascendency.

Meeting with no success, he finally wrote General Townsend, assistant adjutant general, on February 27, 1865:

> "The Navy Department has no copy of the instructions to D. D. Porter and other naval officers under which they cooperated with the expedition of April, 1861, to re-enforce Fort Pickens.
>
> "The President has none, and they have applied to me. My copies, I think, I placed in Hartsuff's hands. . . .
>
> "Please forward the inclosed note to him, and if you have copies let me have for the Navy Department a copy of the President's order to Colonel Brown which required all naval officers to aid him. General Scott knew of the expedition and its orders; and you were acting confidentially with him and may have had custody of those orders *which were kept secret from the Secretaries of War and Navy*, I believe." [1]

After two weeks passed without an answer, Meigs appealed a second time to Townsend:

> "The Navy Department has lately inquired after the orders under which the Fort Pickens expedition was organized and carried out. The instructions to Colonel Brown and to Captain D. D. Porter were prepared by Colonel Keyes and by myself, or the greater part of them were so prepared, and the more important papers were signed by the President. . . .
>
> "This earliest expedition of the war was organized under exceptional circumstances, and its records do not appear to have been preserved in Washington.
>
> "Inquiry at the Navy Department, and at the Executive Mansion, has failed to discover any copies of the orders.
>
> "It was an Executive act, unknown at the time to

[1] *O. R. A.*, Ser. 1, Vol. I, p. 441. Italics supplied.

any but those engaged therein, including General Scott, the Secretary of State, and the President." [2]

Here was indeed a lovely kettle of fish. Little wonder it created a sensation, this revelation that the files in Washington did not contain orders which, in a crisis that threatened disruption of the Union, the president of the United States had personally issued and signed. Diligent digging into the musty records of the navy department, followed by anxious inquiry, first at the war department, then at the executive mansion, had left Meigs dazed. Not one of the originals did he locate; worse still, nowhere did there turn up so much as a copy. Had someone destroyed documents carrying the president's signature? Meigs was thinking of the possibility that the future might bring microscopic examination of the entire program of secretiveness. He knew only too well that the president's orders to him, to Porter, and to Brown would stir exceptional curiosity. "The records do not appear to have been preserved"—what an answer that would be to a skillful cross-examiner in a departmental investigation!

This was serious enough, but in his letter there is something incomparably more important. Intentionally or naively, Major General Meigs contributes to the permanent record an item in the presence of which either destruction or misplacement of original orders and copies fades into triviality. In five simple words, he fixes responsibility: "IT WAS AN EXECUTIVE ACT."

THE SENATE QUESTIONS LINCOLN

The irregularities of the president's actions were threatening to undermine confidence in the administra-

---

[2] *Ibid.,* pp. 441-442. See also Tarbell, *The Life of Abraham Lincoln,* III, 19.

tion. When the steadily rising tide gave warning, Lincoln came to the conclusion that executive comment would be in order. Accordingly, on July 4, 1861, he addressed to congress a message in which he very cautiously touched on the widely discussed, trouble-promising reinforcement incident. The document said:

> "An order was at once directed to be sent for the landing of the troops from the steamship Brooklyn into Fort Pickens. . . . The first return news from the order was received just one week before the fall of Fort Sumter. The news itself was that the officer commanding the Sabine, to which vessel the troops had been transferred from the Brooklyn, acting upon some *quasi* armistice of the late Administration (and of the existence of which the present Administration, up to the time the order was despatched, had only too vague and uncertain rumors to fix attention) had refused to land the troops." [3]

Practically with one accord, informed observers had regarded the reinforcement project as a desperate undertaking, one which jeopardized the peace of the nation. In the arrangement of his expedition, the war and navy departments were not the only governmental agencies to which Lincoln failed to give his full confidence. He did not so much as consult congress, and it so happens the power to declare war reposes in the congress of the United States. Despite his precautions, however, details were leaking out. Members of house and senate were hearing complaints of unexampled executive interference with army and navy operations. The protests were crystallizing even into whispers of one-man government. A ghost rumor that would not down had it that Federal

[3] Appleton's *American Annual Cyclopædia,* 1861, p. 603. See also Crawford, *The Genesis of the Civil War,* pp. 467–468; *A Compilation of the Messages and Papers of the Presidents,* VI, 22.

forces had reinforced Fort Pickens in violation of some sort of agreement which involved the honor of the administration. Now came the first official statement on the subject, the reference in the president's message to a "quasi-armistice."

Instantly, the senate became alert. A quasi-armistice! They knew what an armistice was, but what was a quasi-armistice? And, who were parties to it? Were any of them United States officials who were in a position to pledge the faith of the government? What were its terms? What became of it? A quasi-armistice "of the late administration"! If the late administration authorized it, how could the present administration disregard it? Did a shift of administrations invalidate obligations assumed by the government? And what was the meaning of this reference to the refusal of a naval officer to obey orders, a refusal predicated on his interpretation of the agreement? With the conviction that the seriousness of the situation justified a demand for full disclosure of the facts, on July nineteenth the senate adopted a resolution and sent it to the president. Eleven days later the senators heard his answer:

"*To the Senate of the United States:*
"In answer to the resolution of the Senate of the 19th instant, requesting information concerning the *quasi* armistice alluded to in my message of the 4th instant, I transmit a report from the Secretary of the Navy.

"ABRAHAM LINCOLN
"July 30, 1861"

"NAVY DEPARTMENT
July 29, 1861
"The Secretary of the Navy, to whom was referred the resolution of the Senate of the 19th instant, requesting the President of the United States to

'communicate to the Senate (if not incompatible with
the public interest) the character of the *quasi* armistice to which he refers in his message of the 4th
instant, by reason of which the commander of the
frigate Sabine refused to transfer the United States
troops into Fort Pickens in obedience to his orders;
by whom and when such armistice was entered into;
and if any, and what, action has been taken by the
Government in view of the disobedience of the order
of the President aforesaid,' has the honor to report
that it is believed the communication of the information called for would not, at this time, comport with
the public interest.

"Respectfully submitted,

"GIDEON WELLES." [4]

THE PRESIDENT OF THE UNITED STATES

The one individual best informed, the only person in
the world who knew all the facts the senate called for,
was Abraham Lincoln. Upon his administration rested
sole responsibility for the reinforcement project. The
secret expedition, his personal plan, he had directed by
sealed orders over his signature. Meigs was right: "It
was an Executive act." In the course of the proceedings
Lincoln had gone so far as to admonish subordinate navy
officials that under no circumstances were they to inform
the navy department of what was going on. Now, however, with the appearance of this senate demand for details, he shifted his course. Not only did he eliminate
himself from the picture but he actually placed the duty
of formulating a reply upon the shoulders of the secretary of the navy whom he had so pointedly ignored. The
sum total of information personally transmitted by the
president to the senate was that he was forwarding a
report from the secretary.

[4] *O. R. A.*, Ser. 1, Vol. I, pp. 440-441; *A Compilation of the Messages
and Papers of the Presidents*, VI, 34.

Had the old Puritan conscience ascribed to Welles by John T. Morse, Jr.,[5] only run true to form, what a story he could have unfolded! Lincoln had kept from him parts of the reinforcement plan, but he was conversant with details in abundance to stir up a senate investigation. What if he had rejected the role of scapegoat, nerved himself to tell the truth, the whole truth, and nothing but the truth?

Welles knew all about the armistice and, what was more, he knew what Lincoln knew about it. Now there lay before him the two documents, the president's message and the senate resolution; and he, of all men, was to write the answer. Apart from other embarrassment, the message itself puzzled him. After mentioning the officer's refusal to land the troops, Lincoln, strangely enough, referred to his knowledge of the armistice in these words, "of the existence of which the present administration had only too vague and uncertain rumors to attract attention." The officer in question was of course Captain Adams who on April first had written Welles the whole story of the armistice, solemnly warning against violation of what he described as "the agreement entered into by the United States government with Mr. Mallory and Colonel Chase." Such an official report by the senior naval officer at Pensacola was assuredly not a vague and uncertain rumor. More than this, Welles recalled that, upon receipt of this very letter, he had taken action which his diary set out in the words, "I went immediately to the President with Captain Adams' communication and we both deemed it absolutely essential that a special messenger should be forthwith sent overland with orders to immediately land the troops." [6]

[5] *Diary of Gideon Welles*, I, xxiii.
[6] *Ibid.*, pp. 29-30.

All this, and more, Welles could have told the senate. Under the trying circumstances, he did the best he could. He understood perfectly that the last thing expected of him was to lay bare the facts and thereby blow up a storm which might make shipwreck of the administration. He therefore limited what he saw fit to say to the terse statement, "He has the honor to report that it is believed the communication of the information called for would not, at this time, comport with the public interest."

And so, after Lincoln responded by enclosing the report prepared by Welles, and its members listened to this communication, the senate of the United States knew of the "quasi-armistice" precisely what it had known before.

II. FORT SUMTER

The final outcome at Charleston can be appreciated only after knowledge and understanding of the march of events which ended with the message of the guns of the shore batteries. For the beginnings of the Sumter episode there must, therefore, be a return to the period of the late fall of 1860.

Chapter VII

CONTROL OF CHARLESTON HARBOR

FEDERAL GUNS IN COMMAND

In 1860 Charleston was the main port of South Carolina. Among other defenses it had Castle Pinckney, Fort Moultrie, and Fort Sumter. Their names were redolent of a past glorified by deeds of Carolina patriots. Thomas Pinckney had served with distinction in the War of the Revolution. When, in the same struggle, English warships had entered Charleston harbor and attacked Fort Sullivan, a courageous defense on the part of the garrison under command of Colonel William Moultrie had resulted in the repulse of the fleet. Presently the British had come back with a force which, in addition to taking the city of Charleston, had captured a large portion of the American army south of the Potomac. The colonials had retaliated a few months later, in the battle of King's Mountain, with the near annihilation of an English command. Thus inspirited, under leadership of Sumter, Pickens, and Marion, the Carolinians had added further luster to their record.

With the coming of the fall of 1860, trouble was again brewing for South Carolina. Recent experiences had convinced her people that their future well-being rendered inevitable withdrawal from the Union. As they viewed changed conditions, Federal-garrisoned forts in Charleston harbor were like loaded guns pointed straight at the heart of the state. Secession was not as yet an accomplished fact, but it was on the way and, even prior to separation, it was unpleasant to tolerate the presence of the troops. This they had reconciled themselves to do, but on one point they were insistent; the government must preserve the existing status, must not reinforce the forts and, sooner or later, must relinquish them to the officials of South Carolina.

The commander of the harbor garrison was Major Robert Anderson. His father before him was a soldier, a lieutenant colonel in the continental army. The son, a graduate of West Point, already had to his credit an excellent army record, one revealing recognition for gallantry in action. His translation of French artillery texts for use in instruction of cadets attests the thoroughness of his training. Winning his rank of major in 1857, he was to be promoted in May, 1861, to a brigadier-generalship in the regular army. That destiny should have assigned to him the most appealing role in the opening act of the great drama is another illustration of the capriciousness of fate. He became a pawn in the desperate game being played by North and South, a buffer between irreconcilable and passion-stirred factions, called to stand guard over his flag in an isolated outpost. This Union officer was born in Kentucky, of Virginia ancestry, and had married a Georgia girl. These affiliations, which had not in the least affected his ardent pro-Union principles, rendered ideal his selection as commander at Charleston. Earnestly as he desired reconciliation of the discordant elements, there was never a doubt as to his course in the event of a final rupture.[1] Nevertheless, his complete understanding of Southern temperament won the respect and friendship of the Carolinians.

As early as November, 1860, Major Anderson sensed

[1] *Dictionary of American Biography,* I, 274.

that conditions around him were approaching a critical stage, whereupon he informed Washington that retention of the harbor necessitated the strengthening of his garrison. To the war department he gave the benefit of his belief that as soon as there came to the South Carolinians knowledge of the ordering of reinforcements, an attack on Fort Moultrie would follow.[2]

Realizing that the very smallness of his command might invite attack,[3] he knew equally well that for the Southerners the situation involved more than the mere instinct of self-preservation. He was no stranger to the imperishable memories, the hallowed traditions which were interwoven into the very life of this people. That the historical significance of the names "Sumter" and "Moultrie" was not lost on him he revealed in a letter to Adjutant General Cooper: "There appears to be a romantic desire urging the South Carolinians to *have possession* of this work, which was so nobly defended by their ancestors in 1776." [4] He took occasion to express the hope that the state would not attempt to take the forts by force, but would "resort to diplomacy to secure them." [5] The Carolinians were willing and eager to exhaust the possibilities of diplomacy but were of the opinion that, upon the conclusion of negotiations, the problem would remain. In view of this belief, Governor Gist forwarded to Washington a plain-spoken message that he would not care to be held responsible for consequences if "a single soldier, or another gun, or ammunition" should be sent to the forts.[6]

Weeks prior to the secession of the state, Major Ander-

[2] *O. R. A.,* Ser. 1, Vol. I, p. 75; Crawford, *The Genesis of the Civil War,* p. 62.
[3] *O. R. A.,* Ser. 1, Vol. I, p. 74.
[4] *Ibid.,* p. 78.   [5] *Ibid.,* p. 76.
[6] Crawford, *The Genesis of the Civil War,* p. 31.

son was pressing the government to make a decision as to retention or surrender of the harbor fortifications. To his certain knowledge, a crisis was impending. Interviews with representative Charlestonians, reported to him by members of his staff, led him to write that, whatever else came up for discussion in such conferences, one fact invariably stood out, a determination to have control of the harbor. The secession of the state was, in his view, a mere matter of time. This would place squarely up to Washington the necessity of a definite policy relative to the Charleston forts. His conclusion was that the sooner the government made up its mind, the better it would be for all concerned.[7] Of such importance was the issue that Anderson deemed it worth while to make a personal investigation of the prevailing sentiment. Accordingly, on December fifth, he and Colonel Huger called on the mayor and various other influential citizens. The result was full confirmation of what his staff had said. In consequence, he again gave the department his diagnosis of the existing state of mind on the mainland. Without exception, he wrote, his hosts had manifested determination to exert their full influence to prevent a mob attack on the garrison, but, with equal unanimity, they had expressed an unalterable conviction that, upon the secession of the state, the Federal troops must take their departure.

The import of the adjutant general's reply was that, in view of information from what it regarded as a reliable source, the government believed there was no occasion for apprehension of an early outbreak. Even if a collision were to come, the letter said, it was the desire of the administration that Anderson should be free from fault. To be sure, he was to maintain his position to the

7 *O. R. A.,* Ser. 1, Vol. I, p. 81; Crawford, *The Genesis of the Civil War,* p. 65.

best of his ability against aggression, but the secretary of war was in grave doubt as to the expediency of increasing the garrison because, in the existing state of agitation, this might lead to serious results.[8]

A few days later the department of war sent Major Buell with a memorandum of instructions for Anderson. This reiterated the previously expressed purpose of the secretary to abstain from reinforcing the fort, but it authorized the commander, in case of any tangible evidence of hostile intention, to use his discretion concerning the transfer of his command from one fort to another.[9] Buell's brief stay in Charleston convinced him that the idea of the populace regarding the surrender of the harbor was "as fixed as the act of secession itself." [10] This finding confirmed the view of the secretary of war and the adjutant general who had enjoyed access to inside information provided by almost daily reports from Charleston. They knew the situation and knew it was dangerous. In order to avoid intensifying irritation, they had not only declined to send additional troops but were cautiously refraining from any action which might stir up further dissension. They were lending their influence to the preservation of peace.

What of the Carolinians? Many accounts have shown astonishing lack of appreciation of their attitude. Only the man of poise and judicial temperament possesses capacity to put himself in another's place, get the other's point of view, judge him with fairness. The rareness of such ability perhaps accounts in some part for the widely spread impression of the South Carolinians as a group of irresponsible enthusiasts. In this connection it is a

[8] *O. R. A.,* Ser. 1, Vol. I, pp. 82-83.
[9] *Ibid.,* pp. 89, 90; Crawford, *The Genesis of the Civil War,* p. 73.
[10] *Ibid.,* p. 74.

happy circumstance that General Crawford has gone on
record with testimony, the weight and impartiality of
which his distinguished career and unquestioned loyalty
to the Union assure. A member of Anderson's staff at
Moultrie, very much alive mentally, alert to what was
going on in Charleston, he seized the opportunity closely
to observe the convention which passed the ordinance of
secession. Of it, he gives his impression:

> ". . . A body of men as unanimous in sentiment, as
> calm and deliberate in feeling, as earnest and able,
> as ever assembled in any State of the Union. . . .
> Quietly the convention had met and had been opened
> with prayer to God. There was no excitement. . . .
> There was an element of over-caution in the Con-
> vention, that showed itself abundantly in the shrink-
> ing, temporizing policy in regard to Fort Sumter,
> and in the elaborate and repeated efforts at peaceful
> diplomacy. . . . At this period peaceable separation
> was the undoubted wish of all. . . . The adjournment
> of the Convention was characterized by the same
> dignity that had marked its sessions." [11]

Interestedly watching the operations of another group
of men of the state, General Crawford noted that at about
this time the more conservative element of the South Carolina legislature voted down a motion that the forts be
taken at once.[12] His estimate of convention and legislature leads naturally to the inquiry as to why the Federal
policy relative to retention of the Charleston forts so
profoundly aroused the people of South Carolina. Perhaps the question may be answered by turning away
from a realm overhung by mists of bias or prejudice to
consider a hypothetical situation offering the advantage
of being viewed dispassionately. Indulge the imagination

11 *Ibid.,* pp. 46, 47, 51, 53, 55.
12 *Ibid.,* p. 96.

for the moment. Canada concludes that association with Britain is prejudicial to her interests, announces her intention to become an independent nation, and, with such an end in view, sends to London a commission to arrange peaceable separation. Britain, however, stoutly resists the proposed secession. Presently, feeling in both countries reaches such intensity that war is in immediate prospect. Meanwhile, a fortress manned by British troops dominates the harbor and city of Montreal. Again and again the Canadians protest the presence of the garrison as an irritant jeopardizing the success of pending negotiations. Instead of removing the troops, the English government not only moves at once to recondition the fortress but lets it be understood that it is sending reinforcements of arms, ammunition, and soldiers. Would such an attitude on the part of Downing Street allay or heighten excitement and resentment?

THE FORTS ARE STRENGTHENED

Despite Secretary of War Floyd's opposition to any action which might bring about a clash and his insistence that Anderson should coöperate by maintaining a defensive attitude, Washington willingly countenanced energetic efforts to place the forts in the most effective condition possible. Early in December Captain Foster, of the Federal engineers, wrote that he was increasing the "defensive capacities" of Fort Moultrie, the work occupied by Anderson's command. Employing at this post one hundred and twenty-five men, he had at the same time about one hundred and fifteen at Fort Sumter and thirty at Castle Pinckney.[13] Thus no fewer than two hundred and sixty workmen were busily gearing up these war

13 *O. R. A.*, Ser. 1, Vol. I, p. 86.

machines. Nor were they overlooking offensive equipment. Major Anderson sent word that they were mounting guns at Sumter as rapidly as possible.[14] By December twentieth Colonel De Russy, commander of the corps of engineers in Washington, felt justified in reporting to Secretary Floyd that, "of all the fortifications in the harbor of Charleston, Fort Sumter must be looked upon as far the most important, and it is now in condition, as regards its state of preparation, to resist any attack that will be made upon it, provided it be furnished with a proper garrison." [15]

These activities, it will be noted, were in progress prior to the withdrawal of South Carolina. What was the significance of feverish haste in strengthening the defensive capacities of Moultrie, the rush in mounting guns at Sumter? The people of the state naturally presumed that the sole justification even of the existence of the harbor forts lay in their protection of Charleston. Certainly they knew of no new danger necessitating reinforcement; surely the time was inopportune strongly to reëquip already formidable instrumentalities of war. South Carolina was still as much a member of the Union as Massachusetts. Assuredly, an acrid controversy was in progress between the state and the central government, but this was not unique; the country had weathered other equally stormy crises. True, disaffected sections were threatening secession, but there was nothing new about this. There was a possibility that in time all differences would be ironed out. Such Federal officials as the secretary of war and the adjutant general plainly entertained such a hope and, as General Crawford remarked, this was the undoubted wish of the Charleston convention.

With wondering eyes the Charlestonians viewed all this

14 *Ibid.,* p. 99.　　　　　　　　　　　15 *Ibid.,* p. 100.

Federal-preparedness energy at their very doors. The hurried placing of those additional cannon, guns whose terrifying mouths spoke only a language of destruction and death, indicated that the fort was being made ready for action. To what was all this leading? Was it within the realm of possibility that those in control at Washington were planning that Charleston and its people eventually should supply the target? It is conceivable that protestation that Anderson was restricting the work to an increase of defensive capacities of the forts did not altogether reassure them. When the forts should be stronger defensively, might it not follow that they would possess added power of offense? Furthermore, in the last analysis what practical difference could there be between placing these works in apparently impregnable shape by the mounting of cannon, and reinforcing them by throwing in other troops? However unaccountable, it nevertheless appears that they were content to center their attention on the insistence that there should be no reinforcement from Washington. At any rate, no acute issue arose out of activities inside the walls.

In the meanwhile, steps were being taken of which the Southerners had no knowledge. There was one in particular which, spotlighted, would have chilled the blood of an already disquieted country. Anxious speculation would have followed exposure that on December 12, 1860, Abraham Lincoln, whose assumption of right to interfere in governmental affairs prior to his inauguration was surely open to question, had sent to E. B. Washburne for secret transmittal to General Winfield Scott, commanding general of the army, this message: "Please present my respects to the general, and tell him, confidentially, I shall be obliged to him to be as well prepared

as he can to either *hold* or *retake* the forts, as the case
may require, at and after the inauguration." [16]

ANDERSON MOVES HIS GARRISON INTO FORT SUMTER

In 1773 Josiah Quincy, of Massachusetts, paid a visit
to Charleston. That it proved a pleasant experience his
diary's account reveals: "This town makes a beautiful
appearance as you come up to it and in many respects
a magnificent one. I can only say in general that in
grandeur, splendor of buildings, decorations, equipages,
numbers, commerce, shipping, and indeed everything, it
far surpasses all I ever saw, or ever expect to see, in
America."

The Charlestonians must have given the visiting New
Englander a traditional Southern reception but it happened that Mr. Quincy's visitation was not primarily a
quest for social indulgence. The highhandedness of British rulers was bringing about in some of the colonies a
swelling tide of resentment and his serious mission was
to feel out the Carolinians on the matter of a projected
struggle for American independence. He was not long
in learning that the selfsame winds which had scattered
seeds of discontent elsewhere had blown also across this
fertile soil. What congenial spirits these Southerners
really were, he discovered when the time arrived for
patriots to prove their faith; in addition to sending their
young manhood into the ranks, the sturdy sons of South
Carolina contributed to the cause of the Revolution more
funds than all other colonies combined. Thus they gave
practical expression of their spirit of independence, their
zeal to live their lives in their own way, untrammelled by

[16] Nicolay and Hay, *Lincoln*, III, 250. See also Robert McNutt Mc-
Elroy, *Jefferson Davis; the Unreal and the Real* (2 vols. New York and
London, 1937), I, 278.

outside intermeddling. From the first landing of the Huguenots, they had repeatedly fought for their rights; against Indians, Spaniards, French, English, they had defended their homes.

Nearly a century later, in 1860, the passion for self-determination, a heritage from their fathers, was as alive as ever. It was to come to grips with a new, a sinister issue. An undreamed-of change had come in their relations with their fellow colonists. Returns from the recent presidential election had opened their eyes to the upward swing in power of a bitterly partisan faction, one which had exploited as the campaign keynote its characterization of alleged unspeakable conditions in the slaveholding South. Now that threatened encroachment on the part of an unsympathetic, even hostile, North was placing their future in jeopardy, there stirred memories of the indomitable self-reliance of those whose blood coursed in their arteries. Their forebears had brooked no unfriendly domination; nor would they. Their state was first to act. On December 20, 1860, the Charleston convention passed the ordinance of secession.

Just five days later came Christmas. None knew what the future held in store but, despite faraway rumblings and occasional flashes, Charleston would not have been Charleston to allow constitutional issues to becloud the joyousness of the supreme festival of the year; for, with these folk, religious and festal inclinations ran together in the observance of Christmas. And so, throwing aside the pursuits of the money-changers, closing their eyes to ominous portents, all interests swirled into an eddy of happy abandon. With an intoxicating admixture of holiday relaxation and reverent commemoration of the day when the Child was born in Bethlehem, they celebrated as they had always celebrated the sacred season which symbolized the ideal of peace on earth, good will to men. Little dreamed the celebrants that the mirthfulness of the day was to provide an incongruous prelude for a tomorrow chilled by gloom and fear. On that morrow came staggering intelligence that, seizing the opportunity afforded by the populace's preoccupation with yuletide gaieties, the Federal commanding officer had not only removed his garrison from Moultrie into the stronger Fort Sumter, but had crippled the abandoned post by spiking its guns and burning the gun carriages. Instantly the atmosphere became surcharged with excitement and indignation. The holiday spirit shifted to one of angered resentment. Men rushed to armories, troops marched in the streets, voices shouted threats of immediate retaliation.[17]

Anderson had planned carefully the details of the transfer. Members of his command did not know of the secret arrangements until the hour for action. To cover the removal, the commander left Captain Foster at Moultrie with instructions to use the guns of the fortress on any vessel which attempted to obstruct the garrison's passage to Sumter.[18] There was no opposition except that, when the first boat load of soldiers landed, they came upon "secession" workmen, a few of whom possessed arms. Captain Doubleday ordered his men to fix bayonets and charge, the laborers speedily surrendered, and the fort passed under Anderson's control.[19] Next in order was the hoisting of the national emblem over the work. The garrison made this the occasion of an impressive ceremony. After dress parade, the entire command assembled around the flagstaff; with Anderson kneeling beside him,

---

[17] Crawford, *The Genesis of the Civil War*, p. 108.
[18] *Ibid.*, pp. 105, 106; Nicolay and Hay, *Lincoln*, III, 51.
[19] *B. & L.*, I, 45; Nicolay and Hay, *Lincoln*, III, 53.

the chaplain offered prayer; then, with his own hands, the commander raised the flag. Captain Chester, a witness of the event, was of the opinion that no one present could ever afterward entertain any question as to the Southern-born commander's loyalty to the Union.[20] The following day, December twenty-sixth, Anderson wrote the adjutant general:

> "I have the honor to report that I have just completed, by the blessing of God, the removal to this fort of all my garrison, except the surgeon, four non-commissioned officers, and seven men. . . . I left orders to have all the guns at Fort Moultrie spiked, and the carriages of the 32-pounders, which are old, destroyed. I have sent orders to Captain Foster, who remains at Fort Moultrie, to destroy all the ammunition which he cannot send over. The step which I have taken was, in my opinion, necessary to prevent the effusion of blood." [21]

Here presented itself a new angle of an already troublesome problem. Just four days before, Anderson had warned Washington that the Carolinians would resort to extreme measures to prevent the placing of additional troops in Sumter. He further made clear their determination that the fort should be turned over to the state and expressed his belief that, as soon as they thought there was reasonable ground for doubt as to whether this would be done, an attack would follow.[22] Soon he was to read a telegram from Secretary Floyd revealing that the Federal department of war shared the amazement of the Southerners at the daring strategy of the removal: "Intelligence has reached here this morning that you have abandoned Fort

[20] *B. & L.,* I, 65; Crawford, *The Genesis of the Civil War,* p. 112.
[21] *O. R. A.,* Ser. 1, Vol. I, p. 2; Crawford, *The Genesis of the Civil War,* p. 106.
[22] *O. R. A.,* Ser. 1, Vol. I, p. 105.

Moultrie, spiked your guns, burned the carriages, and gone to Fort Sumter. It is not believed, because there is no order for any such movement. Explain the meaning of this report." [23]

In keeping with his construction of the policy of the administration, the secretary of war had resolutely pursued a course which he hoped would ward off a collision. In view of prior understandings and the department's instructions to Anderson, he found it impossible to credit what he had heard. With intimate knowledge of conditions at Charleston, he fully comprehended the gravity of such action, one later to be chronicled both in Alfred Roman's *Military Operations* and in General Edward P. Alexander's *Military Memoirs* as the first overt act of war.[24] Anderson's coup dumfounded others than the secretary. When the news reached the capital, Mr. Trescott, until a few days before assistant secretary of state, prevailed on Senators Jefferson Davis and R. M. T. Hunter to go with him to the president. When Davis related the occurrence, Buchanan's exasperation burst its bounds: "My God, are calamities . . . never to come singly! I call God to witness, you gentlemen, better than anybody, *know* that this is not only without but against my orders." [25]

Bearing the same date as the secretary of war's demand, and with the added similarity that it wasted no words, Anderson's reply authenticated the report: "The telegram is correct. I abandoned Fort Moultrie because I was certain that if attacked my men would have been

[23] *Ibid.,* p. 3.

[24] *Military Operations of General Beauregard in the War Between the States* (2 vols. New York, 1884), I, 27; *Military Memoirs of a Confederate* (New York, 1907), p. 9.

[25] Crawford, *The Genesis of the Civil War,* pp. 143, 144.

sacrificed, and the control of the harbor lost. . . ." [26] Anderson was a soldier, not a diplomat. Well aware of the
difficult situation, as well as of the negotiations in progress
between Washington and South Carolina, his assignment
was to keep the flag of the United States flying over the
harbor of Charleston. Governors and secretaries of the
cabinet might correspond at their pleasure; he had a
definite task to perform, he could hold his own better
in Sumter than in Moultrie, he was in Sumter, and that
was that. Furthermore, he was of the opinion that his
course had made a contribution to peace. The possessor
of a giant's strength rarely has occasion to use it. One
look at Sumter's forbidding exterior, a glance at the
emblem flying above it would likely cool the enthusiasm
of those who had designs upon it. It was this that he
had in mind in suggesting to the adjutant general that
his being found in such a position that "it would be
madness to attack" him would provide effective insurance
against the possibility of bloodshed.[27]

In spite of plausible excuses, the removal calls for
close inspection. Major Anderson was, of course, subject
to the direction of the secretary of war; from that source
no instruction had come on which he could predicate his
action. The president's impassioned protest left no doubt
that he had flown directly in the teeth of orders from
that dignitary. His position was also untenable in view
of the fact that as late as December first he had learned
that the department of war considered there was little
danger of an assault on Fort Moultrie. No one knew
better than he that the only change since observable in
the status was his own move to condition Fort Sumter.
Unless something had happened which was not being

[26] *O. R. A.,* Ser. 1, Vol. I, p. 3.
[27] *Dictionary of American Biography,* I, 274.

made a matter of record, it is difficult to reconcile Anderson's attitude with his established reputation as an officer of outstanding ability and entire trustworthiness. Groping for the explanation, memory recalls that perplexing communication of only two weeks before in which Lincoln asked General Scott to have everything in readiness for decisive action concerning the forts, "at and after the inauguration." Had Scott passed on to the commander of Fort Sumter this message of the private citizen who, however, within a few months was to become president of the United States? Was the transfer of the garrison, almost as great a surprise in Washington as in Charleston, the result of such a whispered suggestion?

The same day on which he telegraphed his explanation to Secretary Floyd, Anderson reviewed for Adjutant General Cooper an interview which took place shortly after the transfer. The governor of South Carolina had sent one of his aides to demand "courteously but peremptorily" the return of the garrison to Moultrie. This demand Anderson refused. Referring to an understanding between the chief executive of the state and Buchanan that the government would not attempt reinforcement of the forts, particularly of Fort Sumter, the messenger insisted that the Federals had not honored their agreement. Anderson replied that as commander of the harbor it was his privilege to occupy such of the forts as he chose, and he added that the mere transfer of his detachment from one post to another was not a reinforcement. With engaging frankness, he startled his visitor with the admission that he had undertaken the removal of the command "on my own responsibility." [28] The governor in whose behalf the aide appeared was Francis W. Pickens who had assumed his office just eleven days before. That

[28] *O. R. A.,* Ser. 1, Vol. I, p. 3.

Pickens held the confidence of the president is learned from the fact that by Buchanan's appointment he had served as a representative of the United States at the court of St. Petersburg.[29]

General Crawford relates further details of the interview between Anderson and the governor's representatives, Colonel Johnson Pettigrew and Major Ellison Capers. Colonel Pettigrew stated to Anderson that it was part of the understanding that all property of the government within the limits of the state should remain as it was and the status in Charleston harbor was not to be altered. After impressing the governor's earnest desire for peace, he observed that the Sumter coup had brought wholly unexpected complication. The commander answered that he knew nothing of the understanding in question, and that he could get neither positive orders nor information from Washington. Upon his countering with a complaint that armed steamers were threatening his position, Major Capers gave his assurance that the steamer was merely a patrol boat, on duty as much to guard against trouble from disorderly Carolinians as to detect any irregular attempt at reinforcement of the fort. Capers took occasion to disavow any intention to do aught to harass Fort Sumter. At this point of the interview, Anderson politely but firmly brought the matter to a head with the words, "Make my compliments to the Governor, and say to him that I decline to accede to his request; I cannot and will not go back." [30] He added that, while he was a Southern man, his government had assigned him to defend Charleston harbor, and he intended to defend it.[31]

[29] Crawford, *The Genesis of the Civil War*, p. 79.
[30] *Ibid.*, pp. 109-111.
[31] *B. & L.*, I, 46.

Meanwhile, in Washington decided interest attached
to a memorandum of which the record says:

> "The following message was delivered by Lieu-
> tenant-Colonel Lay, aide-de-camp, from the General-
> in-Chief to the President of the United States, in
> person, about 3½ p. m., December 27:
> "Since the formal order, unaccompanied by spe-
> cial instructions, assigning Major Anderson to the
> command of Fort Moultrie, no order, intimation,
> suggestion, or communication for his government
> and guidance has gone to that officer, or to any of
> his subordinates, from the Headquarters of the Army;
> nor have any reports or communications been ad-
> dressed to the General-in-Chief from Fort Moultrie
> later than a letter written by Major Anderson,
> almost immediately after his arrival in Charleston
> Harbor, reporting the then state of the work." [32]

The demand by Secretary of War Floyd for an explanation of Anderson's conduct had stated that, in the
absence of an order for any such movement, the department did not credit the rumor of the transfer. The inevitable inference from the memorandum of the general
in chief is that the commander's performance occasioned
such serious concern as to lead to a demand upon the
general for further investigation and report. The very
wordiness of Scott's reply brings questioning; if no order
had gone to Anderson from headquarters of the army,
why was not it sufficient simply to say so? Is there significance in what is palpably a suggestive overstatement;
namely, "no order, intimation, suggestion or communication . . . has gone to that officer, or to any of his subordinates"? And when was it ever heard that headquarters
of the army was guilty of the irregularity of sending

[32] *O. R. A.,* Ser. 1, Vol. I, p. 111.

orders, intimations, suggestions, or communications to a subordinate?

That something had mightily stirred the president is obvious. A circumstance of interest is that on the same day on which the secretary of war received the message announcing Anderson's removal, Lieutenant Colonel Lay delivered into the hand of Buchanan the report from General Scott. It was indeed a field day for the history-makers; the secretary heard the news, telegraphed for an explanation from Anderson, the answer came, the president forwarded his demand to the general in chief, and that official's aide-de-camp returned his answer to the chief executive—all on the same day, December twenty-seventh!

Properly respected, such an understanding as that insisted on by Colonel Pettigrew in his interview with Major Anderson might have gone far toward a solution of the problem. On December twenty-eighth, in a letter to the president of the South Carolina convention, Governor Pickens referred to the evacuation of Fort Moultrie as a direct violation of the agreement in effect between Washington and the Carolina officials, and characterized the repudiation of the understanding as "bringing on a state of war." [33]

[33] Crawford, *The Genesis of the Civil War*, p. 125.

Chapter VIII

PRESIDENT BUCHANAN AND THE SOUTH
CAROLINA COMMISSIONERS

SOUTH CAROLINA'S PEACE COMMISSION PROTESTS

The record has shown that South Carolina seceded December 20, 1860. Firmly of the conviction that the state had the right to withdraw when further continuance in the Union should prove unhappy for its people, the convention had reached its verdict, "The Union now subsisting between South Carolina and other states under the name of the United States of America is hereby dissolved." [1] Two days later it appointed a commission charged with responsibility for launching peace negotiations with the Federal government. Impressed by the caliber of the commission's personnel, Rhodes comments, "Abler and better members of the convention could not have been selected for this mission." [2] It was indeed a representative group: James H. Adams, alumnus of Yale and former governor of the state; R. W. Barnwell, graduate of Harvard, former college president and United States senator; James L. Orr, once speaker of the national house of representatives.

On the very day on which Anderson abandoned Fort Moultrie, December twenty-sixth, the mediators reached Washington. Still under the spell of the critical initial

[1] Stephens, *A Comprehensive and Popular History of the United States*, p. 560.
[2] *History of the United States*, III, 223.

movement of their state's withdrawal from the Union, they made known their mandate to treat with the Federal government for delivery of United States property within the limits of their state, for apportionment of the public debt, and, generally, "for the continuance of peace and amity between this Commonwealth and the Government at Washington." [3] Here, then, is an introduction to those who were to speak for the Carolinians, as well as to the message they were to present. The keynote of their communication, that they had come to negotiate for a continuance of peace and amity, was no mawkish effusion; it was the thoroughly considered proposition of what General Crawford described as an unquestionably earnest and notably capable body of representatives. Recalling their instructions to spare no effort to insure a "future of good will and harmony," the conciliators directed President Buchanan's attention to a most unexpected turn of affairs "within the last twenty-four hours":

> "We came here, the representatives of an authority which could at any time within the past sixty days have taken possession of the forts in Charleston Harbor, but which, upon pledges given in a manner that we cannot doubt, determined to trust to your honor rather than to its own power. Since our arrival an officer of the United States acting, as we are assured, not only without but against your orders, has dismantled one fort and occupied another, thus altering to a most important extent the condition of affairs under which we came." [4]

Spokesmen of a group with whom, again to use the words of General Crawford, "peaceable separation was the undoubted wish of all," they were wondering as to the state of mind of those back home now that Anderson's

[3] *O. R. A.*, Ser. 1, Vol. I, p. 109.
[4] *Ibid.*, pp. 109-110.

desperate strategy had plunged everything into confusion. The worst of it all was that their people had refrained from action chiefly because of confidence in pledges that the government would not disturb the harbor status. That there was ground for their faith, there seems little question. Nicolay himself concedes that Southerners in the capital had obtained from the president the tacit promise that he would not send reinforcements to Charleston unless the Carolinians should attack Anderson.[5] And Gideon Welles, of the Lincoln cabinet, mentions a reported understanding that the Southerners would make no attack on Fort Sumter, provided the administration did not undertake to reinforce the garrison, adding that this agreement was to govern Buchanan's attitude during the remaining period of his occupancy of the office of president.[6]

The president could not have failed to be impressed by the final words of the message of the commissioners, a plain-spoken, yet respectful, warning that the garrison's presence carried the implication of a threat which might provoke regrettable repercussions. They set forth both the trouble and their proposed solution:

". . . In conclusion, we would urge upon you the immediate withdrawal of the troops from the harbor of Charleston. Under present circumstances they are a standing menace which renders negotiations impossible, and, as our recent experience shows, threatens speedily to bring to a bloody issue questions which ought to be settled with temperance and judgment."[7]

"Peace and amity"—"a future of good will and harmony"—"ought to be settled with temperance and judg-

[5] *The Outbreak of Rebellion,* p. 24.
[6] *Diary of Gideon Welles,* I, 12.
[7] *O. R. A.,* Ser. 1, Vol. I, p. 110.

ment"—such sentiments have not the ring of fire-eating fanaticism. The proffered friendliness on the part of the Carolinians cannot be dismissed as dissimulation without running counter to the salutary admonition against sweeping indictment. Ulterior motives may or may not be attributed, but such accusation should be buttressed by the facts which justify it; here is the record, the account of what they said and did. Any imputation of insincerity, moreover, is in striking contrast with the judgment of the scholarly, distinguished veteran, General Crawford, who, after attending its sessions, voiced his high estimate of the personnel and the proceedings of the convention.

On the very day on which the commissioners wrote their communication to the president, the commanding general of the army was apparently bearing in mind the request made of him by Lincoln just sixteen days before for, in a memorandum of the twenty-eighth, he made some recommendations:

"Lieutenant-General Scott, who has had a bad night, and can scarcely hold up his head this morning, begs to express the hope to the Secretary of War—

"1. That orders may not be given for the evacuation of Fort Sumter;

"2. That one hundred and fifty recruits may instantly be sent from Governor's Island to re-enforce that garrison, with ample supplies of ammunition. . . .

"3. That one or two armed vessels be sent to support the said fort." [8]

Also on December twenty-eighth, Major Anderson received from Governor Pickens a memorandum setting forth certain concessions relative to the transportation of

[8] *Ibid.*, p. 112. See also Crawford, *The Genesis of the Civil War*, p. 169.

mails for the post and the disposition of the women and
children of the garrison. The paper stipulated that "the
kindest regard shall be paid" to the ladies, but it included
also certain prohibitions:

> ". . . for the present there shall be no communica-
> tions of any other kind allowed from the city to the
> fort, or any transportation of arms or ammunition,
> or any supplies, to the fort; and this is done with a
> view to prevent irregular collisions, and to spare the
> unnecessary effusion of blood." [9]

On the same day on which he received it, Major Anderson sent the Pickens memorandum to Adjutant General
Cooper with the comment that the document revealed that
the Carolinians were treating the Sumter command as
enemies. A postscript which he added amply explains
the irritation of the people of Charleston:

> "I do not feel authorized to reply to the memoran-
> dum of the governor, but shall regret very deeply
> his persistence in the course he has taken. He knows
> not how entirely the city of Charleston is in my
> power. I can cut his communication off from the sea,
> and thereby prevent the reception of supplies, and
> close the harbor, even at night, by destroying the
> lighthouses. These things, of course, I would never
> do, unless compelled to do so in self-defense." [10]

Assuredly, here was stimulating food for thought. With
no trace of blustering braggart in his make up, Robert
Anderson was known to the Carolinians as a deeply pious,
highly competent, coolheaded artillery expert. He believed he could do, and the inhabitants of the city feared
he might be ordered to do, just those very acts. Thus
the announcement that he held the city at his mercy

[9] *O. R. A.*, Ser. 1, Vol. I, p. 113.
[10] *Ibid.*

told also the reason why those living under the shadow of Sumter's guns had firmly resolved there should be an end of such potential terrorism.

THE PRESIDENT REPLIES

In his December thirty-first answer to the commissioners, the president said he had desired to submit the whole matter to congress for such disposition by that body, "who alone possess the power," as would prevent an outbreak of civil war. He deeply regretted, he wrote, the belief of the commissioners that "the events of the last twenty-four hours render this impossible." [11] Prior to the arrival of the commissioners, Buchanan had given an audience to a delegation of South Carolina congressmen, and in his reply he enclosed a copy of that group's statement to him. Bearing the date of December ninth and signed by all the congressional representatives of South Carolina, the document read:

> "In compliance with our statement to you yesterday, we now express to you our strong convictions that neither the constituted authority, nor any body of the people of the State of South Carolina, will either attack or molest the United States forts in the harbor of Charleston previously to the action of the convention, and we hope and believe not until an offer has been made, through an accredited representative, to negotiate for an amicable arrangement of all matters between the State and Federal Government, provided that no re-enforcements shall be sent into those forts, and their relative military status shall remain as at present." [12]

[11] *Ibid.,* p. 115.
[12] *Ibid.,* p. 116. See also Crawford, *The Genesis of the Civil War,* p. 38.

In the later discussion with the commissioners, the
president took the position that he had made no commit-
ment. To fortify his stand, he called attention to the fact
that the unofficial status of the congressional delegation
had appeared from acknowledgment by its members that
they were acting merely as individuals. Consequently, he
submitted, it lacked authority to make any agreement
which would bind the state. His construction of the net
result of the conference was that any reference to a pledge
on his part was a palpable overstatement:

> "I considered it as nothing more in effect than
> the promise of highly honorable gentlemen to exert
> their influence for the purpose expressed. The event
> has proven that they have faithfully kept this prom-
> ise. . . . It is well known that it was my determina-
> tion . . . not to re-enforce the forts in the harbor,
> and thus produce a collision, until they had been
> actually attacked, or until I had certain evidence
> that they were about to be attacked. This paper I
> received most cordially, and considered it as a happy
> omen that peace might still be preserved. . . . This
> is the whole foundation for the alleged pledge.
>
> "But I acted in the same manner as I would have
> done had I entered into a . . . formal agreement. . . .
> The world knows that I have never sent any re-
> enforcements to the forts . . . and I have certainly
> never authorized any change to be made in their
> relative military status." [13]

Buchanan's reply made it very plain that he was not
a party to the transfer of the garrison:

> "These were the last instructions transmitted to
> Major Anderson before his removal to Fort Sumter.
> . . . Under these circumstances it is clear that Major
> Anderson acted upon his own responsibility, and

[13] *O. R. A.,* Ser. 1, Vol. I, p. 117.

without authority, unless, indeed, he had 'tangible evidence of a design to proceed to a hostile act' . . . which has not yet been alleged." [14]

Even so, whether denominated a pledge or a gentlemen's agreement, the fact remains that there was at the very least an informal understanding. Without question, Buchanan had no intention to reinforce unless there was proof of contemplated aggressive action. Equally certain it is that he knew of no evidence of such intention. Unhesitatingly, he confided to the commissioners that his first impulse was to order the garrison back to its former post.[15] But he reminded them that the Carolinians themselves had altered the entire outlook when, on the day following Anderson's action, they had seized two of the harbor forts and raised above them the flag of the state. By such retaliatory rashness, he observed, their own people had brought about a strained condition which eliminated from consideration the withdrawal of the garrison from Sumter. This, he asserted with finality, he could not, and he would not, do.

In his *Memoirs*, General E. P. Alexander presents a behind-the-curtain sidelight. His account is that, concluding to order Anderson back to Moultrie, Buchanan mentioned his decision to Stanton, his attorney general. Determined to thwart any such move, the practical politician in Stanton rose to the occasion. He knew what to do. A hurried conference with Dan Sickles, a member of congress from New York and an adept in the art of political pressure, gave rise to wholly unexpected, sensational publicity. In New York and Philadelphia what the press acclaimed as bold strategy and undaunted

[14] *Ibid.,* pp. 117-18.
[15] Nicolay, *The Outbreak of Rebellion,* p. 30; Nicolay and Hay, *Lincoln,* III, 64.

courage on the part of the Sumter commander, the cities honored with a salute of one hundred guns. Sickles knew the technique of another game. Straightway there began pouring into the White House a flood of telegrams commending the chief executive for firmness in dealing with the Charleston crisis, lauding him as a second Jackson, proclaiming him a savior of his country who had scorned to issue an order which would be tantamount to a rebuke to the hero who had saved the day at Charleston. The scheme worked. The order never saw the light of day.[16]

And again the fog closes in. On the selfsame day of the president's reply, General Scott was issuing to the commander of Fort Monroe this order:

> "Prepare and put on board of the sloop-of-war Brooklyn, as soon as the latter can receive them, four companies, making at least two hundred men, destined to re-enforce Fort Sumter. Embark with said companies twenty-five spare stands of arms, complete, and subsistence for the entire detachment for ninety days, or as near that amount as your supplies may furnish. Communicate at once with the commander of the war steamer, learn the earliest moment at which he can receive the troops on board, and do not fail to have them there at that time. Manage everything as secretly and confidentially as possible. *Look to this.*" [17]

In this connection it is well to recall the president's earnest insistence, "The world knows that I have never sent any reinforcements to the forts," as well as his candid admission of the good faith of the congressmen in carrying out their part of the understanding. Scott's headquarters were almost directly across the street from

[16] *Military Memoirs of a Confederate*, p. 11.

[17] *O. R. A.*, Ser. 1, Vol. I, p. 119. See also Crawford, *The Genesis of the Civil War*, pp. 171, 177.

the office of the president. Was not there available in the department of war some messenger who knew the way to the executive office? Or, does the key to the mystery turn up in Scott's admonition to manage the affair as secretly and confidentially as possible? Was he keeping it from Buchanan? Is it possible that here is still another echo of the Lincoln letter of December twelfth?

THE COMMISSIONERS' ANSWER

Conceding his lack of power to coerce a seceding state, Buchanan appeared committed to a policy of exhausting all measures usable in the interest of peace. With this end in view, he did not hesitate to take drastic action when occasion required. When a former commander of Fort Moultrie had resorted to unauthorized procedure to replenish his store of ammunition, his transfer had followed at once. Rather than compromise, the president had accepted the resignation of his secretary of state, Lewis Cass, to whose militant championing of the reinforcement project he had steadfastly declined to yield.[18] Now that he had declined to order Anderson back to Moultrie, the commissioners restated their construction of the agreement: "You received and acted on assurances from the highest official authorities of South Carolina that no attempt would be made to disturb your possession of the forts . . . if you would not disturb their existing condition until commissioners had been sent and the attempt to negotiate had failed." [19]

They reminded the president that he was to have granted them an interview the day following their arrival but that, upon receipt of the news of Anderson's removal,

18 Appleton's *American Annual Cyclopædia,* 1861, p. 100.
19 *O. R. A.,* Ser. 1, Vol. I, p. 122.

he had postponed the audience until the next day. At
this, their first opportunity, they had called upon him
to redeem his pledge. Whether there was such a pledge,
they submitted, could no longer be an open question, for
Secretary of War Floyd had resigned, publicly declaring
his interpretation of Anderson's action as a violation of
the pledged faith of the government. Years afterward,
a letter from former commissioner Orr to General Crawford disclosed the sharp issue raised in this meeting. In
urging that Anderson should be sent back, it relates,
Mr. Barnwell took the liberty of painful frankness, saying, "But, Mr. President, your personal honor is involved
in this matter; the faith you pledged has been violated;
and your personal honor requires you to issue this order."
Finally, according to the Orr letter, Buchanan replied,
"Mr. Barnwell, you are pressing me too importunately;
you don't give me time to consider; you don't give me
time to say my prayers. I always say my prayers when
required to act upon any great State affair." [20]

Reverting to the president's complaint relative to the
state's impetuous action in taking over the remaining
forts, the commissioners asserted that this was beside
the point, inasmuch as prior to that seizure there was
ample time for any decision which the exigency of the
case demanded. After the news of Anderson's coup
reached him, they pointed out, more than twelve hours
intervened, and two cabinet meetings met and adjourned,
before word came of the South Carolina maneuver; in
the interval, they refreshed his memory, influential friends
entreated him to act without delay to correct the Sumter
commander's blunder. The lack of vigilance which provided Anderson's opportunity they explained, asserting
that during the past sixty days, a period in which Sumter

[20] Crawford, *The Genesis of the Civil War,* p. 148.

was without any garrison whatever, their people would have experienced little difficulty in occupying the fort. They said:

"You ought to know better than any man that it would have been taken but for the efforts of those who put their trust in your honor. . . . After . . . reiterated assurances given in your behalf, which we cannot believe unauthorized, they determined to forbear, and in good faith sent on their commissioners to negotiate with you. . . .

"Scarcely had the commissioners left, than Major Anderson . . . abandoned his position, spiked his guns . . . made preparations for the destruction of his post, and withdrew, under cover of the night, to a safer position. This was war. . . .

". . . What the State did was in self-defense. . . .

"And all this without the slightest provocation. . . . You have decided. You have resolved to hold by force what you have obtained through our misplaced confidence. . . . Be the issue what it may, of this we are assured, that if Fort Moultrie has been recorded in history as a memorial of Carolina gallantry, Fort Sumter will live upon the succeeding page as an imperishable testimony of Carolina faith." [21]

Deserved or not, this was intemperate language to address to the chief executive of the nation. It was Nicolay's reaction that even though the commissioners made many points which defied refutation, their attitude overstepped the borderline of propriety. Accordingly, Buchanan wrote across the face of the document, "This paper just presented to the President is of such a character that he declines to receive it," and returned it to its authors.[22] The pledge which the commissioners attributed to the president, if made at all, had its birth in

[21] *O. R. A.*, Ser. 1, Vol. I, p. 124.
[22] Nicolay and Hay, *Lincoln*, III, 86.

Buchanan's December ninth conference. Following that interview, the South Carolina congressional delegation filed with the Charleston convention a report in which they referred to a suggestion made by them during the conference; namely, that Anderson might decide to transfer his garrison to Fort Sumter:

> "We stated that the latter step would be equivalent to re-enforcing the garrison, and would just as certainly as the sending of fresh troops lead to the result which we both desired to avoid. When we rose to go the President said in substance, 'After all, this is a matter of honor among gentlemen. I do not know that any paper or writing is necessary. We understand each other.' " [23]

Already it has appeared that tension in the cabinet, brought about by sharp difference of opinion with reference to what should be done at Sumter, led to the resignation of the secretary of war. In the letter which Secretary Floyd sent to the president, he clearly stated the troublesome issue:

> "I then considered the honor of the Administration pledged to maintain the troops in the position they occupied, for such had been the assurances given to the gentlemen of South Carolina. . . . South Carolina, on the other hand, gave reciprocal pledges that no force should be brought by them against the troops or against the property of the United States. . . . Thus affairs stood until the action of Major Anderson. . . . Our refusal or even delay to place affairs back as they stood under our agreement, invites a collision and must inevitably inaugurate civil war. . . . I deeply regret that I feel myself under the necessity of tendering to you my resignation as Secretary of War, because I can no longer hold it under my convictions of patriotism, nor with

[23] *O. R. A.,* Ser. 1, Vol. I, p. 126.

honor, subjected as I am to a violation of solemn pledges and plighted faith." [24]

Floyd was a native of Virginia, a circumstance which, from the viewpoint of the radical element in the North, did not weigh heavily in his favor. About his head there broke a storm of criticism, some of which he may or may not have deserved. Be that as it may, there was obviously scant excuse for the vitriolic assaults which followed his retirement from the cabinet. His enemies went so far as to endeavor to stain his name with dishonor. The plan was to involve him in an alleged conspiracy to defraud the government. It would be less than fair not to note that, knowing of the strikingly similar attack upon Secretary Toucey,[25] some who suspect that much of this was the outgrowth of political ruthlessness have asked relevant questions. Why, when the District of Columbia Court called the case for trial, did District Attorney Ould ask that the case be dropped? Why did Mr. Ould state his belief that the defendant was not a party to the conspiracy? Why did the presiding judge dismiss the case? [26] Such questioners do not overlook the fact that, had there existed a promising outlook for judicial ascertainment of guilt, there was ready at hand intolerance in abundance to poison the atmosphere of a jury hearing.

His determined foes did not stop here. They attributed to him what they chose to characterize treasonable inclinations, asserting that he was guilty of connivance in the transportation of guns and military supplies to points in the South. As to this, the questioners make the point

[24] Appleton's *American Annual Cyclopædia*, 1861, p. 701. See also Crawford, *The Genesis of the Civil War,* pp. 150-151.

[25] Richard S. West, *The Second Admiral; a Life of David Dixon Porter, 1813-1891* (New York, 1937), p. 77.

[26] Appleton's *American Annual Cyclopædia*, 1861, p. 701.

that, even if true, it did not necessarily involve disloyalty. As indispensable to an impartial consideration of his supposed improper conduct, they urge the following facts. The crux of Northern contention was that the South was a part of the Union, a Union which no faction could be permitted to disrupt. While within the limits of the Southern states there were numerous forts, every one of these was manned by a Federal garrison. If the department sent arms, it consigned them in each instance to commissioned officers of the army of the United States, over which organization the secretary of war assuredly did not exercise arbitrary, sole control. They further observe that while, in the event of final rupture of relations, such guns would be located in the South, they not only would be in the hands of Federal soldiers who would know how to use them, but could be available for Southern appropriation only in case of mass defection of Union garrisons, which was hardly to be considered as within the realm of probability.

Others have thought it worth while to note that such intimated but unproved charges were made against an official who necessarily must have earned a reputation as a man of character and ability. At any rate, they suggest, he owed his place in the cabinet to one who had enjoyed exceptional opportunity to appraise the men of his period; namely, a Pennsylvanian who had served successively as congressman, United States senator, minister to Russia, secretary of state under Polk, minister to England under Pierce, and at the time of his selection of Floyd, was president of the United States, the last Democratic president for a quarter of a century.[27]

27 *Modern Encyclopedia,* p. 185.

CHAPTER IX

SUPPLIES FOR FORT SUMTER

Two days after General Scott issued his December thirty-first order to prepare the sloop-of-war *Brooklyn*, "destined to reinforce Fort Sumter," Lieutenant Colonel Thomas received a memorandum in the handwriting of the general. This directed him to fit out a steamer for sea duty, stipulating that the vessel was to carry two hundred well-instructed men, with three months' subsistence and ample ammunition. He was to notify Major Anderson that, should an attack be made by any battery in the harbor upon a vessel bringing reinforcements or supplies, "the guns of Fort Sumter may be employed to silence such fire." [1] With his eyes wide open, Scott was inviting trouble. His plan for reinforcement, he was bound to know, he was making with utter disregard of the thoroughly understood attitude of the Carolinians. With knowledge of the practical certainty that the batteries would fire on the steamer, he was calmly passing along to an army major the suggestion that his commanding general would not view with disapproval the use of his guns. Here was a perfect prelude to a chapter that would tell of war.

The memorandum contained other items of interest. The fact that the steamer would have on board a large complement of troops Thomas was to keep secret by in-

[1] *O. R. A.,* Ser. 1, Vol. I, p. 128.

structions for "complete concealment" on her approach
to the harbor of Charleston. He was to warn Anderson
to beware of telegrams; further, he was to assure him
that his conduct had met "with the emphatic approval
of the highest in authority," a statement which did not
square with the facts. Lastly, he was to give to the Sumter
commander the promise that additional reinforcements
would be sent him if necessary.[2] All this, to be sure, meant
nothing less than a descent to trickery in order to slip
into the fort troops more than sufficient to double the
strength of the garrison. At least, however, there was
here no evasion of the truth of intention to reinforce. In
his answer of four days later Colonel Thomas wrote the
general that in his opinion the project could be carried
out by the *Star of the West,* a steamer sailing regularly
on the New Orleans route. By the simple ruse of her
clearing for that port, it would be thought she was on
her accustomed voyage; in this way the movement could
be made "without exciting suspicion." [3] That Thomas
was an apt pupil in the Scott scheme of intrigue he revealed in his order of the next day to Lieutenant Woods,
the officer in charge of the detachment which was to sail
on the steamer:

> "The duty upon which you are now placed by
> direction of the General-in-Chief will require great
> care and energy on your part to execute it success-
> fully, for it is important that all your movements
> be kept as secret as possible . . . on approaching the
> Charleston bar, you will place below decks your en-
> tire force, in order that only the ordinary crew may
> be seen by persons from the shore or on boarding
> the vessel." [4]

2 *Ibid,* pp. 128, 129.   3 *Ibid.,* p. 130.
4 *Ibid.,* pp. 131-132.

This leaves an unpleasant sensation. The steamer was to make the approach to Charleston under the guise of a friendly freighter when as a matter of fact her mission was furtively to reinforce Fort Sumter, and all this within less than one week after the president of the United States had dramatically called the world to witness that he had neither sent reinforcements to the Charleston forts nor authorized any change in their relative military status.

On January seventh, after the *Star of the West* had sailed, General Scott forwarded by the warship *Brooklyn* a message for her captain. This was to let him into the secret that the mission of the *Brooklyn* was "to afford aid and succor in case your ship be shattered or injured." [5] The very words betray the writer's knowledge that he was up to mischief. Not only was the steamer to have the support of a sloop of war, but the Federal general in chief clearly understood that, should the Carolinians suspect the nature of her cargo, there would likely be real need for such protection. Crossing Charleston bar on January ninth, the vessel proceeded up the channel opposite the Morris Island batteries. The inevitable happened. First, the cannoneers fired a shot across her bow and, when that warning proved ineffective, they turned their guns squarely on her. Persuaded at last of the deadly earnestness of the Carolinians, the *Star of the West* turned and steamed out of range.[6]

The ship's approach had attracted the attention of the Sumter command and, when the batteries opened on her, Major Anderson seriously considered returning their fire. In the emergency he sought counsel of his staff, announcing that it was his inclination to close the harbor and to fire on any vessel attempting an entrance. Lieu-

[5] *Ibid.*, p. 134.
[6] Evans, *Confederate Military History*, V, 10.

tenant Snyder and Captain Doubleday favored such
instant retaliation, but Lieutenant Davis and Dr. Crawford considered it the wiser course first to call upon
Governor Pickens to disavow responsibility. They adopted
the latter procedure.[7] Immediately, Anderson sent the
governor this message:

> "Two of your batteries fired this morning upon
> an unarmed vessel bearing the flag of my Govern-
> ment. . . . I have the honor, therefore, respectfully
> to ask whether the above mentioned act—one, I be-
> lieve, without a parallel in the history of our country
> or of any other civilized government—was committed
> in obedience to your instructions, and to notify you,
> if it be not disclaimed, that I must regard it as an
> act of war, and that I shall not, after a reasonable
> time for the return of my messenger, permit any
> vessels to pass within the range of the guns of my
> fort. In order to save, as far as in my power, the
> shedding of blood, I beg that you will have due noti-
> fication of this my decision given to all concerned.
> Hoping, however, your answer may be such as will
> justify a further continuance of forbearance on my
> part,
> "I have the honor to be, very respectfully, your
> obedient servant,
> "ROBERT ANDERSON." [8]

Between the lines the message conveys the information,
first, that the *Brooklyn* had not arrived to carry out her
part of the program; second, that Anderson had not received Scott's order with its suggestion of his use of his
guns. Uninformed as to the real mission of the steamer,
Anderson did not know that she was loaded with reinforcements, nor that she was to have a naval convoy.
This accounts for his reference to an unarmed vessel.

[7] Crawford, *The Genesis of the Civil War*, pp. 187, 188.
[8] *O. R. A.,* Ser. 1, Vol. I, p. 134.

The Carolinians knew better. Just how they contrived to ferret out a military secret of which even the commander of the fort knew nothing, does not appear; in any event, as Nicolay remarked, "The effort to keep the expedition an entire secret had not succeeded." [9]

On the day of the receipt of Anderson's letter, January ninth, Governor Pickens replied. He took occasion to emphasize that from the beginning of the controversy he had made very plain to the Federal authorities that the state of South Carolina would regard as an act of hostility any attempted reinforcement of the garrison or change in the status of the forts. "The first act of hostility," he insisted, was that of Anderson himself in his removal to Fort Sumter, an offense which had proved so serious as abruptly to terminate peace negotiations between the state's representatives and the president. Interpreting the sending of the troops on the *Star of the West* as nothing short of an effort at coercion, Governor Pickens came directly to the issue so pointedly made. Anderson's ultimatum brought a significantly unambiguous response:

> "Special agents, therefore, have been off the bar to warn all approaching vessels, if armed or unarmed, and having troops to re-enforce the forts on board, not to enter the harbor of Charleston, and special orders have been given to the commanders of all forts and batteries not to fire at such vessels until a shot fired across their bows would warn them of the prohibition of the State. Under these circumstances, the Star of the West, it is understood, this morning attempted to enter the harbor, with troops on board, and having been notified that she could not enter, was fired into. The act is perfectly justified by me. In regard to your threat in regard to

[9] *The Outbreak of the Rebellion*, p. 33.

vessels in the harbor, it is only necessary to say that
you must judge of your own responsibilities." [10]

Here again were ingredients of serious trouble. As to
just what it was, the record is silent, but Anderson learned
something which cooled his ardor. His next communication to the governor announced that "under the circumstances" he had concluded to refer the whole matter to
Washington and that, pending receipt of official advice
from that quarter, he would defer execution of the threat
contained in his note of that morning.[11] There was another who lost no time in taking up the matter with
Washington; Governor Pickens also had some questions
to ask. On January eleventh he sent a messenger to the
president to inquire whether the sending of the vessel was
by his order and, further, if he considered it his right
to move Federal troops into the state. If Buchanan gave
an affirmative answer, the envoy was to say positively
that "neither will be permitted, and either will be regarded as his declaration of war against the State of
South Carolina." [12]

The *Star of the West* incident stirred additional com-
motion. Secretary of the Interior Thompson handed in
his resignation with a public statement: "I was rejoiced
the vessel was not sunk, but I was still more rejoiced that
the concealed trick, first conceived by General Scott and
adopted by Secretary Holt, but countermanded by the
President when too late, proved a failure." [13] Here, surely,
was no diplomatic resort to euphemism; in the parlance
of the street, the writer was not pulling his punches.
"Concealed trick" relieves all strain upon the imagina-

10 *O. R. A.,* Ser. 1, Vol. I, pp. 135, 136.
11 Nicolay and Hay, *Lincoln,* III, 108.
12 Crawford, *The Genesis of the Civil War,* p. 196.
13 *Ibid.,* p. 183.

tion. And why did the president countermand the strata-gem? Thompson's positive averment that it was the idea of Scott possibly gives the clew; also, there comes to mind the message sent through Mr. Washburne to the general on December twelfth.

The day following the firing on the *Star of the West*, Secretary Holt replied to Anderson's request for instruc-tions. The news had already reached the department of war. Furthermore, the secretary knew, what Anderson did not suspect, the inside story of the *Star of the West* venture. Oddly, he did not see fit to regard seriously the shelling of the steamer:

> "The probability is, from the current rumors of to-day, that this vessel has been fired into by the South Carolinians, and has not been able to reach you. . . .
> ". . . You will continue, as heretofore, to act strictly on the defensive; to avoid, by all means com-patible with the safety of your command, a collision with the hostile forces by which you are sur-rounded." [14]

What manner of reasoning could have resulted in such an utterance? The secretary of the interior had exposed the whole affair as a wily stratagem to which Holt, the secretary of war, was a party. In the face of Anderson's reference to the firing on the vessel as an act of war, Sec-retary Holt, ignoring the matter as if what had occurred was of slight consequence, in effect instructed Anderson to consider the incident closed. How Scott's reinforce-ment effort impressed the officers of the garrison, General Totten learned from Captain Foster four days later, January fourteenth:

> "I do not, however, consider it good policy to send re-enforcements here at this time. We can hold our

[14] *O. R. A.*, Ser. 1, Vol. I, p. 137.

own as long as it is necessary to do so. If any force
is sent here it must have the strength and facilities
for landing and carrying the batteries on Morris or
Sullivan's Island. The former will be the easier operation. But if the whole South is to secede from the
Union, a conflict here and a civil war can only be
avoided by giving up this fort." [15]

Captain Foster was a responsible officer, a member of
Anderson's staff, with the advantage of close touch with
all developments at Charleston. As well as any man, he
foresaw that there were breakers ahead. It was not his
prerogative to say in so many words that the fort should
be abandoned, but he yielded to the impulse to put Washington on notice that arbitrary retention was a more
hazardous program than seemed generally to be understood. Some appreciation of this fact apparently was
dawning upon Federal officials in the capital. Just six
days after his letter of January tenth, Secretary of War
Holt again wrote Major Anderson:

> "You rightly designate the firing into the Star of
> the West as 'an act of war,' and one which was
> actually committed without the slightest provoca-
> tion. . . . Unfortunately, the Government had not
> been able to make known to you that the Star of the
> West had sailed from New York for your relief,
> and hence, when she made her appearance in the
> harbor of Charleston, you did not feel the force of
> the obligation to protect her approach as you would
> naturally have done had this information reached
> you.
> "Your late dispatches . . . have relieved the Gov-
> ernment of the apprehensions previously entertained
> for your safety. In consequence, it is not its purpose
> at present to re-enforce you. The attempt to do so
> would, no doubt, be attended with a collision of arms

[15] *Ibid.*, p. 139.

and the effusion of blood—a national calamity which the President is most anxious, if possible, to avoid." [16]

Obviously this is the writing of a man confused in his thinking, even warped in his judgment. Referring to the attack on the vessel as an act of war, he promptly goes on to say that an attempt to relieve the fort would no doubt be attended by bloodshed. Exposed by the public statement of the secretary of the interior as a co-schemer in a concealed trick, he pronounces judgment that the assault by the batteries was without provocation. It was not the government's purpose to reinforce the fort, he observes, when precisely that and nothing else inspired the *Star of the West* fiasco of just one week before. Apparently unconscious of the significance of his remark that, because Washington had not informed Major Anderson of the coming of the ship, he did not feel "the force of the obligation to protect her approach," he takes up again his theme of the desirability of avoiding an outbreak. There was just one method available to Anderson to give assistance to the *Star of the West* and that was to return the fire of the batteries; this would have meant war.

FOOD SUPPLIES FOR MAJOR ANDERSON'S COMMAND

With few exceptions, writers of the Fort Sumter story have had much to say relative to Major Anderson's food supply. With such unanimity and persistence have they painted a picture of a brave little band whose condition was rapidly approaching desperation that the resulting impression of a "starving garrison" has approximated

16 *Ibid.,* p. 140.

the dignity of established truth. The facts, however, justify a restudy.

Anderson's own testimony on the subject seems not to have received the attention it deserves. On December 26, 1860, in the very letter in which he announced to Washington his transfer of his command to Sumter, he wrote that he had one year's supply of hospital stores and about four months' supply of provisions.[17] On December 29, 1860, Robert N. Gourdin, a leading citizen of Charleston, received from his warm friend, Major Anderson, a message saying, "I have supplies of provisions, of all kinds, to last my command about five months, but it would add to our comfort to be enabled to make purchases of fresh meats and so on, and to shop in the city." [18] Because of what is to follow, this should be carefully fixed in mind. From the pen of the commander, here is incontrovertible evidence that the provisions then on hand would safely carry him over until about May 29, 1861.

Leading officials in Washington were taking cognizance of the Charleston situation. In a letter of January sixteenth to General Winfield Scott, Secretary of State J. S. Black discussed the matter. Observing that the forces of South Carolina had shut off Anderson's communication with his government, he concluded that in the course of a few weeks the exhaustion of his stores of food would make it difficult for the commander to maintain his position. The letter, however, contained the definite statement that Anderson's provisions would "last him very well for two months." [19] Thus, while Black's estimate of the adequacy of the supplies fell short of that given by Anderson, it provided testimony from a high source that,

---

[17] *O. R. A.,* Ser. 1, Vol. I, p. 2.
[18] Crawford, *The Genesis of the Civil War,* pp. 128, 129.
[19] *O. R. A.,* Ser. 1, Vol. I, p. 141.

certainly until March sixteenth, the stock on hand would meet the needs of the garrison. The pertinence and materiality of such admissions will be obvious when, later, there will come harrowing tales of conditions at Sumter at the time of Lincoln's inauguration, March fourth.

When Anderson took advantage of the relaxation incident to the celebration of Christmas to slip his men from Moultrie into Sumter, it created bad feeling, but no reprisal was forthcoming. The more recent questionable attempt secretly to send reinforcements on the *Star of the West* provoked a caustic interchange of notes between the commander of the fort and the governor; but there followed the letter of Secretary of War Holt to Anderson with its renewed assurance of the secretary's desire to avoid a collision. The Southerners proceeded to do their part toward healing the wound. A note from South Carolina Secretary of War Jamison to Anderson, written eleven days after the firing on the steamer, revealed that the Carolinians were willing to treat the matter as closed: "I am instructed by his excellency the governor to inform you that he has directed an officer of the State to procure and carry over with the mails each day to Fort Sumter such supplies of fresh meat and vegetables as you may indicate." [20]

This was what the hint to Mr. Gourdin had brought to pass. Less than two weeks before, Anderson was writing the governor threatening to use his guns to close the harbor. Now that same official was saying that Anderson had but to indicate his needs. Better than this, without any direct request from the commander, the governor was making it the duty of a state officer to see to it that the garrison received supplies daily. On the same day

[20] *Ibid.*, p. 144. See also Crawford, *The Genesis of the Civil War*, p. 201.

on which the offer arrived, January nineteenth, Anderson replied to the friendly overture:

> "I confess that I am at a loss to understand the latter part of this message, as I have not represented in any quarter that we were in need of such supplies. As commandant of a military post, I can only have my troops furnished with fresh beef in the manner prescribed by law, and I am compelled, therefore, with due thanks to his excellency, respectfully to decline his offer. If his suggestion is based upon *a right*, then I must procure the meat as we have been in the habit of doing for years, under an unexpired contract with Mr. McSweeney, a Charleston butcher. . . . If the permission is founded on courtesy and civility, I am compelled respectfully to decline it, with the reiteration of my thanks for having made it. In connection with this subject, I deem it not improper respectfully to suggest that his excellency may do an act of humanity and great kindness if he will permit one of the New York steamers to stop with a lighter and take the women and children of this garrison to that city." [21]

Technically, Anderson was correct in his designation of the source from which properly his supplies should come. He wrote the adjutant general on January twenty-fifth that, if the Carolinians were in earnest in their expressed willingness for the command to enjoy marketing privileges in Charleston, it puzzled him that they should object to the government's sending provisions, groceries, and coal from New York. Doubtless he was not without suspicion that the Southerners were motivated in part by a desire to shut off any excuse for Federal provisioning of the command. Be that as it may, his categorical statement that he had not represented in any quarter his need of such supplies would seem to eliminate

21 *O. R. A.,* Ser. 1, Vol. I, pp. 144-145.

him from authorship of the starving garrison thesis. Sensitive as to whether courtesy or recognition of his right prompted the offer of the governor, he declined the proffered assistance but, strangely, did not hesitate to ask another favor.

Immediately upon receipt of his instructions from the governor, the secretary of war of South Carolina proceeded to make good the offer. He directed Quartermaster General Hatch to inform Major Anderson that he would purchase and take down every day "such provisions from the city market as he may indicate." [22] Hatch at once took action of which he gave due notice to the commander: "Inclosed please find copy of letter from Secretary of War. Not waiting your request, I shall send by the mail-boat in the morning two hundred pounds of beef and a lot of vegetables. I requested Lieutenant Talbot to ask you to let me know this evening what supplies you would wish sent daily." [23]

On the next day, January twentieth, Hatch had his answer: ". . . as no arrangements have been made by me with your government in reference to supplies for this post, I feel compelled to decline the reception of those supplies." [24]

This from the commander of the garrison!

That, nevertheless, the provisions were actually sent to, and immediately sent back by, Major Anderson, is shown by Captain Foster's letter of the next day to General Totten:

"The temper of the authorities seems to have changed for the better since Mr. Hayne and Mr. Gourdin have been in Washington. The proposition to supply fresh meat and vegetables was made by

[22] *Ibid.,* p. 145.   [23] *Ibid.*
[24] *Ibid.,* pp. 145-146.

Governor Pickens on the 19th, but declined by Major
Anderson the following day. A supply of fresh meat
and vegetables that had been sent down yesterday by
the South Carolina quartermaster-general was returned." [25]

The day following, Secretary of War Holt wrote
Messrs. Fitzpatrick, Mallory, and Slidell, Southern senators in Washington. He expressed his gratification in
learning through South Carolina Attorney General
Hayne that the Sumter command was obtaining necessary
provisions, such as fresh meat and vegetables, from the
city of Charleston. It was his conviction, he said, that a
continuation of the "present amicable footing" between
Anderson and the officials of the state would be "the hap-
piest result" that could be attained.[26] While Hayne's announcement was premature, since the arrangement as to
food was not as yet in effect, it is apparent that he knew
what the governor had in mind and had taken for granted
the prompt execution of the plan. Plainly, the Federal
secretary did not share Anderson's hesitation in accepting the aid which the Carolina officials were ready to give.
On January twenty-first, South Carolina Secretary of
War Jamison undertook to assist Major Anderson to
overcome his indecision relative to the matter of the governor's offer:

> "In offering to permit you to purchase in this city,
> through the instrumentality of an officer of the State,
> such fresh supplies of provisions as you might need,
> his excellency the governor was influenced solely by
> considerations of courtesy; and if he had no other
> motive for refusing to any of your garrison free ac-
> cess to the city to procure such supplies, he would
> have been moved by prudential reasons for the safety
> of your people, in preventing a collison between them

[25] *Ibid.,* p. 148.   [26] *Ibid.,* pp. 149, 150.

and our own citizens. As to the manner of procuring your supplies, his excellency is indifferent whether it is done by the officer referred to, . . . or . . . by the butcher whom you say you have before employed." [27]

This seems to have had the desired effect for, the day following, the major was ready to discuss the proposition from a more practical viewpoint:

"I have the honor to acknowledge the receipt of your favor of the 21st instant, and to express my gratification at its tenor. I shall direct my staff officer to write to the contractor in reference to his supplying us with beef, and will communicate with you as soon as the necessary preliminaries are arranged, in order that you may then, if you please, give the requisite instructions for carrying them into effect. Be pleased to express to his excellency the governor my thanks for the kind and prompt manner in which he gave his consent to the proposed transfer of the women and children of this garrison." [28]

On January twenty-seventh, in a letter to the adjutant general in which he discussed certain rumors, Anderson said:

"The object of one, which has been repeated more than once, that we are getting fresh provisions from the Charleston market, is apparent enough, viz, to show they are treating us courteously. *But even that is not a fact.* I send herewith a copy of a letter written to our former beef contractor about furnishing us with meat, &c., to which no reply has yet been received—why, I am unable to ascertain; so that, up to this moment, *we have not derived the least advantage from the Charleston market.*" [29]

[27] *Ibid.,* p. 151.   [28] *Ibid.,* p. 152.
[29] *Ibid.,* p. 154. Italics supplied.

Four days later he wrote that he presumed that the contractor did not dare to send the articles ordered for fear of incurring the displeasure of the people of Charleston.[30] Later, however, on the same day, January thirty-first, a note from him carried the news that subsequent developments had dispelled all suspicion:

> "I hasten to write this letter, to be taken to the city by my friend, the Hon. Robert N. Gourdin, to say that the butcher has sent down a supply of fresh beef, with a note from him stating that he had not received my note, and that he did not, therefore, know of my order to him to continue my supplies. . . . Mr. Gourdin says that his excellency the governor is very desirous that we shall receive our supplies regularly, and thinks that there can be no difficulty in reference to groceries also." [31]

Despite long-strained relations and the tension occasioned by the secret mission of the *Star of the West,* followed by Anderson's laying down conditions under which alone he would avail himself of the governor's aid, the record is clear that the Carolinians were leaving nothing undone in their effort to be courteous and helpful. So, holding to this conciliatory policy, they generously overlooked Anderson's touchiness and made arrangements in strict accord with his stipulated preference; and at last they convinced him that the offer arose out of a sincere desire to promote friendliness. Even Nicolay brought himself to admit that members of the garrison received their mail and had the privilege of making purchases of food in Charleston.[32] Reference to the January thirty-first report discloses that Anderson drew a distinction between fresh meat and supplies on the one hand, and groceries on

---

[30] *O. R. A.,* Ser. 1, Vol. I, pp. 159-160.   [31] *Ibid.,* p. 160.
[32] *Lincoln,* IV, 19.

the other, remarking that Mr. Gourdin thought there would be no objection to an extension of the arrangement so as to have it include groceries. He informed the adjutant general on February second that he had received that morning a letter from Mr. Gourdin saying, "I saw his excellency this evening, and he makes no objection to your groceries being sent you." [33]

Now that they were beneficiaries of this friendly cooperation on the part of the state, Anderson was aware that Federal interference would be a blunder. He went so far as to write Washington, "I do hope that no attempt will be made by our friends to throw supplies in; their doing so would do more harm than good." [34] It was the course of wisdom to leave well enough alone. Their great respect for Anderson, coupled with their full appreciation of the delicacy of his position, influenced the Carolinians to see to it that the command lacked none of the necessities of living. To be sure, they were not undertaking to provide the garrison with implements of war or with strictly military supplies. As early as November, 1860, an effort by Fort Moultrie's commander to replenish his stores of ammunition from the Charleston arsenal met determined opposition; but, upon Captain Seymour's formal application, the mayor permitted even this.[35] True, there were those who vigorously opposed even the sending of provisions, but the governor let it be known that, if occasion required, he would order out a company of soldiers to put them on the boat. That the assistance from the state contributed materially to the well-being of Anderson and his men appears in an observation by General Crawford: "The difficulties in regard to the fresh provi-

---

[33] *O. R. A.*, Ser. 1, Vol. I, p. 162.
[34] *Ibid.*, p. 159.
[35] Crawford, *The Genesis of the Civil War*, pp. 58, 59.

sions had been adjusted; the mails were sent regularly, and the garrison maintained in a high state of health." [36]

It so happened that General Crawford was at the time assistant surgeon at Fort Sumter. Starvation presents no difficulties of diagnosis. This unqualified testimonial to health conditions at the post presents another troublesome item, the inclusion of which would have tended to dim the luridness of the story certain writers have seen fit to tell. Insofar as the period up to February is concerned, there is, therefore, no justification for suggestion of the Sumter command's suffering from lack of adequate food supply. The starving-garrison theory does not read convincingly in the light of Anderson's signed estimate of December twenty-ninth that he had supplies of all kinds to last his command until about May twenty-ninth, an estimate, moreover, which did not take into account the provisions secured from Charleston through the coöperation of the governor. Later the food situation is to come up again.

[36] *Ibid.,* p. 291.

CHAPTER X

NEW HANDS AT THE CONTROLS

COMPENSATION FOR THE RELINQUISHMENT OF SUMTER

The controversy between South Carolina and the national government had roots running deep into the subsoil of ultimate sovereignty. Governor Pickens and his friend, President Buchanan, were upholding diametrically opposed positions. True, the state had ceded to the United States the site for the fortification, but that was done while South Carolina was a constituent part of the Union, with a view to securing additional protection of its own interests. To the governor's way of thinking, now that the state had seceded it was little short of presumption for Washington even to consider the maintenance of a garrison within its borders. The obstinacy of those holding a contrary opinion was getting on his nerves. Convinced that nothing but a face-to-face conference would suffice, he would send to Buchanan a responsible official with a straight-from-the-shoulder message. Accordingly, on January twelfth he wrote the president that Attorney General Hayne would come with instructions to make formal demand for the surrender of the fort. He was taking this action, he added, because of his earnest desire to avoid the bloodshed which would result from Washington's insistence on its present course.[1]

With the passing of two weeks and prior to Hayne's taking up the matter with Buchanan, there dawned upon

[1] *O. R. A.*, Ser. 1, Vol. I, p. 166.

149

Pickens realization that, after all, the United States possibly had in the Sumter plant valid property rights which he had not sufficiently considered. In consequence, he so modified his instructions to Hayne that the attorney general's communication to the president took on an entirely new tone. In its final form the proposition was that, speaking on behalf of the governing powers of South Carolina, he held authority to pledge the faith of the state that, upon the Federal government's relinquishment of the fort, adequate compensation would be made for the property interest of the United States.[2] This was a clear concession that, inasmuch as the fortification represented a substantial investment on the part of the central government, it would be inequitable for the state to fail to make good any money loss entailed by its surrender.[3] There was, therefore, no inclination to ask a gratuitous return of the property.

Distorting this suggestion of adjustment into a proposal "to buy Fort Sumter and contents," President Buchanan, speaking through Secretary of War Holt, hedged from meeting the issue squarely. Predicating his action upon his belief that under the constitution he was without power either to cede or to surrender the fort, he rejected the overture of South Carolina. Coming to the matter of the status at Charleston, he put an end to all uncertainty as to the administration's future course. While there was no present intention to strengthen the garrison, such action would follow immediately should the safety of Anderson and his men require it. Moreover, he gave the governor's messenger to understand that the troops would continue to occupy the post until "com-

[2] *Ibid.*
[3] Nicolay, *The Outbreak of Rebellion,* p. 35; Crawford, *The Genesis of the Civil War,* p. 227.

petent authority" should unravel the tangled skein of the war of words. The fact that he had definitely charted his course along this line was, he maintained, entirely consistent with his sincerely pacific inclinations. Reiterating that the attitude of the Sumter command was neither menacing, nor defiant, nor unfriendly, he outlined its function: "It is acting under orders to stand strictly on the defensive, and the government and people of South Carolina must well know that they can never receive aught but shelter from its guns, unless, in the absence of all provocation, they should assault it, and seek its destruction." [4]

This was news indeed. Here was another enigma to complicate the existing network of confusion. The people of Charleston were growing more and more restive under the threat of high-powered guns which, with only slight tightening of tension, might become hostile. Now from the president they were hearing the consolation that they were beneficiaries of the guardianship of this formidable fighting machine. All this sounded amicable enough, but no foreign power was threatening and they knew of no emergency which necessitated intervention of any nature on the part of the central government. If, in truth, a purpose to police South Carolina interests was motivating Washington's retention of the fortress, surely Sumter's present strength was adequate for any imaginable requirement. Not only was there no occasion for reinforcement, but such a course would inevitably make more difficult an adjustment of troubled relations.

More than this, their recollection of an event of less than one month before somewhat dimmed the persuasiveness of the chief executive's protestations of protection. When the *Star of the West* steamed into the harbor of

[4] *O. R. A.*, Ser. 1, Vol. I, p. 168.

Charleston, loaded to the guards with arms, ammunition, and soldiers, the troops concealed below decks, it made an impression too vivid so soon to be forgotten. If Washington intended this as an additional precaution in the program of shelter for the people of Charleston, unfortunately the Charlestonians did not believe it. The secretiveness of the ship's mission had leaked out and it was common knowledge that her captain abandoned his bold undertaking only when, from the roar of the guns of the shore batteries, he awoke to the realization that Carolina was sovereign in her waters.

What had happened to the *Star of the West* should, it seems, have satisfied all parties that the governor was grimly in earnest in conveying through Hayne the warning that the state would vigorously oppose the sending of reinforcements. Nevertheless, certainly insofar as retention of the work was concerned, the president was firmly standing his ground. The controversy had reached an impasse. The Federal government held the view that the dignity of the nation would be compromised by surrender of one of its forts under pressure of thinly disguised threats. The commonwealth of South Carolina insisted that a sovereign state could not longer countenance the maintenance within its borders of an armed garrison flying the flag of a government whose jurisdiction the state had repudiated.

THE CONFEDERATE GOVERNMENT ASSUMES RESPONSIBILITY

Whereas in 1861 Gustavus V. Fox was only a retired naval captain, in 1865 he was assistant secretary of the navy. Such an exceptional record of promotion leaves the impression that behind it there were of necessity unusual circumstances which focused attention on him. In all likelihood, Fox himself supplies the key to the mystery in a report made by him in 1865 to Secretary of the Navy Welles, a document in which he set out the following details of the 1861 expedition to Fort Sumter. As originator of the plan, he took it up with General Scott. The general not only gave his approval but took Fox to Secretary of War Holt to whom, on February seventh, Fox outlined the planned procedure and made known his willingness "to conduct the party to the fort." So strongly did the project appeal to Holt that he in turn agreed to lay it before President Buchanan that same day. To Fox's chagrin, however, on the following day Scott told him that the administration would probably abandon the idea of reinforcement. "He seemed," the report commented, "much disappointed and astonished." [5]

The record has disclosed a letter of February sixth in which Secretary Holt, on behalf of the president, assured the Carolinians that the presence of the Sumter garrison involved for them naught save protection; yet the Fox report runs up the curtain on a scene of the day following, the spotlight playing on the selfsame secretary in conference with the captain, interestedly drinking in the details of a reinforcement scheme. In the meantime, as shown by a letter from Captain Foster to General Totten, the work of placing Sumter in effective fighting condition was proceeding "with unabating activity." Weak points of the fortress he was strengthening, some with solid walls of stone, others with irons and lumber. It was his belief that within a few days he would have these "as secure as necessary." [6] The Carolinians could not have been altogether ignorant of these activities, knowledge of which naturally did not add to their peace of mind. To this

[5] *O. R. N.,* Ser. 1, Vol. IV, p. 246.
[6] *O. R. A.,* Ser. 1, Vol. I, p. 172.

point they had refrained from any attack on the fort,
great as had been the provocation of the secret transfer of
the command and the visit of the *Star of the West*. Negotiations were in progress and, pending these, they had
agreed not to resort to force unless reinforcement from
the outside should be attempted. They were willing to
strain a point to avoid apparent captiousness in their
construction of what would be considered reinforcement.

Up to this period, the principals in the controversy
were South Carolina and the United States. On the fourth
of February, however, the appearance on the flagpole of
the capitol in Montgomery of a strange new emblem
heralded to the world the organization of the government
of the Confederate States of America. The situation now
took on a different phase. No longer was it necessary for
one isolated state to pit its strength against the overwhelming power of the central government. Within a few
days the Confederate congress adopted a resolution declaring a new policy. Henceforth the Confederate government would assume responsibility in such matters as the
existing problem at Fort Sumter. That issue was too
fraught with danger for any one man to handle it, particularly in view of the fact that Governor Pickens, well
known to be high strung and peppery at best, was unin-
tentionally contributing to a crisis of far-flung potentialities. His patience threadbare, the governor welcomed relief from the heavy burden.

Full information of conditions as he saw them Pickens
transmitted in a letter of February thirteenth to Howell
Cobb, president of the Confederate provisional congress.
He had honestly invoked, he wrote, every form of negotiation consistent with the dignity of the state to the end
that South Carolina should have possession of what was
rightfully hers, the forts in Charleston harbor; all over-

tures had ended in the same blind alley, "a refusal, positive and unqualified." During his state's affiliation with the Union, as a matter of course no one had questioned the right of the United States to police Fort Sumter, particularly since its primary function was protection of the port of Charleston; but, he submitted, with the termination of that association, any such obligation on the part of the Federal government was a thing of the past. Washington's insistence that the status was unchanged, and the president's protestation that the state should continue to regard the garrison as a sentinel standing guard over its interests appeared to him a plain distortion of its real significance. His conclusion was that altered conditions had brought it about that "the sole use of it as a military post is in the control it gives to the United States of the harbor of Charleston." Nor did he find it far to go for a convincing illustration of his point: "Its purpose cannot be otherwise than unfriendly when it can only be to enable the United States to commit to its military subordinates the power to refuse 'to permit any vessels to pass within range of the guns' which are within its walls." [7]

Almost verbatim, he was quoting a passage from Anderson's ultimatum of January ninth. The threat had left its sting and his feathers were still ruffled. The logic of his attitude nevertheless appears formidable. The time had come when it was imperative that there should be at least some definite understanding as to future relations at Charleston. So long as South Carolina had been an integral part of the Union, the presence of the garrison had one meaning; but, now that the state was recognized territory of another sovereignty, it carried an altogether different significance. The citizens of Charleston had hardly believed their ears when they learned of the threat of the

[7] *Ibid.*, pp. 255-256.

commander of the fort that, given adequate provocation, he would use his guns to close the port. It is easy to understand that to them it was unthinkable that they should long endure the existence of such undoubted power; if the garrison was to hold its guns over the city as a menace to its very existence, they must of necessity regard its presence as hostile.

THE SECRET PLAN OF THE COMMANDING GENERAL

It was on February eighth that General Scott had sorely disappointed Captain Fox by the intimation that the administration seemed not to be impressed by schemes to reinforce Sumter. What took place during the ensuing twelve days the record does not disclose but something unusual was in the air for, on the twentieth, the general instructed his aide, Lieutenant Colonel Scott, to notify Captain Ward of the naval receiving ship *North Carolina* to prepare his squadron for immediate service. The aide was further to ascertain what store of provisions would be adequate and also how many troops Ward would need in addition to his marines. Giving away the secret that what Scott was aiming at was the reinforcement of Sumter, as well as revealing that the general was running true to form, the order concluded, "See that he is supplied with everything for Anderson. I shall write to-morrow. No time now. Afraid of the wires." [8] The instruction was rather inexact in its specifications but its use of the word "squadron," the suggestion of additional troops, followed by a blanket requisition of everything for Anderson, leave no question that a business-like movement was in the making. The inevitable vein of secrecy cropped out; tempting

[8] *O. R. A.,* Ser. 1, Vol. I, p. 177.

material for speculation appears in the hesitancy of the commanding general to use the telegraph in time of peace.

Close on the heels of the first, another order followed the next day. From one of the officers at Sumter, General Scott had received a list of articles needed at the fort; Assistant Adjutant General Thomas was writing to say that these also should be procured and delivered to Captain Ward should there be room for them in his ships. Suggesting that the expedition might require a detachment of from fifty to two hundred recruits, Thomas likewise closed his note with a word of caution, "See that they are confidentially prepared for that service." [9] General Scott's new attitude causes confusion. When Fox first made known his idea, the general had not only approved it, but had escorted the captain to the office of the secretary of war. Later he had quieted Fox's enthusiasm by a report that the administration was lukewarm. Now, within less than two weeks, he was not only building up an expedition of his own, but was resorting to extreme caution to cover his tracks. Was he endeavoring to sidetrack Fox? Did he have in mind the reservation for himself and his department of the execution of the reinforcement plan?

In the midst of all this activity, on February twenty-third the secretary of war forwarded to Anderson orders to continue to act "strictly on the defensive," and so to establish the sincerity of the president's assurance that the Carolinians had no reason to apprehend trouble from the Sumter garrison.[10] In the light of the combined circumstances, the impression is inescapable that somebody, somewhere, was being kept in the dark as to what was going on in the headquarters of the army. Further adding to the mystery, it turned out that Fox was not being shunted aside. On February twenty-third, the very day on

[9] *Ibid.*, p. 179.   [10] *Ibid.*, p. 182.

which the secretary of war sent his message to Anderson, Captain Fox was writing Montgomery Blair, outlining his reinforcement project:

"I simply propose three tugs, convoyed by light draft men-of-war. These tugs are seaboats, 6 feet draft, speed 14 knots. The boilers are below, with $3\frac{1}{2}$ feet space on each side, to be filled with coal. The machinery comes up between the wheelhouses, with a gangway on either hand of 5 to 6 feet, enabling us to pack the machinery with two or three thicknesses of bales of cotton or hay. This renders the vulnerable parts of the steamer proof against grape and fragments of shells, but the momentum of a solid shot would probably move the whole mass and disable the engine. The men are below, entirely protected from grape; provisions on deck. The first tug to lead in empty, *to open their fire.* The other two to follow." [11]

Plainly, an expert had worked out the details. Nor was there lack of appreciation of the practical certainty that the effort would provoke attack by the Carolina batteries. Assuredly, this is in colorful contrast with the secretary of war's insistence that Anderson should maintain a defensive policy. The secretary was to make another contribution to the muddle. At his instance, Adjutant General Cooper wrote Anderson on February twenty-eighth that, in view of the contents of the "inclosed slip," the secretary of war wished to express his hope that nothing of a hostile character would occur. The enclosure injected a new note: "The Commissioners from the Southern Confederacy are expected to arrive here before the close of this week. They are accredited to the incoming administration and, pending the efforts to negotiate, nothing will be done calculated to disturb the public peace." [12]

11 *O. R. N.,* Ser. 1, Vol. IV, pp. 224-225. Italics supplied.
12 *O. R. A.,* Ser. 1, Vol. I, p. 187.

The South Carolina commissioners had visited Washington in December—in the interest of peace. The authority of the newly organized Confederate government had now superseded that of the state and a Confederate commission was on the way—in the interest of peace. There were many who preferred peace to war and among these, as revealed by their latest orders, were the secretary of war and the adjutant general. Queries present themselves. Could Secretary of War Holt have known of Scott's order to Captain Ward to put his squadron in readiness as early as possible? Did Adjutant General Cooper know that Assistant Adjutant General Thomas was ordering out recruits for Scott's expedition with the direction that these should be "confidentially prepared"? Was Cooper aware of Fox's detailing to Blair a scheme which he clearly anticipated would open the fire of the Carolina batteries? Could it be that the secretiveness of General Scott and Assistant Adjutant General Thomas was being resorted to in order to hide Scott's maneuvers from Adjutant General Cooper, Secretary Holt, and President Buchanan? Was there an inner clique which, with cynical contempt for the "weakness" of Buchanan, was covertly laying plans for war?

The sequence grips the imagination: February twentieth, the hurried call for Ward's squadron, everything for Anderson, fear of the telegraph—this from Scott; February twenty-first, the assistant adjutant general's communication relative to secret preparation of additional troops; February twenty-third, instructions from the secretary of war enjoining Anderson so to guard his actions as to win back the confidence of the Carolinians; February twenty-third, Fox's unveiling to Blair plans and specifications for a venture which, confessedly, was to end in strife; February twenty-eighth, the earnest ad-

monition of the secretary of war to Anderson that, because
of the expected arrival of the Confederate commissioners,
nothing should be done to jeopardize the success of the
negotiations. Such a chain of circumstances apparently
tells its own story. Somewhere a fine Italian hand was
manipulating strings. Some undercover intrigue was in
the making. The period was propitious. Buchanan and his
official family had not wanted war, but these "weaklings"
were on their way out. Within less than one week the new
administration would assume control and the nation would
feel the power of an army of crusaders inspired by red-
blooded leadership. Bearing in mind that the secretiveness
was that of General Scott, it is perhaps permissible to
speculate as to whether here was another reverberation of
the December twelfth letter from Abraham Lincoln.

BEAUREGARD TAKES COMMAND

The military situation at Charleston soon took on a
more serious aspect. On March third one of the Confederacy's recently appointed brigadier generals, P. G. T.
Beauregard, arrived to take command. Somewhere in the
personnel of the Confederate advisory council there was
someone gifted with uncanny skill in accurate appraisal
of military ability. In consequence, throughout the entire
war the South was singularly happy in its choice of key-
men for difficult posts. Among the first of these assign-
ments was that of Beauregard. The storm of controversy
was rapidly centering on Charleston harbor. It was a
distinct tribute to the new general to be charged with the
weighty responsibility of a command which required exceptional tact and resolution. That duty he was to meet
with the finesse of a man with background. A stream of
good French blood had flowed from the old world into

Louisiana and of this stock came Beauregard. Graduating from West Point at the age of twenty, he had at once entered active service. Eight years later an engineer on General Scott's staff during the operations in Mexico, twice wounded at the taking of the city of Mexico, he had to his credit repeated citations for courage and competence. That he possessed in marked degree the respect and confidence of army officialdom is attested by his elevation in 1860 to the position of superintendent of the United States Military Academy. His occupancy of that post was, however, short-lived, for his openly avowed intention of going with his state, in the event of its secession, brought about his transfer five days after he reported for duty. There followed promptly his resignation from the United States army and his selection as a brigadier general in the army of the Confederacy.

Thus it came to pass that, a short while afterward, Beauregard was in command at Charleston while, a few miles distant across the bay, Anderson was ranking officer at Fort Sumter. Fate had again dipped its brush in irony. When in other days it fell to the lot of Major Anderson to give instruction in artillery technique to the West Point cadets, among those who sat under him was the young Louisianian, Beauregard. The youth's earnestness and promise so appealed to the instructor that, upon his graduation, Anderson was instrumental in having him retained as assistant instructor. Subsequent relations of the two were cordial, even intimate. Now, under different flags, they confronted each other, conscious that there might come a day when pupil would match skill against technique of teacher. Beauregard well knew that one of the army's ablest strategists had whipped Sumter into fighting shape; and, better than anyone, Anderson was in a position to appreciate the caliber of his prospective foeman. Neither had any illusions as to the deadly potentialities of the threatened clash. Neither doubted that, if the dread hour struck, the other would know what to do and would do it with the mastery of an expert. And so, spurred on by the rapidly materializing crisis, the comrades of a few years before feverishly busied themselves in final preparations to blast each other with shot and shell.

A NEW ADMINISTRATION COMES INTO POWER

On March 4, 1861, Abraham Lincoln was inaugurated president of the United States.

Fully cognizant of the task at hand, he devoted his inaugural to an effort to clarify his position. Briefly, it was that he strongly opposed extension of the slavery system and was uncompromisingly committed to the cause of the preservation of the Union. Looking backward, it was his view that the Union, formed in fact by the Articles of Association, matured and continued by the Declaration of Independence, was older than the Constitution. Looking forward, he dared think that the Union of the states was perpetual. Secession ordinances were, therefore, legally void; in consequence he gave his pledge that the laws of the Union should be "faithfully executed in all the states." Brave words these, words echoing the faith of a strong man, the new captain of the ship of state; but, even as he spoke, the foghorn was sounding, and the deck rose and fell with the ominous ground swell of a sullen sea.

Almost concurrently with the inauguration, the atmosphere of the great drama became heavy with an element of hitherto-unfelt apprehension. A strangely discordant note crept into communications. Suggestions for avoiding collision began to give place to undisguised references to war. Premonitions of impending crisis brought general alarm. Sharp differences had arisen between the preceding administration and the South Carolina commissioners but, while Buchanan had refused to withdraw the Sumter command, he had tempered the denial with assurance of continued Federal protection. Now, with the passing of Buchanan, there walked from the wings onto the stage a new figure, one as yet with an untried part, but whose presence injected a strange and disturbing uneasiness.

Immediately upon the conclusion of the inaugural ceremonies, Senator Wigfall of Texas notified Governor Pickens that the address meant war sooner or later and that in all likelihood no time would be lost in sending reinforcements to Fort Sumter.[13] Nor was he alone in his interpretation of the president's meaning. L. Q. Washington, prominent among Southerners in the capital, forwarded to Confederate Secretary of War Walker a message echoing Wigfall's sentiments; war was coming, he said, and its arrival would not be long delayed. This, in his opinion, was Lincoln's program, one which nothing except secession of the border states could have blocked. By way of confirmation of his diagnosis of symptoms observable in the new regime, he set out the finding of a group of Southern men who had conferred in the capital the night before:

> "We all put the same construction on the inaugural, which we carefully went over together. We agreed that it was Lincoln's purpose at once to attempt the collection of the revenue, to re-enforce and hold Forts Sumter and Pickens, and to retake the other places . . .
> "We believe that these plans will be put into ex-

13 *Ibid.*, p. 261.

ecution immediately. I learn five or six United States
ships are in New York Harbor, all ready to start.
The United States steamer Pawnee came here the
other day suddenly from Philadelphia, fully provisioned and ready to go to sea." [14]

Another arresting contrast shows up here; these cheer-
less messages were written less than one week after the
secretary of war of the Buchanan administration had informed Major Anderson of the coming of the Confederate
commissioners and had urged avoidance of any complication which might obstruct the path to possible adjustment. Meantime, what was the outlook at Charleston?
Two days after Lincoln came into office, the adjutant
general heard from Anderson that the Confederates had
landed reinforcements at Cummings Point. The commander's hitherto well-nigh-daily report that all was still
and quiet gave way to the comment that everything indicated activity and determination. The message made clear
his alarm: "God grant that our country may be saved
from the horrors of a fratricidal war!" [15] Anderson had
heard something. Far from a sentimentalist, the distinctly
new tone of his note, the reverent invocation of the Deity,
the unashamed disclosure of profound emotion, leave no
question that he sensed a sharp turn for the worse had
come. Renewed activity on the part of the Southerners in
turn indicated that they likewise had received news which
had stirred them to the depths. Even so, there was no cessation of courtesy. Captain Foster wrote General Totten
on March ninth that, the day before, an officer arrived
from Cummings Point with a white flag and a letter from
Colonel Gregg offering ample apology for the firing toward Sumter of a gun which the practicing artillerymen
did not know "was shotted." [16]

[14] *Ibid.,* p. 263.   [15] *Ibid.,* p. 191.   [16] *Ibid.,* pp. 192-193.

In Washington, too, they were closely watching developments. Edward Bates, the attorney general, kept a diary in which he set down that on March ninth Lincoln held a cabinet meeting to consider the desirability of sending a reinforcement expedition to Charleston. Concerning this project, he noted, army men informed the president and his advisers that they considered destruction of such an expedition almost inevitable, whereas it was the contention of the naval experts that the danger was but slight. The diary reveals that both groups impressed Bates: "The naval men have convinced me fully that the thing can be done, and yet as the doing of it would be almost certain to begin the war . . . I am willing to yield to the military counsel and evacuate Fort Sumter." [17]

It is noteworthy that Bates, a finished lawyer, trained in accurate use of language, did not write that the undertaking would likely begin war. He spoke of its precipitating "the war," words perhaps betraying a conviction that it was merely a question of time when hostilities would flare forth. It leaked out that other cabinet members were questioning the wisdom of retention of the Federal garrison in Sumter. Furthermore, something had altered the former, pessimistic views of Senator Wigfall for, on March eleventh, he telegraphed Beauregard of the opinion current in Washington that Anderson would be ordered to evacuate within five days; he added that this was certainly informally agreed on in the cabinet the preceding Saturday night. This was comforting news but he was, nevertheless, proceeding cautiously: "May have been done as a ruse to throw you off your guard and enable them to re-enforce." [18] At that very moment the Confed-

[17] Nicolay and Hay, *Lincoln,* III, 380-381.
[18] *O. R. A.,* Ser. 1, Vol. I, p. 273.

erate commissioners were in Washington. Senator Wigfall's telegram preceded by only one day their first formal
communication to Seward. While the senator was not inclined altogether to trust the new administration, it seemed
to him that the developments justified an inference that
Lincoln would possibly adopt the peace policy of the
Buchanan regime.

Only a few weeks had passed since Captain Fox's interview with General Scott in which he learned that Buchanan's administration seemed not to favor his proposed
expedition to reinforce Fort Sumter. In the report made
by Fox in 1865, reviewing the events of 1861, he explained that with the incoming of the Lincoln government
there was a revival of his reinforcement dream. On March
twelfth of that year, the document says, Postmaster-
General Blair telegraphed him to come to Washington.
Having assumed office only eight days before, Lincoln
was in the throes of acquainting himself with his manifold
duties. Nevertheless, despite the failure to carry the point
with the preceding administration and although he knew
that General Scott had advised surrender of the fort,
Blair had an idea that the time was opportune to reopen
the discussion. There was no difficulty in securing a hearing; in Fox's words, "Mr. Blair took me at once to the
White House, and I explained the plan to the President." [19] Nicolay tells of the interview, saying that Captain Fox convinced Lincoln and a majority of the cabinet
that he could "in a dark night throw a small quantity of
provisions and a few men into the fort." [20] Because of its
bearing on the true purpose of the Charleston expedition,
it is well to take note of the expression "provisions and
men." They did not, however, adopt the plan. So keenly

[19] *O. R. N.,* Ser. 1, Vol. IV, p. 246.
[20] *The Outbreak of Rebellion,* p. 51.

did Blair resent the reluctance of his associates to unite behind the Fox program that he offered to resign.[21]

The danger incident to any effort at reinforcement was being more and more understood. There were, of course, extremists who were indifferent to consequences, but a large element of the people were in favor of concession to avoid strife. This public sentiment was being reflected in the attitude of members of the Lincoln cabinet who, while convinced of the feasibility of the desperate Fox plan, were, nevertheless, shying from assumption of responsibility for sponsoring its execution. Frustrated for the time, Fox was nothing if not resourceful. Those who thought they had eliminated him were to learn that he was as capable a politician as a soldier. Unruffled, he at once set about to see to it that final determination of the issue was postponed. He had not played his last card. His report reveals his hand:

> "Finding that there was great opposition to any attempt at relieving Fort Sumter, and that Mr. Blair alone sustained the President in his policy of refusing to yield, I judged that my arguments in favor of sending in supplies would be strengthened by a visit to . . . the fort. The President readily agreed to my visit if the Secretary of War and General Scott raised no objections.[22]

The Federal officers in Sumter little dreamed that the administration was regarding with favor the Fox maneuver. How little they did know, Captain Foster revealed in his note of March fourteenth to General Totten:

> "The news received yesterday by telegraph, to the effect that orders were issued to evacuate this fort, seems to have caused an almost entire cessation of

[21] *Diary of Gideon Welles,* 1, 13.
[22] *O. R. N.,* Ser. 1, Vol. IV, p. 247.

work on the batteries around us. I am not ceasing
work on the preparations, although I am taking an
inventory of the materials on hand, and otherwise
getting ready for such orders should they actually
arrive . . .

"Unless otherwise directed I shall discharge my
force when the orders for evacuation arrive, and leave
with the command, with my associates, and report to
you at Washington." [23]

General Totten, chief of engineers of the United States
army, located in Washington, was presumably in close
touch with the administration. Before him was this letter
from one of his responsible officers at Sumter, plainly
taking for granted the early abandonment of the fort.
Captain Foster was going so far as to detail his intended
subsequent movements. What explanation is there for
General Totten's failure immediately to inform Foster
that there was no foundation for the report?

Capital gossip soon had it that Lincoln was about to
send a special messenger to Charleston. The rumor reached
the ears of the Confederate commissioners, but they
missed completely the significance of the anticipated step.
On March fourteenth, Commissioner Forsyth wrote Governor Pickens that he confidently believed Sumter was to
be evacuated and that a government representative was
on his way with the necessary orders for Anderson.[24] The
fact that the mission of the president's envoy became
known even to the commissioners brings to light one of
the main difficulties with which Lincoln was contending.
He was uncertain whom to trust, and surely surrounding
conditions justified his perplexity. In consequence, he
limited more and more the circle of those whom he felt he

[23] *O. R. A.*, Ser. 1, Vol. I, p. 196. See also Crawford, *The Genesis
of the Civil War,* p. 300.
[24] *O. R. A.*, Ser. 1, Vol. I, p. 275.

could take into his confidence. Even more than in earlier life he exhibited the excessive reticence described by Herndon in the words, "He was the most secretive—reticent—shut-mouthed man that ever lived." [25]

Whatever the cause, a haze of uncertainty pervaded the capital, a haze that obscured the vision not only of the populace, not only of the Southern commissioners, but also of such consequential officers as the chief of army engineers.

[25] W. H. Herndon's letter to Remsberg in *Journal of Southern History,* Vol. III, No. 3, p. 265.

Chapter XI

PLANS TO "PROVISION" FORT SUMTER

THE PRESIDENT IS INFORMED THAT REINFORCEMENT MEANS WAR

On March fifteenth, the very next day after the commissioners wrote Governor Pickens of their belief that orders were en route for the abandonment of Sumter, President Lincoln made an unusual request of each member of his cabinet. It was that there be prepared and submitted to him in writing an opinion on the following question, "Assuming it to be possible to now provision Fort Sumter, under all the circumstances is it wise to attempt it?" [1] They were his official counselors, but the usual cabinet discussion would not suffice. The Charleston problem was rapidly reaching troublesome proportions, and he wanted the advice in such form that it could be read and studied. Secretary of War Cameron answered the same day. From the first mention of the subject of the expedition, he had understood that, as a mere matter of routine, most likely there would be placed squarely up to his department responsibility for seeing it through. Reluctantly he advised against the attempt, basing his counsel upon his knowledge of concurrence in this view of all officers at Fort Sumter, and of General Scott and General Totten. Taking into account the professional qualification, the high rank of both commanding general and chief of engineers of the army, as well as their sources of inside information,

[1] *O. R. A.,* Ser. 1, Vol. I, p. 196.

the secretary went so far as to venture the suggestion that the president would not be justified in disregarding such high authority. He very definitely expressed his own reaction:

> "Whatever might have been done as late as a month ago, it is too sadly evident that it cannot now be done without the sacrifice of life and treasure not at all commensurate with the object to be attained; and as the abandonment of the fort in a few weeks . . . appears to be an inevitable necessity, it seems to me that the sooner it is done the better." [2]

Conversant with Fox's project, Cameron was bearing in mind that, by the captain's own admission, it was part of his calculation that the approach of the leading tug would open the fire of the Carolina batteries. Of the practically certain consequences of such recklessness, the secretary was outspokenly apprehensive:

> "The proposition presented by Mr. Fox, so sincerely entertained and ably advocated, would be entitled to my favorable consideration if, with all the light before me and in the face of so many distinguished military authorities on the other side, I did not believe that the attempt to carry it into effect would initiate a bloody and protracted conflict." [3]

These were startlingly plain words. In effect, the head of the department of war was saying to the president that, if he wanted war, this was the way to get it. With his answer Cameron enclosed memoranda from Generals Scott and Totten. Through the almost daily reports of Captain Foster of the engineering force at Sumter, General Totten knew intimately conditions at the post. His memorandum recorded his familiarity with, as well as his

[2] *Ibid.,* pp. 196-198.   [3] *Ibid.,* p. 198.

emphatic disapproval of, the Fox program. "We know," it said, "that guard boats and steamers are active during the night; and think they have all the means of intercepting with certainty this little expedition, and overpowering it by boarding—a commencement of war." Nor did he limit his objections to the scheme proposed by Captain Fox for, he continued, "this attempt, like any other, will inevitably involve a collision." [4] There, again, was plain language; once more, and from an outstanding military expert, the deliberate warning—a commencement of war.

General Scott's memorandum took a wider range. According to information which had come to him, there were friendly Southerners who held the view that the evacuation of Forts Sumter and Pickens would strongly impress the eight remaining slaveholding states and so "render their cordial adherence to the Union perpetual." It might even result, the general dared think, that the friendly gesture of withdrawal of the garrisons would bring back into the fold the states on whose soil the two fortifications stood. He was inclined to advise that it would be excellent strategy on the part of the Federal government openly to adopt such a conciliatory, even magnanimous, attitude as to regain the confidence of the disaffected sections and thereby break the back of the whole secession movement. Referring to the Fox movement, he unhesitatingly passed judgment that any such venture verged on sheer daredeviltry:

> "It seems from the opinions of the Army officers who have expressed themselves on the subject—all within Fort Sumter, together with Generals Scott and Totten—that it is perhaps now impossible to succor that fort substantially, if at all, without cap-

[4] *Ibid.,* p. 200.

turing, by means of a large expedition of ships of war and troops, all the opposing batteries of South Carolina. . . . An abandonment of the fort in a few weeks, sooner or later, would appear, therefore, to be a sure necessity, and if so, the sooner the more graceful on the part of the Government." [5]

Cameron, Scott, Totten were the three officials on whom would fall the burden of any military movement. All three abruptly predicted that the Fox venture was heading the nation straight into war. What of the other cabinet members? Blair and Chase favored the plan but Chase was qualifying his approval by a reservation; if the probability was that the attempt would provoke war, he could not give it his sanction. Nicolay says that further reflection convinced Chase that conflict could be averted if only the administration would disarm suspicion by a policy of liberality and kindliness toward the South. He therefore returned an affirmative answer.[6] Welles was of the opinion that the continued friction at Charleston had reconciled the public mind to the withdrawal of the garrison. Smith argued that retention of Sumter was not essential to any of the duties of the government. As Bates saw it, the hazard involved outweighed any possible gain. Seward reiterated his prediction that the program would provoke combat and open civil war. According to General Crawford, he took pains feelingly to explain the positiveness of his position: "I would not initiate a war to regain a useless and unnecessary position on the soil of the seceding States. I would not provoke war in any way *now*." [7]

These were the men whom the president had brought to Washington as advisers on whom he could safely lean.

[5] *Ibid.,* p. 200, 201.   [6] *Lincoln,* III, 385.
[7] Crawford, *The Genesis of the Civil War,* p. 353. See also Nicolay and Hay, *Lincoln,* III, 385-388.

It was anything but heartening that at such a time
as this only two of them were upholding his hand.[8] And,
most disconcerting of all, what was he to think of the
attitude of Seward, the man on whom he had conferred
the highest honor at his disposal? It was an impressive
line-up: Scott, Totten, the entire Sumter staff, every
member of the cabinet except two. Such unanimity of
judgment would, it seems, have given pause even to a
president sincerely seeking advice. Can it be that this
was one of those instances when counsel is asked with
expectation that it will secure backing for a predeter-
mined course? Here was a gesture of consulting military
authorities and his own official family; is it possible that,
whatever his friends and advisers said or thought, he was
driving straight ahead toward a planned objective?

Even so, it was hardly Lincoln's preference to present
the bald aspect of a one-man project. With skilful handling, might not it be possible to bring his associates
into line? Obviously some such thought came into his
mind for, on March nineteenth, Secretary Cameron notified General Scott that the president desired accurate
information as to the real conditions surrounding Major
Anderson's command. The general was, therefore, to
select and send immediately to Charleston a competent
observer with instructions to bring back a detailed report
of the existing status.[9] On its face this seemed reasonable
enough; in so crucial a matter no one could object to the
gathering of all possible information. And surely the
forthcoming report could hardly be other than fair inasmuch as Scott, whose opposition to Fox's suggested procedure was a matter of record, was to name the investigator.

[8] Crawford, *The Genesis of the Civil War*, p. 357.
[9] *O. R. A.*, Ser. 1, Vol. I, p. 208.

Why, then, should there promptly show up another angle to this ostensibly open and neutral conduct? When the order reached the files of the war department, there was on it an indorsement by the secretary of war saying that General Scott selected Captain Fox as the messenger and that his choice was "approved by the president." [10] All this brings again to the fore Fox's observation that his arguments would be strengthened by a visit to the fort. The proponent of the scheme, the officer later to command the expedition, would, it seems, have been the last man Scott would think of as one to conduct an impartial investigation. Fox was partisan to the last degree, but Scott decided upon Fox, and the selection met with the "approval" of the president.

On the next day, March twentieth, the Confederate commissioners telegraphed General Beauregard to ask, first, if the garrison had left Sumter; second, if there was any action on the part of Anderson indicating likelihood of such a course. [11] And on the same day all three Confederate commissioners signed a communication to remind the Confederate secretary of state that time was essential to a peaceful issue of their mission. Far from losing hope, they confidently asserted that, if there was faith in man, reliance could be placed on the assurances they had received. [12] Encouraged by what he had heard, the next day Confederate Secretary of War Walker wrote Beauregard that semiofficial rumors justified the inference that in all probability Anderson would shortly leave Sumter. How strongly Walker believed in the imminence of evacuation he revealed by including in his note the suggestion that it would be in order to provide for Major Anderson and his men a safe exit from the harbor. [13]

[10] *Ibid.*, p. 209.
[12] *Ibid.*

[11] *Ibid.*, p. 277.
[13] *Ibid.*, p. 279.

An expression which now was becoming hackneyed
opened Captain Foster's March twenty-second report to
General Totten. Everything, he said, appeared to be
quiet that morning in the batteries around them. This
time, however, the captain had other news. On the preceding night, his message said, a special messenger, Mr.
Fox, arrived at the fort under escort of Captain Hartstene and, after a confidential interview with Major Anderson, left immediately for Washington.[14] The details
of this visit Fox set out in his 1865 report. Reaching
Charleston he sought out Captain Hartstene, formerly
an officer in the United States navy, through whom he
secured an introduction to Governor Pickens. He presented his credentials and the governor authorized Hartstene to take him to Fort Sumter. While preparations
for the trip were being made, he had a conversation with
General Beauregard. Of his later conference with Anderson and his subsequent report to Lincoln, Fox wrote:

"Major Anderson seemed to think it was too late
to relieve the fort by any other means than by landing an army on Morris Island. He agreed with General Scott that an entrance from the sea was impossible; but as we looked out upon the water from the
parapet it seemed very feasible, more especially as
we heard the oars of a boat near to the fort, which
the sentry hailed, but we could not see her through
the darkness until she almost touched the landing. I
found the garrison getting short of supplies, and it
was agreed that I might report that the 15th of
April at noon would be the period beyond which he
could not hold the fort unless supplies were furnished. I made no arrangements with Major Anderson for reenforcing or supplying the fort, nor did
I inform him of my plan.

"Upon my return I had the honor to be called

14 *Ibid.*, p. 211.

frequently before the President and in the presence
of different members of his Cabinet to answer the
objections presented by Lieutenant-General Scott
and the military authorities. . . . I maintained the
proposition and suggested that it was a naval plan
and should be decided by naval officers. The President asked me if there was any naval officer of high
authority in Washington who would sustain me,
and if so to bring him to the White House. I knew
that Commodore Stringham was at that time filling
the position of detailing officer in the Navy Department and I took him to the President, where in the
presence of Lieutenant-General Scott he not only
confirmed my views, but said that he had that morning held a conversation with Commodore Stewart,
who declared that Fort Sumter could be easily re-
enforced and provisioned with boats at night." [15]

All this again focuses attention on Lincoln's approval
of Scott's selection of Fox as the investigator of conditions at Sumter. The mission completed, Fox returned to
the capital for conferences in which the president called
upon him to refute the objections of the military authorities, particularly those of General Scott, the very man
to whom, ostensibly, he owed his assignment. To say the
least this is somewhat confusing. Furthermore, it is
noticeable that Fox wrote that he had made no arrangements for reinforcing the fort; true, he added the words
"or supplying," a camouflage which was quite the vogue,
the inappropriateness of which appears by his own disclosure that what they did discuss, Major Anderson
thought they could not accomplish by any procedure
short of the landing of an army. Also calling for explanation is Anderson's note to Washington the day following
his interview with Fox, which he opened with the statement that he had examined the point alluded to by Fox

[15] *O. R. N.*, Ser. 1, Vol. IV, pp. 247-248.

the night before. Observing that a vessel lying at the point in question would be at the mercy of Moultrie's thirteen guns, he shifted to the department of war the burden of making its own decision as to what would be the chances of a safe debarkation and unloading under the circumstances.[16] If Fox's version of the conference with Anderson is worth face value, a question presents itself: what, then, was the commander talking about?

Other details had faded from Fox's memory. He overlooked mentioning what General Crawford relates; namely, that Major Anderson took pains to impress on Captain Fox the fact that the arrival of reinforcements would instantly precipitate a collision and bring on civil war.[17] Clearly, it was not an enduring impression. At any rate, the record is silent as to whether, on his frequent appearances before the president, Fox was able to recall this memorable feature of the conversation. In his record of the conference between Fox and Pickens, General Crawford tells that, just before the two separated, Pickens remarked that he understood the object of the visit to the fort to be peaceful, a characterization in which Fox acquiesced.[18] There was one of Fox's hosts who was not sure that his errand was one of peace, who was suspicious both of messenger and of mission. After the return from Sumter, Beauregard inquired of Captain Hartstene whether he was with Captain Fox all the time during his visit, to which Hartstene replied that they were together with the exception of a brief period when Fox was with Major Anderson; whereupon the seasoned soldier observed, "I fear that we shall have occasion to regret that short period." [19] In the midst of all this manipulation,

16 *O. R. A.,* Ser. 1, Vol. I, p. 211.
17 *The Genesis of the Civil War,* p. 371.
18 *Ibid.,* pp. 370, 387.   19 *Ibid.,* p. 372 n.

on March twenty-sixth General Totten wrote Captain
Foster:

> "It is hoped that in case of the evacuation of Fort
> Sumter you will be able to bring away the books,
> drawings, papers, and perhaps light articles of value
> in your care, but it can hardly be expected that you
> can secure the heavy articles of property. You
> should, however, do so if you can.
>
> "Should the fort be evacuated, you will . . . leave
> with the command, and report in person, with your
> assistants, Lieutenants Snyder and Meade, at this
> Department." [20]

So, just seventeen days prior to the bombardment of
Sumter, the army's chief of engineers was writing instructions predicated upon his expectation of the withdrawal of the garrison. There were those in the administration orchestra whom the conductor was not supplying
with the score.

MORE LIGHT AS TO THE "STARVING GARRISON"

If the plan to reinforce Fort Sumter was to succeed,
there was another detail which called for attention. In
view of the almost unanimity of advice that the undertaking would end disastrously, it was desirable to present
it in another light than that of simple aggression, the use
of the armed force of the United States government to
overawe a seceding state. From immemorial time, when
one group has coveted the possessions of a neighbor, or
has seen fit to unloose its legions to enforce its will upon
a weaker people, it has unblushingly made resort to hoary,
accepted diplomatic technique; thereupon, a puzzled
world has listened to the prospective aggressor's complaint of brutal mistreatment of its nationals residing

[20] *O. R. A.*, Ser. 1, Vol. I, p. 217.

within the boundaries of the contemplated victim. When
it is deemed profitable to arouse the war spirit, nations
have found no method comparable to this humanitarian
appeal to go to the rescue of those of their own blood.

So, in this instance, it was unwise to proceed until
back of the movement there was a united sentiment. One
obstacle was that many Northerners, alarmed by the
prospect of an open break, were even going so far as
emphatically to disapprove any measure which might
bear the taint of coercion. No one, however, could overlook the fact that the little garrison at Sumter, sym-
bolizing the sovereign power of the United States, had
no alternative but to stand its ground until orders came
to abandon the post. Should it be made to appear that,
by reason of its position of isolation and its numerical
weakness, the command was being harshly discriminated
against, enduring grave hardship, even confronting possible martyrdom, the North as one man would rise in
response to such a poignant appeal. Apparently indicating that at this juncture the old technique was not being
overlooked, Miss Ida Tarbell writes in her biography of
Lincoln:

> "Almost the first thing brought to his [Lincoln's]
> attention on the morning of his first full day in office
> was a letter from Major Anderson, the officer in
> command of Fort Sumter, saying that he had *but a
> week's provisions*, and that if the place was to be
> reinforced so that it could be held, it would take
> 20,000 good and well-disciplined men to do it. . . .
> What was to be done? *The garrison must not be
> allowed to starve.*" [21]

Gideon Welles, Lincoln's secretary of the navy, made
a contribution toward the creation of a similar impres-

[21] *The Life of Abraham Lincoln,* III, 14-15. Italics supplied.

sion. He records that on March 6, 1861, General Scott
disclosed to him, Secretary of War Holt, and General
Totten "certain intelligence of a distressing character
from Major Anderson at Fort Sumter, stating that his
supplies were almost exhausted, *that he could get no provisions in Charleston,* and that he with his small command would be wholly destitute in about six weeks." [22]

John T. Morse, Jr., added a powerfully stirring narrative in his life of Lincoln: "On the same day [March 4,
1861] there came a letter from Major Anderson. . . .
There were shut up in the fort together a certain number of men and *a certain quantity of biscuit and of pork;*
when the men should have eaten the biscuit and the pork,
which they would probably do in about four weeks, they
would have to go away. The problem thus became direct,
simple, and urgent." [23]

Here, indeed, was a blood-chilling canvas, a picture
of a spectacle which, according to these writers, be-
numbed the new president on the occasion of his inauguration: a brave and hungry little garrison, reduced to a
fast-diminishing ration of biscuit and pork, facing the
stark reality of being utterly destitute within a week,
starvation creeping closer and closer, while only a few
miles distant across the bay there lay the city of Charleston with unlimited quantities of food, a community from
which they could get no provisions, and which, callously
enough, had decreed that no relief from other sources
would be tolerated. Here was the antidote for Northern
apathy to the administration program. Breathed there a
man with soul so dead as not to feel an onrush of red
blood under the stimulus of the new-found slogan, "The

[22] *Diary of Gideon Welles,* I, 4. Italics supplied.
[23] *Abraham Lincoln* in the "American Statesmen Series" (2 vols.
Boston and New York, 1899), I, 244. Italics supplied.

garrison must not be allowed to starve"? What would
history say of a people who sent their soldiers to a faraway post and failed to reach out a rescuing arm when
they faced the extremity of threatening starvation?

The new rallying cry had as its source of inspiration
the purported letter from Major Anderson, a document
represented as coming to Lincoln's notice not later than
March fourth or fifth. Reported as disclosing acute distress at Sumter, it served the purpose of a dynamo of
patriotism, one sending its electric thrill of sympathy
and indignation into the heart of the North. The vital
significance of such a message renders the more striking
an element of mystery which surrounds it. The writers
who made such effective use of it give a reference which
neither discloses the statements they set forth, nor can
be warped to support their theory of the garrison's March
fifth privation. As careful a student as Professor Ramsdell, who has made a thorough study of the episode, says
simply, "Anderson's letter has not been located." [24] In
such a situation, it is in order to have a look at the
Official Records, and, by use of these documents, to call
to the stand the one witness who beyond peradventure
knew the exact facts—Major Robert Anderson.

Reverting to what the record has already revealed, as
far back as December 26, 1860, Anderson reported to
his adjutant general that he had on hand a "year's supply of hospital stores and about four months' supply of
provisions." [25] Thus his own estimate was that the provisions then at the post would last the command until
about April twenty-sixth, one month and twenty-two
days later than the date to which Tarbell, Welles, and

[24] Charles W. Ramsdell, "Lincoln and Fort Sumter," *Journal of
Southern History*, III (August, 1937), 266. For further discussion of
the Anderson letter, see Appendix II.

[25] *O. R. A.*, Ser. 1, Vol. I, p. 2.

Morse refer. On December 29, 1860, he wrote Gourdin, his Charleston friend, that he possessed stores of provisions "of all kinds" to meet the needs of the command about five months, or until about May 29, 1861, which was two months and twenty-five days after the date of the inauguration.[26]

On January 19, 1861, according to the record, Governor Pickens offered to send over daily to Fort Sumter fresh meat and vegetables, to which proposal the major replied that he was at a loss to understand the latter part of the message—the offer of supplies—inasmuch as he had not represented in any quarter that the garrison was in need of such provisions.[27] Suiting his action to his word, when the South Carolina governor delivered the provisions to the fort, the commander promptly sent them back.[28] This was on January twentieth, only some six weeks prior to the period named by the depicters of the garrison's distress. Anderson made known that he desired to procure his beef in the accustomed manner— from a Charleston butcher—whereupon Governor Pickens readily acceded to his preference and gave the necessary instructions for coöperation on the part of the state. A letter of January thirty-first from Anderson to Gourdin proves that the proposed plan was being carried out and indicates the governor's willingness to include groceries among the articles the command would be at liberty to procure from the city.[29] The new arrangement completed, Anderson wrote Washington, "I do hope that no attempt will be made by our friends to throw supplies in." [30]

All this was, of course, prior to the inauguration of Lincoln, the date of the garrison's supposed privation.

[26] Crawford, *The Genesis of the Civil War*, pp. 128, 129.
[27] *O. R. A.*, Ser. 1, Vol. I, pp. 144-145.
[28] *Ibid.*, p. 149.   [29] *Ibid.*, pp. 160, 162.   [30] *Ibid.*, p. 159.

The record, fortunately, does not close at this point. In a report of March twenty-sixth, Major Anderson gave information throwing additional light on the arrangement entered into by him and Governor Pickens. On March thirteenth he said, he had written the governor of his failure to receive "some boxes of solidified milk" which to his knowledge had reached Charleston; this failure he had attributed to some interference with the governor's own instructions. He added, however, that on March fifteenth Mr. Jamison had given his assurance not only that Governor Pickens' attitude was unchanged but that an investigation would be made of the alleged interference. The report further brings into the open the revelation that on March seventeenth, thirteen days after Lincoln took office, Anderson wrote Jamison a letter in which he referred specifically to the coöperation of the South Carolina officials in enabling him to secure his provisions, saying, "I hasten to ask you to refer to my letter to his excellency, and you will see that I did not solicit any modification of his original permission about receiving supplies of fresh meat and vegetables. *I am satisfied with the existing arrangement,* and only called attention to a reported interference of it." [31]

If, then, in time for Lincoln to read it on March fourth or fifth, Anderson wrote a letter saying that his supplies "were almost exhausted and that he could get no provisions in Charleston," or that "there were shut up in the fort a certain number of men and a certain quantity of biscuit and pork," or that "he had but a week's provisions," there is presented a problem which defies explanation. His own statement, dated March seventeenth, that he did not solicit any "modification" of the original permission as to provisions, surely leaves

31 *Ibid.,* p. 220. Italics supplied.

no vestige of doubt that his and the governor's agreed plan was in operation. What was more, clearly the commander had no change to suggest; the arrangement was working to his entire satisfaction. What else is needed to demonstrate either that Anderson did not write the letter upon which the utterances of Welles, Tarbell, and Morse relied, or that the interpreters of such communication as he did make woefully misconstrued his meaning? If such a conclusion is not accepted, there is left the unpleasant intimation that Robert Anderson was putting on a Jekyll and Hyde act, stooping to twofacedness the likelihood of which his whole record challenges. He may or may not have written the letter referred to as detailing his desperate situation. If he did, it is something of a coincidence that as important a document as this, one which emitted the spark which started a patriotic conflagration in the North, should not have been preserved. Be that as it may, the March seventeenth letter shows up in the official record prepared by the United States government. All this injects into accounts of the garrison's March fifth privation an element of grave improbability. Certainly it makes a hard bed either for Anderson, or for Scott and Welles, sponsors of the "could get no provisions in Charleston" story.[32]

[32] While testimony from Northern sources is purposely being given preference, an exception may be indulged in for a sidelight contributed by Lieutenant Colonel A. R. Chisolm, one of General Beauregard's aides. That the occurrence he relates took place later than March 3, 1861, is obvious, inasmuch as it was not until that date that Beauregard assumed command at Charleston. Colonel Chisolm writes: "Having visited Fort Sumter five times under a flag of truce, and once after the surrender, I became well acquainted with most of its officers. During a visit in company with Captain Samuel W. Ferguson, the officers jokingly complained of being short of cigars and like luxuries. With General Beauregard's approval, the next time duty called us to the fort we presented them with several cases of claret and boxes of cigars."—*B. & L.,* I, 82.

The record, however, tells more. It uncovers a report from Anderson to his adjutant general as late as April first which proves that his supply department had actually been selling pork, flour, bread, coffee, and sugar to Captain Foster "for the subsistence of his *employes* in his department at this post." This report included another prepared by Lieutenant Norman J. Hall, dated April 1, 1861, and addressed to Major Anderson. Hall's statement detailed the supplies sold, referred to them as being necessarily "consumed by others," estimated the various periods for which each of the sold supplies would have lasted had they been issued only to members of the command, and concluded with the words, "or, with what is now on hand, at least thirty-five days of comfortable subsistence for the command." [33]

Finally there turns up a letter of April third from Anderson to the adjutant general in which, after mention of the governor's failure to send permission for the engineer employes to leave the fort, he made this comment: "To-day notice has been received that no butter can be sent down and only one quarter of a box of soap. These little matters indicate, *perhaps*, an intention to stop our supplies entirely. I must, *therefore*, most respectfully and urgently ask . . . what I am to do *as soon as* my provisions are exhausted. Our bread will last four or five days." [34]

The cumulative effect of these several statements over Anderson's own signature renders inescapable two conclusions. First, among the supplies from Charleston were not only fresh meat and vegetables, but also such articles as boxes of solidified milk, groceries, butter, and soap. Second, beyond question, not only at the time of Lincoln's

[33] *O. R. A.,* Ser. 1, Vol. I, pp. 230-231.
[34] *Ibid.,* p. 232. Italics supplied.

inauguration, but as late as April third, the Carolina officials were still coöperating.

As a matter of course, by this time Anderson was bound to know that the Southerners were not ignorant of activities in Washington. They had reason to suspect some hostile movement and it was only natural they should take all precautions. It was not lost on him that this, likely, afforded explanation of the governor's refusal to permit the engineer employes to leave the post. He understood that, if hostilities were in the offing, it would not be the course of prudence for either force to tolerate unrestricted coming and going between the city and the fort. Curious eyes might be on the alert and, with military secrets to be guarded, it would be stupid to leave open a gate for espionage. Anderson needed no telling that the Confederates would hardly continue to coöperate in providing supplies for a garrison which within a few days might develop into a menace; what he was conveying to Washington was information that already there were indications of a slowing down of the flow of supplies and that, with the arrival of the day when the Charleston market should be closed to him, the command would occupy a precarious position. When, on April seventh, the food supplies from the city were entirely shut off, no one understood better than Anderson that this order was the direct result of news that Washington was about to send warships, troops, arms, ammunition, and supplies to Fort Sumter.

THE PRESIDENT WITHHOLDS VITAL INFORMATION

Major Anderson was careful to keep in close touch with the department of war. His was the responsibility to keep constantly before his superior officers a true picture of his surroundings. Conscious that he held the respect of those in command, he did not hesitate to speak freely what was in his mind. As early as November, 1860, he warned that reinforcement would precipitate an attack. The following month he wrote again of the determination of the people of the state to prevent any increase of his garrison. In the same month his report recorded the mounting of guns in Sumter as rapidly as possible. Secretary of War Holt notified Anderson in January, 1861, that it was not the government's purpose to reinforce Fort Sumter. Also in that month Anderson again protested against any endeavor to throw in supplies. By way of explanation, he informed the department that Governor Pickens had interested himself in seeing that the garrison should regularly receive food from Charleston. A few weeks later President Buchanan, speaking through Secretary Holt, saw fit to give out the comforting assurance that the people of South Carolina ought to know that they would never receive anything but protection from Sumter's guns. In March one of Anderson's notes ended with a fervent expression of his hope that the country might be saved from the horrors of a fratricidal war.

Such excerpts are illustrative of the correspondence between the Sumter commander and the department of war. The net result was mutual recognition of two facts— any sending of supplies from Washington would cause trouble; attempted reinforcement would almost inevitably end in a clash. In consequence, the instructions to Anderson unfailingly emphasized the advisability of acting entirely on the defensive.

In the capital, conditions were becoming more and more confused. It was an open secret that in numerous cabinet meetings discussion had centered on Fort Sumter. Close observers inferred that some momentous movement was on foot. The general impression was that, while the president leaned to reinforcement, he was not receiving from the cabinet the support which he had expected. Presently, according to Miss Tarbell, excitement was spreading in Washington like a fever.[35] And something else had occurred. A Washington dispatch of March fifteenth to the Charleston *Courier* said:

> "The senate had a long executive session today. General Scott (a most unusual thing) was admitted and consulted in regard to the status of all Southern forts. Important military measures were considered. General Scott reiterated his opinion that Major Anderson must be withdrawn. Questions were put to him and the matter discussed minutely in all its bearings." [36]

The senate of the United States was not blind to conditions. With the state of affairs rapidly moving toward a crisis, an injudicious move might bring the curse of war. Not altogether persuaded that those in high position were competently handling delicate questions, it was endeavoring to inform itself to the end that there might be on its part not only intelligent appreciation of the ramifications of the troublesome problem, but understanding coöperation should the president invoke its assistance. With this in mind, on March twenty-fifth the senate passed a resolution asking Lincoln for certain information. In particular, the senators wished to have a look at recent reports from the commander of the Sumter garrison. After all, it was a modest request. What objection could there be to turning over to the highest deliberative body of the nation an army major's correspondence with the war department?

[35] *The Life of Abraham Lincoln*, III, 17.
[36] Quoted in the Montgomery *Weekly Post*, March 27, 1861.

Surely the president of the United States was aware
that only congress could declare war. He knew it was
open to him to adopt the simplest of procedures; namely,
to call congress into extra session, to lay before it Anderson's correspondence along with other pertinent information, and thus to bring it to share responsibility of
the fateful hour. There was, to be sure, a possibility that
congress might take action which would throw his entire
plan out of gear. It was not his temperament to brook
opposition. One of his intimates, Herndon, has mentioned
the stubbornness which nothing could penetrate once he
made up his mind, as well as the intellectual arrogance
and unconscious assumption of superiority which was a
source of irritation to Chase and Sumner.[37] Mr. Hay
says that on frequent occasions, when difference of opinion arose between him and his advisers, the president
was wont to observe that he knew more about it than
any of them.[38]

Lincoln knew something else. Just eleven days prior
to the date of the senate resolution, Senator Douglas
had said in that body:

"I take it for granted no man will deny the proposition that whoever permanently holds Charleston
and South Carolina, is entitled to the possession of
Fort Sumter. . . .

". . . We cannot deny that there is a Southern
Confederacy, *de facto,* in existence, with its Capital
at Montgomery. We may regret it. I regret it most
profoundly; but I cannot deny the truth of the fact,
painful and mortifying as it is. . . . I proclaim boldly
the policy of those with whom I act. We are for
peace." [39]

[37] Edgar Lee Masters, *Lincoln, the Man* (New York, 1931), pp. 389,
400, 401.   [38] *Ibid.,* p. 400.
[39] Stephens, *Constitutional View of the Late War Between the States,*
II, 352-353.

The senator was speaking to his own resolution, one calling for the evacuation of all forts in the South except those at Key West and Tortugas. What was more disconcerting, eleven members of the senate had voted for that resolution. Again, it was common knowledge that the senate had called General Scott for vigorous questioning. The cross-examination had taken wide scope, the status of all Southern forts, and from him had come the admission that the transfer of the Sumter garrison was imperative. Now, to cap all, on Lincoln's desk there lay a request from these same senators for Anderson's correspondence. On the day following, he sent this answer:

"WASHINGTON, D. C., March 26, 1861
"TO THE SENATE OF THE UNITED STATES:
"I have received a copy of a resolution of the senate passed on the twenty-fifth instant, requesting me, if in my opinion not incompatible with the public interest, to communicate to the senate the dispatches of Major Robert Anderson to the war department during the time he has been in command at Fort Sumter.
"On examining the correspondence thus called for, I have, with the highest esteem for the senate, come to the conclusion that at the present moment the publication of it would be inexpedient.
"ABRAHAM LINCOLN" [40]

ANOTHER MESSENGER FROM LINCOLN

Captain Fox, special messenger of the president of the United States, had honored Fort Sumter with a visit. Arriving on the night of March twenty-first, he had obtained an interview with Major Anderson, after which he immediately returned to Washington. Just four days

[40] *A Compilation of Messages and Papers of the Presidents,* VI, 2. See also Tarbell, *The Life of Abraham Lincoln,* III, 17.

later, the honor was repeated. On March twenty-sixth
Captain Foster wrote General Totten:

> "A messenger from the President of the United
> States arrived yesterday about 2 o'clock, and after
> delivering his dispatches and having an interview
> with Major Anderson, departed about 3 o'clock.
> Mr. Lamon, I understand, was the gentleman's
> name, and he was escorted to the fort from the city
> by Colonel Duryea, of the governor's staff." [41]

Two visits, within five days, of presidential envoys
were enough to cause the Southerners to stop, look, and
listen. Naturally, concerning the Fox incident both speculation and suspicion were rife. They were still in the
dark as to what went on in his interview at the fort, but
they knew enough to excite their belief that his object
was not what he represented it to the governor. The
second messenger was also clearly on urgent business for,
after traveling all the way from Washington, he arrived
at the fort, had his conference with the commander, and
took his departure, all within one hour. There was no
difficulty in understanding the nature of his mission.
Colonel Lamon, a former law partner of Lincoln's, in-
troduced himself to Governor Pickens as a confidential
agent of the president and declared openly that he had
come to arrange for the removal of the command.[42] As
in the case of Fox, the governor was scrupulously careful
to extend all courtesy to Lamon, detailing a staff officer
to act as escort.

The frank disclosure of the object of his visit, the
welcome intelligence that he was the bearer of a message
which would go far toward a solution of the Sumter
muddle, allayed the suspicion Fox had stirred and tinged

[41] *O. R. A.,* Ser. 1, Vol. I, p. 221.
[42] Crawford, *The Genesis of the Civil War,* p. 374.

the horizon with a roseate hue. Could it be, the Southerners asked themselves, that Washington at last realized the reasonableness of their contention that they could not tolerate the presence of an armed Federal garrison in a work commanding the approaches to Charleston? Lamon's visit aroused hope that the prospect of war was fading. Beauregard immediately transmitted to Secretary of War Walker at Montgomery the inspiriting news.[43] On the same day there was an interchange of letters between Anderson and Beauregard, copies of which Anderson forwarded to Washington. Beauregard's letter to Anderson said:

> "Having been informed that Mr. Lamon, the authorized agent of the President of the United States, advised Governor Pickens, after his interview with you at Fort Sumter, that yourself and command would be transferred to another post in a few days, and understanding that you are under the impression that I intended under all circumstances to require of you a formal surrender or capitulation, I hasten to disabuse you, and to inform you that our countries not being at war, and wishing as far as lies in my power to avoid the latter calamity, no such condition will be exacted of you, unless brought about as the natural result of hostilities." [44]

The Confederate commander thus assumed as a fact the early withdrawal of the garrison. He also gladly corrected a rumor which he understood had offended Anderson, but this act of thoughtfulness proved unnecessary, for Anderson replied: "I . . . hasten to say that I needed no denial from you of the expression attributed to you. The moment I heard that you had said that I should not leave this fort without surrendering I re-

[43] *O. R. A.*, Ser. 1, Vol. I, p. 282.
[44] *Ibid.*, p. 222.

marked that it was not true, and that I knew you had not said so." [45]

Beauregard's message and Anderson's response bring into the foreground two arresting facts: first, Beauregard referred to Lamon as the authorized agent of the president, and this evoked no denial from Anderson; second, Beauregard mentioned his information that the president's messenger had conveyed to the governor news of the intended transfer of the garrison. If Anderson understood otherwise, this clearly called for comment, but none was forthcoming. Nor is Anderson's silence to be attributed either to reserve or to hostility. In his note disclaiming intention to exact a formal surrender, Beauregard suggested other conditions which, it seems, deeply wounded his opponent. Upon learning this, the Confederate general promptly disavowed any purpose to offend "so gallant an officer," offered an apology, and closed his message, "I remain, dear major, yours very truly." [46] Thereupon, Anderson "hastened" to reply to his "kind and satisfactory note," ending his letter, "I am, dear general, yours sincerely." [47]

The removal of the Sumter command would of course have eliminated the main source of irritation. Whether, therefore, as responsible a messenger as Mr. Lamon carried such a message to Charleston readily appears a matter of importance. The record shows that Beauregard wrote not only the Confederate secretary of war but Anderson as well that Lamon said just that. Any effort to discount this because of Beauregard's Confederate connection brings up another problem. Anderson sent to Adjutant General Thomas, Beauregard's letter containing Lamon's statement; had Thomas known differently, would not he have informed Anderson that there

45 *Ibid.*　　　　　　46 *Ibid.,* p. 223.　　　　　　47 *Ibid.*

was no authorization of such an announcement? Furthermore, on March twenty-eighth, the day following that
of his communication to Thomas, the Sumter commander
wrote Beauregard of his hope that in the near future
the two of them would "be placed in a position which will
be more agreeable and acceptable . . . than the anomalous
one we now occupy." [48] There is no escaping the import
of those words. If, however, there remains any question
as to whether Lamon created the impression of the early
abandonment of Sumter, an answer is provided in Anderson's own words in a letter of April fourth to Adjutant
General Thomas: "The remarks made to me by Colonel
Lamon, taken in connection with the tenor of newspaper
articles, have induced me, as stated in previous communications, to believe that orders would soon be issued for
my abandoning this work." [49]

How is this to be reconciled with the undisputed fact
that, just two weeks before, on March twenty-first, a
former messenger from the president had visited the fort
with the express purpose of carrying back information
with which to stimulate the reinforcement sentiment?
Both Fox and Lamon had come to Charleston within a
period of five days. They came on missions, the respective
purposes of which were diametrically opposed. They gave
out statements and left impressions which were hope-
lessly irreconcilable. What about all this?

Somebody was either quite naive, or quite crafty.

Something was wrong.

[48] *Ibid.*, p. 226.

[49] *Ibid.*, p. 237. See also Crawford, *The Genesis of the Civil War*,
p. 378.

CHAPTER XII

CLEARING THE DECKS FOR ACTION

"EVERYTHING STILL AND QUIET"

The nightmare of war was fraying the nerves of the nation. Fathers and mothers were peering anxiously into the future, wondering how soon the day would come when their sons would be called to march forth as prospective targets. There were many in the North who held the view that it might be very well for the Federal government temporarily to remove its troops from Sumter. A great nation, it seemed, might best reveal its true greatness by willingness to make even great sacrifices for the common good. Turning the fortification over to the Southerners might involve some compromise of dignity but even this would not be too large a price to pay for relief from tension that was leading straight to war. The odds were impressive that such a magnanimous gesture would quiet excitement long enough to provide a breathing spell. Time for reflection might bring to the disaffected states realization of the far-reaching consequences incident to permanent separation from the Union. It might even result in their ultimately resuming their respective places as units of the republic. The seceders, on the other hand, had visions of a government all their own and were contending that, as a matter of right, the United States should voluntarily relinquish such forts as stood on their soil. In both groups Lamon's announcement inspired hope almost too thrilling to be true.

196

So, after these months of dread, this was to be the joyous awakening from a bad dream. That Anderson himself shared the feeling of relief, he revealed in his note to Beauregard, written three days after Lamon's visit, in which he expressed the hope that in the near future they would find themselves in a more acceptable position than the anomalous one they then occupied. To the Sumter commander, worn down under the strain, the news was as welcome as the first faint glow of dawn to a tired watcher of the night. He would get out, the Confederates would move in, and for the time at least the crisis would be at an end. His dream, however, was vain; there were developments of which he had not so much as an intimation. The solution of the problem was not to be as simple as that. The very next day after his optimistic note to Beauregard, March twenty-ninth, Lincoln sent over to the secretary of war a formidable document:

"I desire that an expedition, to move by sea, be got ready to sail as early as the 6th of April next, the whole according to memorandum attached, and that you co-operate with the Secretary of the Navy for that object.

"A. LINCOLN

[Enclosure No. 1.]
"NAVY DEPARTMENT. *Preliminary orders.*— Steamers Pocahontas at Norfolk, Pawnee at Washington, Harriet Lane at New York (Treasury Department), to be under sailing orders for sea, with stores, &c., for one month. Three hundred men to be kept ready for departure from on board the receiving ships at New York.

[Enclosure No. 2.]
"WAR DEPARTMENT. *Preliminary.*—Two hundred men to be ready to leave Governor's Island in New

York. Supplies for twelve months for one hundred men to be put into portable shape, ready for instant shipping. A large steamer and three tugs conditionally engaged." [1]

Fox had won. Here was the fruition of his efforts. In his February 23rd letter to Montgomery Blair, he had said that he proposed three tugs with naval convoy. Lincoln had a more ambitious conception—to enlarge Fox's plan by the addition of five hundred soldiers, a "large steamer" which turned out to be the transport *Baltic*, and three other "steamers." It was all very well for the secretiveness of the scheme to use for the *Pocahontas*, the *Pawnee*, and the *Harriet Lane* the same designation applied to the *Baltic*—"steamers." As a matter of fact, the *Pocahontas* and the *Pawnee* were warships, the *Harriet Lane* an armed cutter.[2]

The president of the United States personally issued and signed this order. There was little leeway for exercise of discretion or judgment on the part of the secretaries of war and the navy. Before the document left the executive mansion, someone had worked out all the details: the number, names, present location, of the men-of-war; the complement of troops the ships were to carry and precisely from what places they were to come; the quantity of supplies they would require; the date of sailing. To a marked extent, the president was playing a lone hand. On March fifteenth his plan had met discouraging opposition from the cabinet but, with the passing of two weeks, sentiment in the official family was now

[1] *O. R. A.*, Ser. 1, Vol. I, pp. 226, 227. See also Nicolay and Hay, *Lincoln*, III, 433.

[2] Rhodes, *A History of the United States*, III, 350; Nicolay, *The Outbreak of Rebellion*, p. 59; *Diary of Gideon Welles*, I, 16; Robert S. Henry, *The Story of the Confederacy* (Indianapolis [c. 1931]), pp. 69, 233.

more favorable. It developed, however, that the president was ignoring the views of his chosen advisers. According to Nicolay, it was on the day preceding the cabinet meeting of March twenty-eighth that Lincoln asked, not any official of the departments of war or navy, nor Scott, nor Totten, but Captain Fox to prepare the skeleton of such an order as he deemed desirable.[3] Another of the Lincoln biographers, John T. Morse, Jr., gives a behind-the-curtain glimpse of the cabinet session:

> "Was it courtesy or curiosity that induced the President to sit and listen to this warm debate between his chosen advisers? They would have been angry had they known they were bringing their counsel to a chief who had already made his decision. . . . He had already, the day before the meeting, directed Fox to draw up an order. . . . When the meeting broke up, he at once issued formal orders to the secretaries of the Navy and of War to enter upon the necessary preparation."[4]

A number of years later, Montgomery Blair wrote of his personal contribution toward nerving the president to make his decision. Fearing that Scott's argument was causing Lincoln to waver, Blair roundly denounced Scott and proclaimed that his ideas were those of a politician, not a general. His boldness stiffened the Lincoln backbone. In his account he said:

> ". . . the President saw that he was misled, and immediately ordered the *reinforcement* of Fort Sumter. It is impossible to exaggerate the importance and merit of this act. It was an *irrevocable decision* that the Union should be maintained by *force of arms*. It was assuming the greatest responsibility ever assumed by any man."[5]

[3] *Lincoln*, III, 433.   [4] *Lincoln*, I, 246-247.
[5] Crawford, *The Genesis of the Civil War*, pp. 365-366. Italics supplied.

All this, as well as Lincoln's appreciation of the seriousness of the step he was about to take, is confirmed by Miss Tarbell who, referring to the president's agitation on the evening of March twenty-eighth, intimates that he was not unaware that the order he was to give the next day might plunge the nation into civil war. She adds that he gave the order.[6]

On the same day on which Lincoln ordered the expedition, the adjutant general learned from Anderson that he had "the honor to report everything quiet." [7] And, on the day following, Captain Foster of the engineers reported to his chief, General Totten, "Everything is quiet." [8] On March thirtieth, Gideon Welles, secretary of the navy, issued private orders to commandants of the navy yards at New York, Washington, and Norfolk, respectively, directing the preparation for sea service on or before the sixth of April of the ships designated by the president.[9] The Fox report of 1865 supplies additional information as to the activities of the period, mentioning, among other details, that Lincoln sent Fox himself to New York on a mission thus described:

> "I met by previous arrangement Messrs. William H. Aspinwall and Charles H. Marshall, for the purpose of making with them preliminary arrangements for the voyage. Mr. Marshall declined to aid me upon the ground that the attempt to relieve Fort Sumter would kill the proposed loan and bring on civil war, and that the people had made up their minds to abandon Sumter and make the stand upon Fort Pickens." [10]

So, to the secretary of war, the general in chief, the chief of engineers, the officers in Fort Sumter, let alone

[6] Tarbell, *The Life of Abraham Lincoln,* III, 19.
[7] *O. R. A.,* Ser. 1, Vol. I, p. 227.   [8] *Ibid.*
[9] *O. R. N.,* Ser. 1, Vol. IV, p. 228.   [10] *Ibid.,* p. 248.

other distinguished military experts mentioned in Cameron's March fifteenth report, all of whom regarded the Fox project as visionary and dangerous, Mr. Marshall added himself and "the people." Here, again, from an anticipated source of sympathy and help, Lincoln and Fox heard the sinister prophecy—civil war.[11] In the meantime, was there any appreciable change in conditions at Sumter? Adjutant General Thomas heard from Anderson on April first:

> "I have the honor to report that everything is still and quiet. . . . The South Carolina Secretary of War has not sent the authority, asked for yesterday, to enable me to send off the discharged laborers. Having been in daily expectation, since the return of Colonel Lamon to Washington, of receiving orders to vacate this post, I have kept these men here as long as I could; but now, having nearly completed the important work of cleaning up the area, &c., I am compelled, in consequence of the small supply of provisions on hand, to discharge them. An examination of the accompanying report of the A. A. C. S. will show that the supply of provisions brought over would, *had the issues been limited to my command*, have lasted for a longer period than that mentioned in my letter of December 26, 1860." [12]

The report's testimony to the continued tranquillity of Charleston is significant, but the high light is its revelation that Anderson daily expected orders to leave. Furthermore, it means something that the commander of the Sumter garrison conveyed this eye-opening information to the adjutant general. It so happens that the adjutant general is the principal staff officer of the army, the right-hand man of the commanding general, through

[11] Crawford, *The Genesis of the Civil War,* p. 404.
[12] *O. R. A.,* Ser. 1, Vol. I, p. 230. Italics supplied.

whom communications are received and orders issued. What is the inference from Thomas' failure at once to inform Anderson that there was no ground for the rumor as to the issuance of such instructions? Surely if, with knowledge that the report was not authentic, he learned that Anderson was laboring under a delusion, Thomas' day's work included no duty comparable in importance to that of setting the commander right on so grave a matter. In view of the bewildering exposure that the veil of secrecy overhanging the White House blinded high-ranking army officials, there is little occasion for astonishment that the conduct of affairs in the capital was mystifying and irritating the Southerners. Confederate Secretary of War Walker wrote Beauregard on April second that, in view of "the delays and apparent vacillations" of the Washington government, he considered that the time had arrived for a cessation of the courtesy of permitting the garrison to secure supplies from Charleston.[13] The secretary's suggestion did not, however, bring immediate action.

In almost the identical language of the report of the preceding day, Anderson informed Adjutant General Thomas on April second that everything was quiet, adding the comment that, as far as he could see, the Confederates were doing no work.[14] This was the status at Charleston, but everything was not quiet in Washington. The Confederate commissioners were keeping their eyes open and what they were witnessing was puzzlingly at variance with the pacific assurances being sent them by Lincoln's secretary of state. On April third they gave Confederate Secretary of State Toombs the benefit of their observations. Federal war and navy departments were humming with activity. Warships, troops, and sup-

[13] *Ibid.*, p. 285.   [14] *Ibid.*, p. 232.

plies were being hurriedly assembled. Precisely what it was all about the commissioners did not know, but they were confident trouble was brewing and in a letter of April fifth to Toombs they said in their judgment it might be just as well for the Confederate government to be on the alert.[15]

On April third something happened to supply further, if entirely unintended, proof of the mastery with which the administration was carrying out its campaign of secretiveness. From one Washington office to another a message went—the writer General Totten, the recipient the secretary of war. The secretary must have smiled indulgently as he perused these earnest words from the general, "If we do not evacuate Fort Sumter it will be wrested from us by force." [16] What more is required to make clear that the chief of engineers of the army, regularly informed by Captain Foster as to affairs at Sumter, was in utter ignorance of the order issued by the president of the United States just six days before?

AN OLD SOLDIER SCORNS TO EQUIVOCATE

The administration decided on April fourth to break to Major Anderson the thrilling news that the expedition would sail. Simon Cameron forwarded the communication over his own name, but the fact is, Lincoln himself drafted the "confidential letter": [17]

> "Your letter of the 1st instant occasions some anxiety to the President.
> "On the information of Captain Fox he had supposed you could hold out till the 15th instant without any great inconvenience; and had prepared an expedition to relieve you before that period.

[15] *Ibid.*, p. 286.   [16] *Ibid.*, p. 233.
[17] Nicolay, *The Outbreak of Rebellion*, p. 58; Nicolay and Hay, *Lincoln,* IV, 40.

"Hoping still that you will be able to sustain yourself till the 11th or 12th instant, the expedition will go forward; and, finding your flag flying, will attempt to provision you, and, in case the effort is resisted, will endeavor also to re-enforce you.

"You will therefore hold out, if possible, till the arrival of the expedition." [18]

The letter referred to as causing the anxiety was Anderson's report of April first in which he mentioned that he was daily looking for orders to vacate his post, an expectation based on information brought from Washington by Colonel Lamon.[19] In this communication, after mentioning his decision to discharge the laborers employed at the fort, Anderson had made the observation that, had he limited the issues of supplies to members of his command, his provisions would have lasted for even a longer period than he estimated in his letter of December 26, 1860. In that letter he had said that he had one year's supply of hospital stores and provisions for about four months. This meant that the *provisions on hand* on December twenty-sixth would, *unreplenished*, be adequate for the needs of the garrison until about April 26, 1861.[20] And this, to be sure, is to be considered in the light of another fact. Since the writing of the December letter, the officials of the state of South Carolina had, on their own initiative, perfected arrangements enabling him regularly to supplement his provisions with supplies from the city of Charleston, these including such articles as fresh meat, vegetables, groceries, butter, and soap. It was these arrangements with which, on March seventeenth, Anderson had expressed himself as being satisfied.[21]

[18] *O. R. A.,* Ser. 1, Vol. I, p. 235: Crawford, *The Genesis of the Civil War,* p. 382.

[19] *O. R. A.,* Ser. 1, Vol. I, p. 230.   [20] *Ibid.,* p. 2.   [21] *Ibid.,* p. 220.

The president's reply divulges that Fox reported that the garrison could hold its own until April fifteenth without any great inconvenience. Of itself, this would seem to provide rather conclusive evidence on the matter of food supplies. No less charged with veiled meaning was the expressed hope that Anderson might maintain his position until the eleventh or twelfth. It was something more than a coincidence that the eleventh or twelfth was the date named for the armada to drop anchor off Charleston bar. Further import of the suggestion as to holding out until the fifteenth later developments are to bring out. It is well to bear in mind that Major Anderson did not receive the president's communication until April seventh. Meanwhile, the expedition was making ready to sail. The furtiveness which cloaked the undertaking, Captain Fox himself reveals in the 1865 report:

> "Delays which belong to the *secret history of the period* prevented a decision until the afternoon of the 4th of April, when *the President sent for me* and said that *he had decided to let the expedition go*, and that a messenger . . . would be sent to the authorities of Charleston before I could possibly get there, to notify them that no troops would be thrown into Sumter if provisions were allowed peacefully to be sent to the garrison." [22]

The president was to time the arrival of his messenger so that the notice would just precede the appearance of the fleet. On its face, such notification leaves the impression of an act of fairness. This conclusion, unhappily, runs counter to a well-established fact; General Scott, General Totten, all the officers in Fort Sumter knew, Lincoln was bound to know, that any Federal attempt to provision the fort would meet certain and determined

[22] *O. R. N.,* Ser. 1, Vol. IV, p. 248. Italics supplied.

resistance. In the light of this, the president's protestation that no troops would be thrown in if the Southerners retreated from their attitude relative to the sending of provisions consciously ignored the real issue. Be that as it may, the administration was closing its eyes to consequences. The day on which Lincoln drafted his letter to Anderson, Fox heard from the war department. The transports for the expedition were lying in New York harbor already loaded with supplies and troops. Fox was to take charge of these and proceed to Charleston where a naval squadron would await him. There he was to make an effort "to deliver his subsistence"; should there be any movement to stop him, he was to make his needs known to the senior naval officer, who would be in possession of orders from the secretary of the navy "to use his entire force to open a passage." [23] Can that have any meaning other than that, if the Southerners dared to make trouble, the warships would blast an entrance into the harbor with their guns?

The highly publicized plan to "provision" the fort and to throw in reinforcements only in case of resistance came in for a somewhat different characterization when General Scott had occasion to deal with it. On April fourth the general gave to Lieutenant Colonel Scott the following instructions:

"This letter will be handed to you by Captain G. V. Fox, ex-officer of the Navy, and a gentleman of high standing, as well as possessed of extraordinary nautical ability. He is charged by high authority here with the command of an expedition, under cover of certain ships of war, whose object is to re-enforce Fort Sumter.

"To embark with Captain Fox you will cause a detachment of recruits, say about two hundred, to

[23] *O. R. A.,* Ser. 1, Vol. I, pp. 235-236.

be immediately organized at Fort Columbus, with a competent number of officers, arms, ammunition, and subsistence." [24]

There spoke the soldier. A veteran of the age of seventy-five years, he had won his spurs in the War of 1812. During the war with Mexico he had received his promotion to the rank of commander in chief of the army of the United States. Grown gray in the service, with the bluntness of the old-timer, the general came out flatly with the truth. He knew who was responsible for the movement; "he is charged by high authority here." He did not refer to the ships as steamers; he knew perfectly well what they were and gave them their proper designation, "ships of war." He neither wasted words about provisioning only, nor hedged as to the goal of the expedition; he knew what it was and stated it with disarming directness, "whose object is to reinforce Fort Sumter."

If it should be thought that General Scott was unconsciously magnifying the military feature of the movement, a resort to the diary of a member of the cabinet will supply ample confirmation of the accuracy of the old soldier's terminology. Gideon Welles was not so dextrous as some of his colleagues in the use of camouflage such as "relieving," or "succoring," or "provisioning" the fort. According to his *Diary*, in the first White House conference following Lincoln's inauguration "there was a very general and very determined opinion expressed that Fort Sumter ought to be and should be reinforced." The *Diary* tells that when Postmaster General Blair warned that the abandonment of Sumter would be considered as treason to the country, "the President decided from that moment that an attempt should be made to

[24] *Ibid.,* p. 236.

convey supplies to Major Anderson, and that he would reinforce Sumter." Of Fox's optimism Welles writes that the captain was confident he could reinforce the garrison with men and supply it with provisions. Relative to the confusion which followed when Lincoln diverted the *Powhatan* from the Charleston to the Pensacola squadron, he says in so many words that the reinforcements were "stolen away" from Sumter and sent to Pickens. Deserving of repetition is his characterization of Seward's assurances to the Confederate commissioners that the fort would not be supplied without notice, "when at the very moment he knew the whole energies of the War and Navy Departments were engaged by order of the President in preparations to forward supplies and reinforcements to Sumter." [25]

With all this preparation in progress in Washington, what was the status at Charleston? On April third a merchant vessel made an attempt to enter the harbor and the Morris Island batteries fired on her. Reporting the incident to Governor Pickens, Major Anderson expressed regret that there were no boats to warn the vessel, thereby disclosing his knowledge of the South Carolina policy of stopping all vessels at the harbor entrance and prescribing conditions under which they could proceed. Indicating again his expectation of orders to leave, as well as his kindly feeling for the governor, he closed his message, "still hoping that God will so direct the counsels of all in authority that we shall soon be relieved of our unpleasant position, I have the honor to remain, with sincere regard, your obedient servant, ROBERT ANDERSON, *Major*." [26]

All the while, the Confederate commissioners were keep-

[25] *Diary of Gideon Welles*, I, 5, 6, 13-14, 15, 26, 27.
[26] *O. R. A.*, Ser. 1, Vol. I, p. 239.

ing close watch on the turmoil in the capital. Despite Seward's promise and their knowledge of the nature of the message Lamon had carried to Charleston, they were more and more impressed by the feverish unrest. With the assembling of troops, the hurried conditioning of war-ships, the prevailing air of mystery, none but the blind could have failed to sense that something was amiss. There were words in abundance, reassuring words, but actions of the administration were shouting a contradiction of what they were hearing. They therefore wrote Confederate Secretary of State Toombs that there was certainly on foot some important move. Mistrusting explanations which impressed them as specious, they observed:

"The statement that this armament is intended for St. Domingo may be a mere ruse.

"We are, however, most creditably informed that Commodore Stringham, who takes charge of the squadron, sails for St. Domingo.

"Having no confidence in the administration, we say, be ever on your guard. Glad to hear that you are ready. The notice promised us will come at the last moment if the fleet be intended for our waters." [27]

THE NOTICE IS GIVEN AT THE LAST MOMENT

The question as to the expediency of aggressive action at Sumter had for weeks dwarfed other issues in the capital. Just seven days after Lincoln gave his order for the expedition, his secretary of the navy forwarded confidential instructions to Captain Mercer of the man-of-war *Powhatan*. From these the captain learned that he was to assemble the *Pawnee*, the *Powhatan*, the *Pocahontas*, and the *Harriet Lane* into a naval force which under his command was to sail in time to arrive off

[27] *Ibid.*, p. 286.

Charleston bar on the morning of April eleventh. There
the squadron was "to aid in carrying out the objects"
of the Lincoln expedition. The seriousness of the assignment came out when, to Mercer's astonishment, he read
further that, if opposition developed, his warships were
to protect the transports, "repelling by force, if necessary, all obstructions towards provisioning the fort and
re-enforcing it"; for, the order made known, "in case of
resistance to the peaceable primary object of the expedition a re-enforcement of the garrison will also be attempted." [28]

What would have been the reaction of Secretary Welles
had he known when he issued his order that Lincoln had
personally arranged to send the *Powhatan* to Pensacola,
had summarily removed Captain Mercer, and had placed
Lieutenant Porter in command of the ship? What emotions would have stirred within him had someone whispered that the president had explicitly instructed that
under no circumstances was the department of the navy
to be informed of what he was doing? The fact, however,
that Welles did not so much as suspect that Lincoln was
sending sealed orders to naval ships of war in no wise
lessens the significance of secret instructions to Captain
Mercer to have his squadron in position off Charleston
on April eleventh [29] and to resort to his guns if gunfire
should be necessary to insure success for the provisioning venture; all of which, insofar as it involved reference
to "provisioning," was beside the point. Over and over
again Anderson had warned the administration that,
whatever it chose to christen its project, more than likely
it would end in tragedy.

[28] *Ibid.*, p. 240; *O. R. N.*, Ser. 1, Vol. IV, p. 235.
[29] *O. R. A.*, Ser. 1, Vol. I, p. 240; Crawford, *The Genesis of the Civil
War*, p. 406. These orders were sent on April 1. See pp. 42-48, *supra*.

Southern speculation as to the implications of the mysterious pressure being exerted in the capital had brought scant satisfaction; the situation at Charleston was more jumbled than ever. Mr. Crawford of the Confederate commission telegraphed Governor Pickens, expressing his opinion that the president intended to shift the responsibility upon Major Anderson by the simple expedient of taking no action whatever.[30] To a messenger sent by Anderson on April fourth, Governor Pickens remarked that orders had come from Montgomery to deny to the occupants of the post permission to leave the premises and to withdraw the garrison's privilege of securing supplies in the city. By way of explanation the governor exhibited the telegram in which Crawford stated that he felt authorized to say no reinforcement would be undertaken, but that "Mr. Lincoln would not order Major Anderson to withdraw from Fort Sumter, and would leave him to act for himself." [31] Like a blow in the face, this intimation stirred the resentment of the ordinarily coolheaded commander. He knew that Crawford had for many years served his state in congress and regarded him as entirely responsible. For months Anderson had chafed under Washington's apparent neglect. This most recent suggestion was the last straw, and he lost no time in forwarding to the department of war on April fifth a plain-spoken protest:

"I have the honor to report everything still and quiet. . . .

"I cannot but think that Mr. Crawford has misunderstood what he has heard in Washington, as I cannot think that the Government would abandon, without instructions and without advice, a command which has tried to do all its duty to our country. . . .

[30] *Ibid.,* p. 391.　　　　[31] *O. R. A.,* Ser. 1, Vol. I, p. 242.

"I am sure that I shall not be left without instructions, even though they may be confidential. After thirty odd years of service I do not wish it to be said that I have treasonably abandoned a post and turned over to unauthorized persons public property intrusted to my charge. I am entitled to this act of justice at the hands of my Government, and I feel confident that I shall not be disappointed. What to do with the public property, and where to take my command, are questions to which answers will, I hope, be at once returned. Unless we receive supplies I shall be compelled to stay here without food or to abandon this post very early next week." [32]

In a time of unexampled stress, his superior officers had given him this assignment at what both they and he were aware was a strategic and difficult post. When he arrived in Charleston, he understood that he was assuming a responsibility which would test his mettle. Patiently he had surmounted one crisis after another; he felt that he was still master of the situation. Nevertheless, the uncertainty of his position was fast upsetting his equilibrium; the fog of rumor was bad enough, but what was he to think when one, accredited as a messenger of the president, flatly contradicted apparently authentic information brought by a former presidential envoy of only a few days before? Why was he, bearing the brunt of it all, being excluded from the confidence of those whose orders he was obligated to await? At the time of all times when close coöperation was imperative, when he desperately needed detailed instructions, the silence of the administration was jangling his nerves.

The tone of his letter demonstrates that strange forebodings were creeping into his mind. What of this latest

32 *Ibid.*, p. 241; Crawford, *The Genesis of the Civil War*, p. 392.

intimation in the Crawford telegram? Was he to credit
the suggestion that the president's plan was simply to
step off the stage without saying a word, and so to leave
him the unsupported actor in the great drama? What if
his supplies from the city should be cut off? What if the
Confederates demanded surrender of the fort? Was he to
lower his flag without a fight? On the other hand, if his
superiors expected him to protect his position, were they
going to leave him to make the attempt with a pitiful
force of less than one hundred men, surrounded as he was
by Confederate batteries and faced by an experienced
Confederate general with an overwhelmingly superior
force? Whether orders came to leave or to fight, his
soldier-training had taught him what to do, but to be
standing guard over a perilous outpost, seemingly ignored
or forgotten, was rather too much. Knowledge of what
was in the air would have redoubled his uneasiness. All
unknown to him, Washington was preparing still another
surprise. On April sixth, the day after he wrote his earnest protest, Lincoln gave the final order that the expedition should proceed on its mission,[33] and at once Secretary
of War Cameron placed in the hands of Captain Talbot
this order:

"You will proceed directly to Charleston, S. C.,
and if on your arrival the flag of the United States
shall be flying over Fort Sumter, and the fort shall
not have been attacked, you will procure an interview with Governor Pickens, and read to him as
follows:
" 'I am directed by the President of the United
States to notify [you] to expect an attempt will be
made to supply Fort Sumter with provisions only,
and that if such attempt be not resisted, no effort to
throw in provisions, arms, or ammunition will be

[33] Nicolay and Hay, *Lincoln,* IV, 62, 1.

made, without further notice or in case of an attack upon the fort.' " [34]

In view of the fact that Lincoln's own hand wrote this notice,[35] its involved phraseology challenges study; again the now familiar phrase, "to supply with provisions only." The president was carefully choosing his cards to create the impression that the mission of the expedition was peaceable. It was unfortunate that its sponsors appeared to have overlooked the inconsistency of this in the light of the circumstance that all arrangements were perfected to make it what Welles described as a military expedition with naval aid and coöperation. As a matter of fact, this was responsible for some speculation within the cabinet. The talk of provisioning only puzzled Lincoln's secretary of the treasury; in the cabinet discussions, according to Hart, "Chase drew the deduction that the simple provisioning of a fort ought not to lead, and would not lead, to civil war." [36] Would the secretary have made such an observation had he known, as surely he should have known, of the plan to provide a convoy of warships?

Gideon Welles, Chase's associate in the cabinet, was a realist of the first water. For the life of him he could conjure up no rational excuse for the Confederacy's being notified at all of the government's intentions, for the reason, extremely simple as it appeared to him, that thereby the Southerners would be given ample time to prepare a fitting reception for the squadron. Nevertheless, with a subtlety which Welles could not penetrate, Lincoln drove straight down the course, gave the notice just as he had planned, and, while sorely perplexing the secretary,

[34] *O. R. A.*, Ser. 1, Vol. I, p. 245. See also Rhodes, *A History of the United States*, III, 338.
[35] Tarbell, *The Life of Abraham Lincoln*, III, 19.
[36] Hart, *Salmon Porter Chase*, p. 209.

played his well-considered game of irritation adroitly and, as it turned out, successfully. It seems not to have occurred to Welles that, if the South was not already braced for the impact, a notice given concurrently with the sailing of the fleet would hardly afford opportunity for adequate preparation to withstand an attack by the combined forces of the Sumter garrison and the naval squadron.[37]

By this time the conclusion seems unavoidable that talk of "supplying with provisions only" has the ring of sounding brass. The secretary of war of the United States, in his letter to the Southern senators, quoted Mr. Hayne as saying that for months Anderson had received from Charleston "all necessary supplies." The date of this letter, however, was January twenty-second. Nevertheless, other and more effective testimony of subsequent date has come to view ending with Major Anderson's utterance of April third that certain little matters perhaps indicated an intention to stop entirely his supplies from Charleston.[38] This brings squarely up the question: When did the Confederates shut off Anderson's supplies?

Major Anderson wrote the adjutant general on April 7, 1861, "You will see by the inclosed letter just received from Brigadier-General Beauregard that we shall not get any more supplies from the city of Charleston."[39] He was referring to a message also dated April seventh in which Beauregard said, "In consequence of the delays and apparent vacillations of the United States Government . . . relative to the evacuation of Fort Sumter, no

[37] McElroy, *Jefferson Davis*, I, 282.
[38] *O. R. A.*, Ser. 1, Vol. I, p. 232.
[39] *Ibid.*, p. 248.

further communications for the purposes of supply from this city . . . will be permitted from and after this day." [40]

On April eighth Beauregard wrote the Confederate secretary of war, enclosing a copy of his letter to Anderson stopping his provisions from the city. He reported also his calling out an additional number of men, a measure which he found necessary because of the warlike preparations being made by the Federal government "with so much mystery." [41]

In his *Reminiscences* General Doubleday, a captain in the Sumter garrison in 1861, records April seventh as the date on which the Confederates put a stop to the command's Charleston marketing. Nor was the general without his suspicion as to what lay behind the drastic order. He writes, "The rebels knew, and *perhaps* he [Anderson] knew, that on the 6th and 7th of April a number of naval vessels had left New York and Norfolk with sealed orders. Their destination could hardly be doubted." [42] The "rebels" did not have quite as definite information as General Doubleday thought but, from dependable sources, they were receiving reports of ominous activities in Washington, and they had their own ideas as to the main event of which these were the preliminaries. As long as there was even slight hope of amicable adjustment, they had willingly contributed to the comfort of the Sumter group, but they were hardly unimaginative enough to continue such a course now that it was becoming increasingly evident that events were shaping for a showdown.

It was on April fourth that Lincoln assured Captain Fox that he would send notice to Charleston that no

[40] *Ibid.* See also George Lunt, *The Origin of the Late War* (New York, 1866), p. 443.   [41] *O. R. A.*, Ser. 1, Vol. I, p. 290.

[42] Quoted in Roman, *Military Operations of General Beauregard,* I, 37, 38.

troops would be thrown into Sumter unless there was opposition to the delivery of the provisions. Cameron's letter to Anderson, announcing the sailing of the expedition "to provision you," bore the same date. On April sixth Cameron instructed Captain Talbot to give to Governor Pickens the "with provisions only" notice. And yet here is the actual testimony of the leading participants at Charleston, Federal and Confederate alike; Anderson's official report to Washington, Beauregard's official report to the Confederate secretary of war, General Doubleday's account, each telling the same story, all making a permanent record—that the Confederates did not shut off the supplies from Charleston until April 7, 1861.

"MILITARY AND NAVAL MOVEMENTS OF EXTRAORDINARY SECRECY"

Turning back to April sixth, it is apparent that the mystifying attitude of Washington had caused Major Anderson's indignation to flare up again. Just the day before, he had written what amounted very nearly to a demand for instructions, asserting his right to this act of justice at the hands of his government. In a letter of the sixth to Adjutant General Thomas, he laid bare his poignant dissatisfaction, his mortification at being left alone with his "hands tied" in an inadequately manned and under-equipped fort. Bluntly he set forth his own conclusion, "The truth is that the sooner we are out of this harbor the better." [43]

At practically the same time Anderson was writing his letter, General Scott was forwarding to the officer in charge at Fort Columbus an order directing immediate organization of two companies of one hundred recruits each, these to be made ready to sail on the eighth.[44]

[43] *O. R. A.,* Ser. 1, Vol. I, p. 245.   [44] *Ibid.*

Meanwhile, at Charleston the opposing commands were punctiliously observing the amenities; upon Anderson's protest that a shell from one of the Confederate batteries had exploded dangerously near the fort, Beauregard replied that the happening was unintentional and there would be no recurrence of the annoyance. "Let me assure you, major," the note continued, "that nothing shall be wanting on my part to preserve the friendly relations and impressions which have existed between us for so many years." [45] Such frank and cordial relations were strangely variant from those prevailing between Washington and Southern leaders. Conflicting rumors, contradictory advices were confounding confusion. Restive under the suspense, on April seventh Governor Pickens telegraphed the commissioners in Washington: "We have so many extraordinary telegrams I would be glad to know from you if it is true that they have determined to re-enforce Sumter, and if a naval force is sent to our harbor." [46]

The reply of the commissioners the next day opened inauspiciously, "The military and naval movements are conducted with extraordinary secrecy." Nevertheless, they expressed confidence in the promise to evacuate.[47] This contrasts singularly with a later observation by Gideon Welles that "the Rebels of Charleston were strangely prepared and warned of the intended expedition." [48] Can it be Welles did not know that less than two weeks before none other than Lincoln's former law partner had left in Charleston the definite impression of an early transfer of the garrison, thereby confirming what Secretary of State Seward was repeatedly saying

45 *Ibid.*, p. 247.
46 *O. R. N.*, Ser. 1, Vol. IV, p. 258.   47 *Ibid.*, p. 259.
48 *Diary of Gideon Welles*, I, 32.

to the commissioners? Whatever may have been the extent of Welles' information, there were some who were of the opinion that, at least to some extent, the situation was clearing up. The New York *Herald* carried the following Washington dispatch, dated April seventh:

"Dispatches received here to-day from Montgomery render it perfectly certain that no attack will be made by the Confederate troops on either Fort Sumter or Fort Pickens. President Davis is determined that this administration shall not place him in a false position, by making it appear to the world that the South is the aggressor. This has been and still is the policy of Mr. Lincoln. It will not be successful. Unless Mr. Lincoln's administration makes the first demonstration and attack, President Davis says there will be no collision or bloodshed. *With the Lincoln administration, therefore, rests the responsibility of precipitating a collision,* and the fearful evils of protracted civil war." [49]

The next day, April eighth, Mr. Crawford of the commission wrote Beauregard that the constant vacillation of the Washington administration rendered everything uncertain. Only the day before, he said, the commissioners were in receipt of further assurance that no action would be taken concerning Sumter without prior notice to Governor Pickens. He took occasion to add that he and his associates placed no faith in the promise. They were experiencing the process of disillusionment. The manifest incongruity between what they were hearing with their ears and what they were seeing with their eyes had resulted in a state of bewilderment. Crawford's message ended on a discordant note, "The war policy prevails in the Cabinet at this hour." [50] Nor was there lacking tan-

[49] Quoted in Lunt, *Origin of the Late War,* p. 446.
[50] *O. R. A.,* Ser. 1, Vol. I, p. 289.

gible evidence of the accuracy of this view. Eventful developments were crowding one another. The same day heralded a memorable occasion in Charleston. Captain Talbot, special messenger of the president of the United States, the third such envoy to arrive within a period of less than three weeks, made his appearance in the office of Governor Pickens to read to the governor and General Beauregard the notice which Cameron had entrusted to him. Following the interview, Beauregard telegraphed Confederate Secretary of State Walker, "Authorized messenger from Lincoln just informed Governor Pickens and myself that provisions would be sent to Sumter peaceably, otherwise by force." [51] A like message from Beauregard to the Confederate commissioners inspired an enlightening comment by Nicolay. Noting that the Beauregard telegram was the commissioners' first information of Talbot's delivery of the notice, he remarked that this showed "the success of the government in keeping its secrets." [52]

The president's message which Secretary Cameron forwarded to Anderson on April fourth expressed the hope that the commander would be able to maintain himself until April eleventh or twelfth. Secretary Welles instructed Captain Mercer on April fifth to leave with his squadron in time to arrive off Charleston bar on the morning of April eleventh. Lincoln's notice to Governor Pickens reached Charleston on April eighth. The significance of all this is transparent. The commissioners apparently knew of what they were talking when they warned that the notice would come at the last moment. Until it arrived, the Southerners did not know definitely

[51] *Ibid.* See also Albert B. Hart, *American History Told by Contemporaries* (5 vols. New York and London, 1897-1929), IV, 213; Appleton's *American Annual Cyclopædia*, 1861, p. 132.

[52] *Lincoln*, IV, 3.

that the expedition was to come. For that matter, Major Anderson did not learn of it until April seventh. Here again Secretary Welles contributes an illuminating passage; with the introductory statement, "the preparations for the Fort Sumter expedition were carried forward with all the energy which the department could command," he thus outlined the make-up and the program:

". . . the supplies and troops for reinforcement being from the army, the expedition was made a military and not a naval one, but with naval aid and coöperation. The transports which the War Department was to charter were to rendezvous off Charleston with the naval vessels, which would act as convoy, and render such assistance as would be required of them." [53]

Promptly on receipt of the information of the notice given by Talbot, on April eighth the Confederate secretary of war telegraphed Beauregard, "Under no circumstances are you to allow provisions to be sent to Fort Sumter." [54] Had Lincoln's own hand written this message, it could not have more perfectly fitted in with his plans. The anticipated refusal to permit delivery of supplies was, it appeared, to be the excuse for further action. At no time had the South adopted the extreme view proclaimed by Wendell Phillips, "Abraham Lincoln has no right to a soldier in Fort Sumter," [55] but the administration needed no telling that on one point the Confederates would remain adamant; even though euphemistically masked as "provisioning," there was to be no reinforcement. That same day, it so happened, the general in chief of the Union army notified Lieutenant Hudson

[53] *Diary of Gideon Welles*, I, 15. See also *ibid.*, p. 22.
[54] *O. R. A.*, Ser. 1, Vol. I, p. 289.
[55] Channing, *A Students' History of the United States*, p. 504.

that the troops embarked on the transport *Baltic* were
destined for Fort Sumter, mentioning further that "high
authority" in Washington had charged Captain Fox
with command of the expedition "under cover of certain
ships of war." [56] The high authority was, to be sure, no
less a personage than the president. The climax of a
notable day's activities came in a formal notice from
Beauregard to Anderson: "I have the honor to inform
you that from and after this day no mails will be allowed
to go or come from Fort Sumter until further instructions from the Confederate Government at Montgomery." [57]

[56] *O. R. A.,* Ser. 1, Vol. I, p. 248.
[57] *Ibid.,* p. 250.

CHAPTER XIII

STORM SIGNALS UP

ANDERSON LEARNS OF THE COMING OF THE EXPEDITION

It was a nerve-racking suspense which Anderson had endured for weeks. Whether for some undivulged reason the administration felt it would be unwise to take him into its confidence, or was simply so engrossed in its own plans as more or less unconsciously to overlook a mere army major, it adds up to the same result: Anderson was utterly in the dark. When the expedition was ready to sail there was no point in further effort to conceal the project from him and so, in Cameron's name, Lincoln wrote the April fourth letter. When on the seventh Anderson read it, the shock left him dazed. The day following, he mailed to Colonel Thomas, adjutant general of the United States army, a letter, the historical significance of which many writers, discreetly or indiscreetly, have overlooked:

"I had the honor to receive by yesterday's mail the letter of the honorable Secretary of War, dated April 4, and confess that what he there states surprises me very greatly, following as it does and contradicting so positively the assurance Mr. Crawford telegraphed he was authorized to make. I trust that this matter will be at once put in a correct light, as a movement made now, when the South has been erroneously informed that none such will be attempted, would produce most disastrous results throughout our country. . . .

"We have not oil enough to keep a light in the lantern for one night. The boats will have, therefore, to rely at night entirely upon other marks. I ought to have been informed that this expedition was to come. Colonel Lamon's remark convinced me that the idea, merely hinted at to me by Captain Fox, would not be carried out. We shall strive to do our duty, though I frankly say that my heart is not in the war which I see is to be thus commenced. That God will still avert it, and cause us to resort to pacific measures to maintain our rights, is my ardent prayer." [1]

After all that had occurred, the veritable maze of conflicting rumors and contradictory messages from Washington, culminating in conferences with two special messengers of the president, that with Lamon resulting in a directly opposite impression from that with Fox, it is easy to comprehend that Lincoln's communication stunned Anderson. His own reply, likewise, struck from the shoulder. A stranger to dissimulation, he spoke with candor. They who were giving him advice should receive some. Without so much as consultation with him, blind to danger signals, they were heading straight into the path of a hurricane. The leaders should do something about it, and do it at once. They had led the Southerners to believe that they anticipated no such action, and he was in a position to know that the assurance caused the Confederates to suspend work on their batteries. Day after day, he had reported everything still and quiet. With the appearance of this armada, he knew there would be a different story to relate. There was, moreover, something else to give him concern; not only he, but Beauregard, expected the transfer of his garrison,

---

[1] *O. R. A.*, Ser. 1, Vol. I, p. 294. See also Crawford, *The Genesis of the Civil War*, p. 385; Nicolay and Hay, *Lincoln*, IV, 40.

and he was uncomfortable in the realization that he had innocently contributed to the deception of the Confederate general whose respect and trust he prized.

"That God will still avert it, and cause us to resort to pacific measures to maintain our rights, is my ardent prayer." He knew what war was, and in the depths of his soul he felt that nothing justified its tragedy until contending factions had patiently tried every honorable recourse. What he was saying was closely akin to the sentiment of an editorial of the London *Times* of a few days before:

> "When civil war is as imminent as it appears to be at this moment in America, it is well to admit the only possible alternative, that of hearing what terms the South is ready to propose in order to avert so dreadful a calamity. The last alternative always remains, and the fratricidal sword will not have lost its edge by remaining in the sheath a few weeks longer." [2]

"We shall strive to do our duty." He was a soldier, and it was a soldier's duty to obey orders, not to reason why. Nevertheless, his fort was the hub of the whole delicate situation and, better than anyone in Washington, he foresaw what the end of it all would be. It was sheer foolhardiness, he thought, to resort to such recklessness without counting the cost. The politicians and swivel-chair warriors would be hundreds of miles away when the heavy guns of Moultrie and the shore batteries threw their shells into Fort Sumter, and he knew over whose heads those shells would explode. Orders or no orders, he owed something to the men of his command; discretion or no discretion, he would open Washington's eyes.

[2] Quoted in Selma (Ala.) *Morning Reporter*, April 9, 1861.

"I frankly say that my heart is not in the war which I see is to be thus commenced." History is written in those plain-spoken words, words which for more than a half-century have stood out on the printed page. They record the testimony of the witness best informed as to the exact facts. Is there any occasion for wonder that many writers of the story of the period have left such an adjudication severely alone? Can it be they have reached a common conclusion; namely, the less said of this, the better? One exception to this discreetly silent group, Nicolay, brings himself to venture the opinion that, had Anderson understood "he was replying indirectly to President Lincoln himself, he might have used other language." [3] And again, from the same author, "One of the few faults chargeable to Anderson is that to this thoughtful and considerate instruction, framed by Lincoln himself (but which he supposed to be the language of Cameron), he replied in a petulant and ill-natured spirit, writing, 'I frankly say that my heart is not in the war which I see is to be thus commenced.' " [4]

Nicolay's pronouncement of judgment upon Anderson inspires a comparison. Revert to Anderson's record: the son of a sire who had served as a lieutenant colonel under General Washington; born in Kentucky; his background steeped in the traditions of Virginia; a graduate of the United States Military Academy and, later, a member of the faculty; a Southerner whose loyalty to the Union was unshakable; attaining the rank of major in 1857 and promoted to a brigadier-generalship in the same year in which he wrote the letter Nicolay condemns. Reflect, then, on the story of John George Nicolay: born in Essingen, Germany, in 1832; getting his first view

[3] *Lincoln,* IV, 40.
[4] *The Outbreak of Rebellion,* p. 58.

of American shores in 1838; and so, on the date of the
letter in question, only twenty-three years removed from
the time when as a child-immigrant he landed at the port
of New Orleans. Despite the efforts of Nicolay and others
to undermine the significance of Anderson's transparently
courageous statement, regardless of the success with which
partisan writers have implanted a different impression,
there can be no blinking the truth that his letter returns
the verdict of the man whose name stands out as the
unrivaled hero of the cast in the tragedy that is Sumter.
In the light of such a finding, the concluding paragraph
of Lincoln's fourth annual message to congress, dated
December 6, 1864, takes on a deeper interest: "In stating a simple condition of peace, I mean simply to say
that the war will cease on the part of the Government
whenever it shall have ceased on the part of those who
began it." [5]

FOX'S DOUBLE DEALING

Assistant Adjutant General Talbot, whom Secretary
Cameron detailed to deliver Lincoln's notice, made his
report on April twelfth. On the evening of April eighth,
he wrote the secretary, he arrived in Charleston accompanied by B. S. Chew. Governor Pickens granted their
request for an immediate interview and they read to him
the message from the president. Upon learning the nature
of the document, the governor said that, inasmuch as
General Beauregard was in charge of the defenses and
was near at hand, he preferred that he should be present.
Chew and Talbot agreed; Pickens summoned Beauregard
and read the notice to him. With silent dignity and severe

[5] *A Compilation of the Messages and Papers of the Presidents,* VI,
255.

self-restraint, the Southerners listened to the ostensibly innocent, pretendedly friendly performance. They were hearing what to them was the equivalent of an ultimatum. Nevertheless, despite conviction that the Federals had delayed the communication until the last moment, although, even as the message was being delivered, there was reason to believe that a Union fleet was headed for Charleston, they tacitly conceded that notice even so belated was more honorable than no notice at all.

Talbot and Chew appreciated as well as Pickens and Beauregard the seriousness of the occasion. The interview concluded, they announced their desire to leave that night for Washington, whereupon both their hosts not only replied that there would be no obstruction to their departure, but provided a staff officer to escort them to the railroad station.[6] For one, Chew thoroughly comprehended that his mission might be regarded as a preliminary to hostilities. He was visibly uneasy regarding the attitude toward him of the people on the streets. His hosts reassured him. The crowd surrounding the building, they explained, was present only to learn the news. Beauregard remarked, "You may go among them, repeat what you have here said, and not a word of insult will be offered you." [7]

The day after the Confederates shut off the Sumter mails, Pickens wrote the president of the Confederate States that Major Anderson was not only protesting to Beauregard against this action, but was asking the return of seized letters. Intercepting the mail, the Confederates had forwarded the official correspondence to the Confederate government, because, as the governor set forth, "rumors, well established, indicated that Mr. Fox had

6 *O. R. A.,* Ser. 1, Vol. I, pp. 251-252.
7 Roman, *Military Operations of General Beauregard,* I, 33.

violated his faith to me in visiting the fort. . . . The
pledge was that he visited Major Anderson by authority,
for pacific purposes entirely. You see that the present
scheme for supplying the fort is Mr. Fox's." [8] This means
that Fox had taken advantage of the governor's confidence in his integrity to carry out what in time of war
would be classed an affair of espionage. What the seizure
brought to light appears from Pickens' letter of April
ninth to the Confederate secretary of war:

> "I took possession of the mails this morning from
> Sumter, and retained the packages marked 'official.'
> These are all sent you. The private letters are all
> sent, as directed, to their owners. I did this because
> I consider a state of war is now inaugurated by the
> authorities at Washington, and all information of
> a public nature was necessary to us. . . .
> "You will see by these letters of Major Anderson
> how it is intended to supply the fort; but by God's
> providence we will, I trust, be prepared for them;
> and if they approach with war vessels also, I think
> you will hear of as bloody a fight as ever oc-
> curred. . . .
> "There has just arrived . . . a fine rifled cannon
> from Liverpool. . . . It throws a shell or twelve-
> pound shot with the accuracy of a dueling-pistol." [9]

The Confederates had taken their action at a most
opportune moment. There, among the official communications, lay a letter, dated April eighth, addressed to
the adjutant general of the United States army, signed
by Major Anderson, referring in explicit terms to "the
expedition" which "was to come." Now the curtain was
up and the secret was out. No longer was the sailing of
an armed fleet a matter of rumor; Anderson's own word

[8] *O. R. A.,* Ser. 1, Vol. I, p. 292.   [9] *Ibid.*

for it, the threatened reinforcement was at last on the way. More than this, there was to come direct from Washington news which tended further to darken the sky. On the same day, April ninth, Mr. Crawford of the commission telegraphed Beauregard that the notice given by Captain Talbot was doubtless authentic. The closing words of the message were disheartening: "Diplomacy has failed. The sword must now preserve our independence." [10]

Incidentally this telegram is a reminder that only three days prior to the tragedy of Sumter, official representatives of the South were still in the nation's capital whither they had gone weeks before with instructions from the Confederate government to seek a friendly adjustment. Their negotiations had encountered a deadlock. Diplomacy had failed.

An editorial in the New York *Tribune* of April tenth said, "We are enabled to state, *with positive certainty,* that the principal object of the military and naval expedition which has sailed from this harbor, within the past four days, is *the relief of Fort Sumter.*" [11] The reference to a military and naval expedition indicates that prattle of provisioning only had not deceived the *Tribune;* its editors were not so artless as to chronicle the departure of the armada as a peaceable project. As soon as the editorial came to the notice of the commissioners, they telegraphed Beauregard: "The Tribune of to-day declares the main object of the expedition to be the relief of Sumter, and that a force will be landed which will overcome all opposition." [12]

[10] *Ibid.,* p. 297.
[11] Quoted in Lunt, *Origin of the Late War,* p. 447.
[12] *O. R. N.,* Ser. 1, Vol. IV, p. 259.

THE SOUTH'S RELUCTANCE TO OPEN FIRE

Recent experiences had led the officials of the Confederate government to be rather circumspect in their attitude toward self-announced special messengers of President Lincoln. On April eighth Captain Talbot had come as the third such agent to appear on the scene since March twenty-first. Three weeks was too brief a period in which to forget the puzzling performances of Fox and Lamon. How much reliance should they place in Talbot's representation? Were they to accept his notice as authorized by Lincoln, or were they to expect a later envoy bringing directly contradictory assurances? When on April ninth Mr. Crawford telegraphed that he regarded the Talbot notice as authentic, and the commissioners followed this the same day with the announcement of the failure of their peace negotiations, Confederate Secretary of War Walker felt that the time had come for action. He telegraphed Beauregard: "If you have no doubt of the authorized character of the agent who communicated to you the intention of the Washington Government to supply Fort Sumter by force you will at once demand its evacuation, and if this is refused proceed, in such manner as you may determine, to reduce it. Answer." [13]

The next day the Confederate commander selected Colonel James Chesnut, a former United States senator, and Captain Stephen D. Lee, a graduate of West Point, as bearers of this message to Major Anderson:

"The Government of the Confederate States has hitherto forborne from any hostile demonstration against Fort Sumter, in the hope that the Government of the United States, with a view to the amica-

[13] *O. R. A.,* Ser. 1, Vol. I, p. 297.

ble adjustment of all questions between the two Governments, and to avert the calamities of war, would voluntarily evacuate it.

"There was reason at one time to believe that such would be the course pursued by the Government of the United States, and under that impression my Government has refrained from making any demand for the surrender of the fort. But the Confederate States can no longer delay assuming actual possession of a fortification commanding the entrance of one of their harbors, and necessary to its defense and security.

"I am ordered by the Government of the Confederate States to demand the evacuation of Fort Sumter. . . . All proper facilities will be afforded for the removal of yourself and command, together with company arms and property, and all private property, to any post in the United States which you may select. The flag which you have upheld so long and with so much fortitude . . . may be saluted by you upon taking it down." [14]

The officers who delivered the message brought back Anderson's reply:

"I have the honor to acknowledge the receipt of your communication demanding the evacuation of this fort, and to say, in reply thereto, that it is a demand with which I regret that my sense of honor, and of my obligations to my Government, prevent my compliance. Thanking you for the fair, manly, and courteous terms proposed, and for the compliment paid me,

"I am, general, very respectfully, your obedient servant,

"ROBERT ANDERSON." [15]

Neither Beauregard nor Anderson needed to be told that, barring a miracle, it was likely only a matter of

[14] *Ibid.,* p. 13.   [15] *Ibid.*

hours when their guns would speak their messages. In spite of this, with the further realization on the part of each that his opponent was performing a painful duty, their correspondence exhibits unfailing courtesy. Even so, there was no escaping the dread consciousness that they were girding themselves for the final move. Beauregard had made a demand for evacuation; Anderson had answered with an unqualified refusal. At the climax of these grim exchanges, however, there cropped out one of those touches which establish the kinship of humanity; handing his formal reply to the aides, Anderson had remarked, "I will await the first shot, and if you do not batter us to pieces we will be starved out in a few days." [16]

This was something else.

Anderson's opponents had sprung from a stock which held in contempt a man who would shoot a bird on the ground. Now a veteran officer was saying that, the honor of his garrison and himself being involved, they would do their duty in full knowledge that resistance was hopeless, that the lives of every man of them might be the price of loyalty. It was one thing to give battle to an antagonist so situated as to be able to meet his enemy on equal terms; it was an entirely different matter to open fire on one who was admitting his doom from the start. Colonel Chesnut asked permission to repeat the remark to General Beauregard.[17] Such an acknowledgment from his comrade of former years deeply affected the Southern general; nor was he the only Confederate official to whom the plight of an honored foeman appealed. That Anderson's statement gave pause also to Confederate Secretary of War Walker, that official's reply of April eleventh discloses:

[16] *Ibid.*, p. 301. See also *B. & L.*, I, 75.
[17] Crawford, *The Genesis of the Civil War*, p. 424.

"Do not desire needlessly to bombard Fort Sumter. If Major Anderson will state the time at which, as indicated by him, he will evacuate, and agree that in the mean time he will not use his guns against us unless ours should be employed against Fort Sumter, you are authorized thus to avoid the effusion of blood. If this or its equivalent be refused, reduce the fort as your judgment decides to be most practicable." [18]

On the day on which Secretary Walker wrote, Anderson had said in a report to Adjutant General Thomas:

". . . these people are expecting the arrival of a hostile force, and they are making the most judicious arrangements to prevent the landing of any supplies at this fort. . . .
". . . had they been in possession of the information contained in your letter of the 4th instant, they could not have made better arrangements than those they have made, and are making, to thwart the contemplated scheme." [19]

As matters stood on the date of the demand for evacuation, the Confederates were confident they held such an advantage as to leave no reasonable question of the result of an engagement. Warning had come, however, that a naval squadron was en route to Charleston and, it so happened, the information was authentic. The record shows that the *Harriet Lane* sailed April eighth, the *Pawnee*, two tugs, and the *Baltic* on the ninth, the *Pocahontas* on the tenth.[20] The Southerners were of course perfectly aware that a combination of the fighting force

[18] *O. R. A.*, Ser. 1, Vol. I, p. 301. See also Hart, *American History as Told by Contemporaries*, IV, 215; *B. & L.*, I, 75; Nicolay and Hay, *Lincoln*, IV, 46.
[19] *O. R. A.*, Ser. 1, Vol. I, pp. 250-251.
[20] *O. R. N.*, Ser. 1, Vol. IV, pp. 243, 244, 249, 253, 254; Crawford, *The Genesis of the Civil War*, p. 416.

of the fleet and the power of Fort Sumter would make a critically dangerous difference in their problem. Despite all this, the Confederate secretary of war countermanded his order for action and suggested to Beauregard that he should give Anderson the privilege of naming his own date for withdrawal. Secretary Walker's action might well be described in the words with which General Pierre Bosquet evaluated the charge of the Light Brigade, "That is magnificent, but that is not war." [21] While contravening fundamentals of military procedure, his revocation of the former order did credit to a Confederate cabinet officer who flinched at the prospect of slaughtering a confessedly hopeless band of men cooped up in a fortress from which there was practically no chance of escape. Is not here definitely established the Confederate government's reluctance to fire on Fort Sumter? Does this sustain or does it scuttle the propaganda that the South recklessly fired on the flag? Practically in Secretary Walker's own words, Beauregard informed Major Anderson of the new proposal:

> "In consequence of the verbal observation made by you to my aides, Messrs. Chesnut and Lee, in relation to the condition of your supplies, and that you would in a few days be starved out if our guns did not batter you to pieces, or words to that effect, and desiring no useless effusion of blood, I communicated both the verbal observations and your written answer to my communications to my Government.
>
> "If you will state the time at which you will evacuate Fort Sumter, and agree that in the mean time you will not use your guns against us unless ours shall be employed against Fort Sumter, we will abstain from opening fire upon you." [22]

[21] Thomas B. Harbottle & Colonel Philip H. Dalbiac, *Dictionary of Quotations* (Fr. and It. London and New York, 1901), p. 18.
[22] *O. R. A.,* Ser. 1, Vol. I, pp. 13-14.

Early on the morning of April twelfth, Major Anderson handed to the aides of General Beauregard this reply:

> ". . . I will, if provided with the necessary and proper means of transportation, evacuate Fort Sumter by noon of the 15th instant, and I will not in the mean time open my fires upon your forces unless compelled to do so by some hostile act against this fort or the flag of my Government by the forces under your command, or by some portion of them, or by the perpetration of some act showing a hostile intention on your part against this fort or the flag it bears, should I not receive prior to that time controlling instructions from my Government or additional supplies." [23]

The concluding words carried a proviso which closed the door. A proposition with such a reservation of right to repudiate it left matters where they were before. More than this, Anderson may or may not have had it in mind, but the date named by him coincided rather significantly with that mentioned by Secretary of War Cameron in his letter of April fourth; there the secretary had written that, on the information of Captain Fox, Lincoln had supposed the garrison could hold out until the fifteenth of April without any great inconvenience and had prepared an expedition which would arrive at the fort before that date.[24] That the forecast of the squadron's movements was the result of expert calculation, Fox himself reveals: "At 3 a.m. of the 12th we reached the rendezvous off Charleston and communicated with the *Harriet Lane*, the only vessel which had arrived; at 6 a.m. the *Pawnee* was seen standing in." [25] Fox was on the *Baltic*, which was carrying the supplies and reinforcements. Thus, on the very morning on which Anderson

[23] *Ibid.,* p. 14.   [24] *Ibid.,* p. 235.
[25] *O. R. N.,* Ser. 1, Vol. IV, p. 249.

gave his answer, a portion of the fleet, a transport, an
armed cutter, and a warship, was at Charleston; another
man-of-war, the *Pocahontas*, steamed in the next day.
The date of Anderson's answer was April twelfth, the
day he named for his evacuation was April fifteenth;
therefore, had Beauregard accepted his proposition, the
Federals would have had three days' leeway to throw into
the fort the supplies, arms, ammunition, and troops.

Two telegrams brought to a close the efforts amicably
to secure possession of the fort. The first was from the
Confederate secretary of war:

"MONTGOMERY, ALA., *April* 12, 1861
"GENERAL BEAUREGARD, *Charleston, S. C.*
"What was Major Anderson's reply to the propo-
sition contained in my dispatch of last night?
"L. P. WALKER" [26]

As soon as the wires could carry it, Beauregard's reply
was in Walker's hands. It told its story in just seven
words:

"CHARLESTON, S. C., *April* 12, 1861
"L. P. WALKER:
"He would not consent. I write to-day.
"G. T. BEAUREGARD" [27]

[26] *O. R. A.,* Ser. 1, Vol. I, p. 305.
[27] *Ibid.*

CHAPTER XIV

THE TRAGEDY OF THE CENTURY

THE CONFEDERATE GUNS SPEAK

To those who had hoped against hope that some kind fate would intervene to brake the trend toward war there had come at last cruel disillusion. All negotiations had ended in a blind alley. Plainly it was of no use further to attempt the untangling of the network of irreconcilable theories. One of the authoritative voices of the period, Appleton's *American Annual Cyclopædia* for 1861, reviewed the recent past, took cognizance of the present impasse, and gave as its conclusion that, if the Confederate government was in earnest in what it had done, the hour had come when the sword must be drawn.[1] This expressed the view also of the Confederate leaders. Further procrastination was dangerous. The dread hour was come. To Pickens and Beauregard, Talbot had brought Lincoln's notification. Anderson had refused Beauregard's demand for evacuation and had returned an impossible answer to Walker's compromise suggestion. Now, in turn, there was in order a formal communication from the Confederate general to Major Anderson. Beauregard's aides, James Chesnut and Stephen D. Lee, wrote and personally delivered to the Sumter commander at 3:20 o'clock on the morning of April twelfth their general's message:

[1] I, 132.

"Sɪʀ: By authority of Brigadier-General Beauregard, commanding the Provisional Forces of the
Confederate States, we have the honor to notify
you that he will open the fire of his batteries on Fort
Sumter within one hour from this time.

"We have the honor to be, very respectfully, your
obedient servants,

"Jᴀᴍᴇꜱ Cʜᴇꜱɴᴜᴛ, Jʀ.,
"*Aide-de-Camp*
"Sᴛᴇᴘʜᴇɴ D. Lᴇᴇ,
"*Captain C. S. Army, Aide-de-Camp*" ²

There was no bitterness. For all concerned it was a
sorrowful moment. Anderson walked with the aides to
their boat, cordially pressed their hands in farewell, and
remarked, "If we never meet in this world again, God
grant that we may meet in the next." ³ After months
of suspense and anxiety, the curtain was going up on
the tragedy of the century. At 4:30 ᴀ.ᴍ., April 12, 1861,
the Confederate batteries opened fire.

The garrison was defending a powerful fortress, one,
however, unfortunately so vulnerable that the surrounding batteries could throw their shells inside it. Furthermore, within the walls there was wood construction to
an extent presenting a grave element of risk. A well-
directed attack might result in setting the interior of
the work on fire, in which event there was likelihood of
the command's being caught in a trap. To create a situation still more fraught with peril, the powder magazine
occupied such a position as to become a terrifying menace
should flames make such headway as to get beyond control. Inside that magazine were thousands of pounds of
powder which, being set off by a chance spark, would
inevitably strew the surrounding sea with wreckage of

² *O. R. A.,* Ser. 1, Vol. I, p. 14.   ³ *B. & L.,* I, 76.

fort and fragments of bodies. Many of the Southerners, personal friends of the men in Sumter, blanched at the thought of what was in store for the garrison. As well as Anderson and his men they knew that bombardment created for the besieged a hazard which called for cool heads and brave hearts.

All day long on the twelfth the batteries directed a steady rain of shells on the fort. On the following day they resumed the bombardment. In addition to the shells, they poured into the walls hot shot, prepared by heating the balls in a furnace. Then it was that the dread possibility developed into reality. Presently, the fort's interior was ablaze and soon dense clouds of black smoke indicated a serious conflagration. At intervals the gases became so noxious that the defenders of the fort had no alternative but to lie prone on the ground to escape suffocation. Next the shells, laid out for convenience, began to explode from the heat. In the words of General Crawford, a witness of it all, "the scene was wellnigh indescribable." [4] With knowledge of conditions within the fort, the Confederate general watched the scene with mingled feelings of satisfaction and alarm. The attack was progressing satisfactorily, but there was something else to be considered. Before his eyes the gameness of the garrison was demonstrating the accuracy of Jefferson Davis' statement that "only fools doubted the courage of the Yankees"; [5] but these soldiers were confronting the probability of annihilation and no one knew this better than Beauregard. Victory was sweet, but the man prevailed over the soldier. His subsequent conduct is learned from his report of April sixteenth to the Confederate secretary of war:

[4] *The Genesis of the Civil War,* p. 437.
[5] McElroy, *Jefferson Davis,* I, 273.

"On the morning of the 13th, the action was prose-
cuted with renewed vigor, and about 7½ o'clock it
was discovered our shells had set fire to the barracks
in the fort. Speedily volumes of smoke indicated an
extensive conflagration, and apprehending some terrible calamity to the garrison I immediately dispatched an offer of assistance to Major Anderson,
which, however, with grateful acknowledgments, he
declined." [6]

The aides sent to confer with Anderson were James
Chesnut, John L. Manning, and A. R. Chisolm. Their
report of April fifteenth to the Confederate adjutant
general tells the story:

"On our arrival at Fort Sumter, we were met by
Dr. Crawford . . . who directed us to avoid the wharf,
as it was in danger of blowing up at any moment
from its mines. . . . We found the barracks totally
destroyed by fire, occasioned by our shells and hot
shot. We stated to Major Anderson that we had
been sent to Fort Sumter by General Beauregard
with a fire engine, to offer assistance to extinguish
his fire and to render any other assistance he might
require, and also Surgeon-General Gibbes of South
Carolina, and assistants were present to administer
to any wounded he might have. The major replied
that he thanked the general for his kindness, but
that his fire was almost burned out, and that he had
but one man wounded, and he not seriously. We
asked him if the magazine was safe. He replied he
thought the lower magazine safe, though it was
amid the burning ruins, and that he had thrown
about one hundred barrels of powder into the water
from the upper magazine during the action, for the
safety of his command. We again asked him if he
did not think it best to use the engine which accom-

[6] *O. R. A.,* Ser. 1, Vol. I, p. 29. See also *B. & L.,* I, 77-78; Appleton's
American Annual Cyclopædia, 1861, I, 668.

panied us on the steamer, which lay out in the stream. He replied no—that he thought everything had been consumed that would burn.

"Major Anderson expressed great satisfaction when we told him that we had no casualties on our side, and again asked us to thank General Beauregard for his kindness; and, on leaving, the major accompanied us himself as far as our small boat." [7]

At about two o'clock in the afternoon, there occurred a strange incident. Colonel Wigfall, whom Beauregard had assigned for duty at Morris Island under Brigadier General Simons, noticed that Anderson's flag was down. By order of Simons, the colonel entered an open boat with one companion and, under heavy fire, crossed over to Fort Sumter with the object of ascertaining whether the lowered flag meant surrender. His conference with Anderson resulted in a misunderstanding. Anderson construed what Wigfall said as an offer of the same terms which Beauregard had outlined on the eleventh; Wigfall received the impression that Anderson was ready to surrender unconditionally and to trust Beauregard to deal fairly with him. Before General Beauregard learned of what had taken place, hearing that a white flag was flying over the fort, he sent Major Jones, his chief of staff, with an offer of terms substantially the same as that of the eleventh. The message, however, made no mention of according to the Sumter commander the privilege of saluting his flag. Anderson stated to Major Jones that it would be exceedingly gratifying to him and to his command if such a concession could be made but that he would not urge the point, being willing to leave the decision to Beauregard. He soon learned that

[7] *O. R. A.,* Ser. 1, Vol. I, p. 62.

he had made no error of judgment, for the Southern commander cheerfully granted the request.[8] Under these conditions, Major Anderson surrendered on April 13, 1861. Beauregard's report said:

"Meanwhile, being informed about 2 o'clock that a white flag was displayed from Sumter, I dispatched two of my aides to Major Anderson with terms of evacuation. In recognition of the gallantry exhibited by the garrison I cheerfully agreed that on surrendering the fort the commanding officer might salute his flag.

"By 8 o'clock the terms of evacuation were definitely accepted. Major Anderson having expressed a desire to communicate with the United States vessels lying off the harbor, with a view to arrange for the transportation of his command to some port in the United States, one of his officers, accompanied by Captain Hartstene and three of my aides, was permitted to visit the officer in command of the squadron to make provision for that object. Because of an unavoidable delay the formal transfer of the fort to our possession did not take place until 4 o'clock in the afternoon of the 14th instant. At that hour, the place having been evacuated by the United States garrison, our troops occupied it, and the Confederate flag was hoisted on the ramparts of Sumter with a salute from the various batteries." [9]

General Beauregard telegraphed the Confederate secretary of war:

"CHARLESTON, *April* 13, 1861
"HON. L. P. WALKER, *Secretary of War:*
"We take possession of Fort Sumter to-morrow morning. I allow him the privilege of saluting his flag. No one killed on our side.
"G. T. BEAUREGARD" [10]

[8] *Ibid.,* pp. 32, 33.   [9] *Ibid.,* p. 29.
[10] *Ibid.,* p. 310.

Secretary Walker replied:

"MONTGOMERY, *April* 13, 1861
"GENERAL BEAUREGARD, *Charleston:*
"Accept my congratulations. You have won your spurs. How many guns can you spare for Pensacola?
"L. P. WALKER" [11]

From the official point of view, this would have fittingly closed the correspondence of the day. There was, however, another telegram for the victorious Confederate general. Opening it, he read:

"MONTGOMERY, ALA., *April* 13*th*, 1861
"To General G. T. BEAUREGARD:
"Thanks for your achievement and for your courtesy to the garrison of Sumter. If occasion offers, tender my friendly remembrance to Major Anderson.
"JEFFERSON DAVIS" [12]

The Charleston *Mercury* of April 13, 1861, featured the story of the first day's bombardment:

"FT. SUMTER BOMBARDMENT
SPLENDID PYROTECHNIC EXHIBITION
FORT MOULTRIE IMPREGNABLE
THE FLOATING BATTERY AND STEVENS'
BATTERY A SUCCESS
NOBODY HURT ON OUR SIDE

"As may have been anticipated from our notice of the military movements in our city yesterday, the bombardment of Fort Sumter, so long and anx-

11 *Ibid.*
12 Roman, *Military Operations of General Beauregard,* I, 52.

iously expected, has at length become an accomplished fact. The restless activity of the night before was gradually worn down, the citizens who thronged the Battery through the night, anxious and weary, had sought their homes; the Mounted Guard which had kept watch over the city, with the first grey streaks of morning were preparing to retire, when two guns in quick succession from Fort Johnson announced the opening of the drama.

"Upon that signal, the circle of batteries with which the grim fortress of Fort Sumter is beleaguered opened fire. The outline of this great volcanic crater was illuminated with a line of twinkling lights; the clustering shells illuminated the sky above it; our citizens, aroused to a forgetfulness of their fatigue, rushed again to points of observation; and so, at the break of day, amidst the bursting of bombs and roaring of ordinance, and before thousands of spectators whose homes and liberties and lives were at stake, was enacted this first great scene in the opening drama of what, it is presumed, will be a most momentous military act. It may be a drama of but a single act. The madness which inspires it may depart with this single paroxysm. It is certain that the people of the North have rankling at their hearts no sense of wrong to be avenged. . . . The administration of the old government may abandon at once and forever its vain hope of forcible control over the Confederate States. But it may not be so; they may persist in the assertion of their power, and if so, they will arouse an independent spirit in the South which will exact a merciless and fearful retribution.

"It were vain to attempt an exhibition of the enthusiasm and fearless intrepidity of our citizens. . . . Boats passed from post to post without the slightest hesitation under the guns of Sumter, and, with high and low, old and young, rich and poor, in uniform or without, the common wish and constant effort were to reach the posts of action. . . .

It is a most remarkable circumstance that, so far
as we have been able to learn from the most careful inquiry, not the slightest injury has been sus-
tained by the defenders of their country.

"It may be added, as an incident that contributed
no little interest to the action of the day that from
early in the forenoon, three vessels of war, two of
them supposed to be the Harriet Lane and the
Pawnee, lay just below the bar, inactive spectators
of the contest. Whether they will attempt to enter
during the night and encounter the batteries on
either side that line of the shore, is yet to be determined; if so, we will present the record of a bloody
issue in our next. Fort Sumter did not return the
fire of our batteries for over two hours and ceased
firing at 7 o'clock, p.m., though our men continued
to the hour of our going to press, etc." [13]

After the battle was over, under the caption "Glory
Enough For One Day," an editorial in the Montgomery
Advertiser said: "The intelligence that Fort Sumter surrendered to the Confederate forces yesterday sent a thrill
of joy to the heart of every true friend of the South.
The face of every Southern man was brighter, his step
lighter, and his bearing prouder, than it had been before." [14]

Exultant over the victory, the people of Charleston
gave free vent to their emotions, singing and dancing
in the streets. The citizens of Montgomery received the
welcome tidings with equal fervor.[15] A thrill of triumph
electrified the whole South. Little reckoned they the dread
significance of it all. Surely it was high tragedy, this
utter lack of realization that those booming guns at

[13] Quoted in Montgomery *Weekly Post,* April 16, 1861.
[14] Issue of April 14, 1861.
[15] Raphael Semmes, *Memoirs of Service Afloat, during the War between the States* (Baltimore, 1869), p. 89.

Charleston had tolled in advance the knell of their proud civilization, that the smoke from those shells would hang like a pall over their lives, the lives of their children, even those of their children's children.

AN IMPERATIVE NECESSITY

The day after Beauregard raised the Confederate flag above the ramparts of Sumter, President Lincoln issued his proclamation calling for seventy-five thousand troops. The document opened with the words, "Whereas the laws of the United States have been for some time past, and now are opposed, and the execution thereof obstructed, in the states of South Carolina, Georgia, Alabama, Florida, Mississippi, Louisiana, and Texas." This tells that when the Confederates assaulted and took Fort Sumter, only seven states made up the Confederate government which was challenging the might of the United States. In the light of the comparative strength of the opposing sections, such an attack approximated sheer recklessness. The Federals had a strong government, well-ordered state, war, navy, treasury, justice departments, ministers in every foreign court, the army, the navy, better transportation facilities, practically all manufactures, overwhelming advantage in population, incomparably superior resources in practically every field.

The Southern leaders who sanctioned the bombardment were not blind. Beauregard, Pickens, Walker, Davis—all were involved. The seeming foolhardiness necessarily presupposes a feeling of desperation. Behind this there was a long chain of causes, but the immediate source of exasperation was news that, under the now trite pretext of provisioning, the administration was preparing to reinforce the garrison. This one thing the Southerners had resolutely set themselves to prevent, whatever the consequences. Because of what they had heard, on April seventh Beauregard had closed to the Sumter command the doors of the Charleston market. They knew that the reason for this action was no secret to those who for weeks had busied themselves in what was plainly preparation for the use of force. It was Union General Doubleday, then a member of Anderson's staff, who was later to give, as the explanation of the prohibition of further supplies, the fact that war vessels were sailing from New York and Norfolk under sealed orders. Better than anyone else, Lincoln understood why Beauregard had issued the order and the Southerners knew that he understood it.

History credits Lincoln with a keen sense of humor. Assuming for the moment that he was sincere in his protestations of "supplying with provisions only," was he, a graduate of the rough and tumble school of practical politics, so ingenuous as not to detect a touch of the ludicrous in his sending food supplies under an escort of warships? Would not it likely cause comment should the grocer boy turn up at the kitchen door, flanked by a cordon of police armed with muskets and supported by a battery of artillery? Whether the absurdity of that procedure was apparent to the president does not clearly appear, but his special message of July 4, 1861, to congress discloses that, after reciting the notice to Governor Pickens, he recorded a complaint: "Whereupon the fort was attacked and bombarded to its fall, *without even awaiting the arrival* of the provisioning expedition." [16]

Such an utterance was the very essence either of naivete or of guile. Was the president in earnest in his implication that the Confederates should have sat with

[16] *A Compilation of Messages and Papers of the Presidents,* VI, 22. Italics supplied.

folded hands until, to the heavy artillery of the fort, there came the support of the eight nine-inch guns of the *Pawnee*, the one eight-inch gun and four thirty-two-pounders of the *Harriet Lane*, the formidable armament of the *Pocahontas*, let alone the arms, ammunition, and troops on board the transport *Baltic?* [17] On April tenth Senator Wigfall had telegraphed Jefferson Davis urging the capture of Fort Sumter before the coming of the day when the Confederates would have to fight the fleet and the fort.[18] Davis' thoughts were running in the same channel. In his report of the events of April eleventh and twelfth, Beauregard further interprets the Confederate government's decision:

> "As, in consequence of a communication from the President of the United States to the governor of South Carolina, we were in momentary expectation of an attempt to re-enforce Fort Sumter, or of a descent upon our coast to that end from the United States fleet then lying at the entrance of the harbor, it was manifestly an imperative necessity to reduce the fort as speedily as possible, and not to wait until the ships and the fort should unite in a combined attack upon us." [19]

In the North there were representative people who wondered at the Federal government's lack of judgment in so inciting hostilities. In his work, *Origin of the Late War*, published in 1866, George Lunt, of Massachusetts, indicates that he shared this feeling. At the time the fleet dropped anchor off Charleston, he says, it was common belief that other transports and warships had put to sea from Northern ports. Noting that preparation

[17] *B. & L.,* I, 78 n.
[18] Louise (Wigfall) "Mrs. D. Giraud" Wright, *A Southern Girl in '61* (New York, 1905), p. 36.
[19] *O. R. A.,* Ser. 1, Vol. I, p. 31.

of these warlike expeditions necessarily had required a considerable period, he gives as his personal reaction, "It bore the aspect, certainly, of a manoeuvre which military persons and, sometimes, metaphorically, politicians denominate 'stealing a march.' " [20] Referring to Seward's April eighth assurance that faith as to Sumter would be fully kept, and observing that on that same day Lincoln gave his notice to Governor Pickens, Matthew Page Andrews writes that President Davis accepted as an act of war the Federal government's sending the naval squadron to Charleston.[21] More and more, students are acknowledging the difficulty of Davis' position; one of these admits openly that, after Lincoln had actually ordered the expedition to sail, his secretary of state was still telling the commissioners from the South that they need fear no effort to relieve Fort Sumter.[22]

The report of General Beauregard made reference to the fleet then lying at the harbor entrance. Captain Fox, who was on the *Baltic* and in charge of the expedition, tells in his 1865 report that this vessel reached the appointed rendezvous at three o'clock on the morning of the twelfth. This was one hour and thirty minutes before the shore batteries fired the first gun of the engagement. He found there the *Harriet Lane*, and the *Pawnee* came in at six o'clock. The secretary of war had given him to understand that, arriving at Charleston, he had but to make his needs known to the senior naval officer who would be there with orders to use, if need be, his entire force to open a passage. Boarding the *Pawnee*, he informed the commander of his instructions and asked that

[20] P. 446.

[21] *History of the United States* (Philadelphia and London, 1914), pp. 270, 271.

[22] James Truslow Adams, *The March of Democracy* (2 vols. New York and London, 1932-33), II, 15.

he "stand in to the bar" with him. Obviously, neither Fox nor his instructions made sufficient impression, for, replying that his orders were to await the arrival of the *Powhatan*, the captain of the warship brought Fox up with a jolt by calmly observing that "he was not going in there to inaugurate civil war." [23] So Fox was not the only victim of the demoralization in Washington. The *Pawnee's* captain was awaiting the *Powhatan*. Here was another case of too many cooks; Lincoln had secretly sent the *Powhatan* to Pensacola. Returning to the *Baltic*, Fox "stood in toward the bar, followed by the *Harriet Lane*, Captain Faunce, who cheerfully accompanied" [24] him. As the shore line came into view, the dull rumble of heavy guns greeted their ears, "and the smoke and shells from the batteries . . . were distinctly visible." [25] In a former report to the secretary of the navy, dated April 19, 1861, Fox had written: "I stood in with the *Baltic* to execute my orders by offering, in the first place, to carry provisions to Fort Sumter. Nearing the bar, it was observed that war had commenced, and, therefore, the pacific offer of provisions was void." [26]

The naval maneuver had not caught the Confederates napping. Alert ears had heard rumors and the intended surprise party had encountered an unexpected welcome. On the afternoon of April twelfth, Major Whiting, adjutant general of South Carolina, reported his observations relative to the squadron: "The Pawnee, Harriet Lane (certain), and the Baltic (conjectured, from my knowledge of her build) are at anchor close at the North Channel. . . . The ships may try to send boats in. Already guns are trained and ranged for night firing on

[23] *O. R. N.*, Ser. 1, Vol. IV, p. 249.   [24] *Ibid.*
[25] *Ibid.* See also Roman, *Military Operations of General Beauregard*, I, 45.   [26] *O. R. N.*, Ser. 1, Vol. IV, p. 244.

the landing. It is doubtful if the ships will try it. They may." [27]

General Crawford, present through it all, testifies to the fleet's nearness to the scene of hostilities: "The bombardment was now at its height; the quarters were in flames, and the flash of Anderson's guns could be distinctly seen from the fleet. . . . There was no movement for his relief. . . . The fleet's flags could be seen from Fort Sumter." [28]

As may easily be imagined, on both sides there was speculation as to just what to expect from the fleet. The garrison believed that help would be forthcoming.[29] Sumter's flag "dipped" to the fleet off the bar, and the ships returned the salute.[30] Anderson's signaling was in vain, and a sentry stationed on the walls to report any activity discovered no activity to report. Captain Fox on the *Baltic* "cheerfully accompanied" by the *Harriet Lane*, "stood in toward the bar," but that was all.[31] The *Pocahontas*, the third of the war vessels assigned by Lincoln to the expedition, failed to put in an appearance on the twelfth. The April fourteenth report of her commander says: "I have the honor to report the arrival of this vessel at the anchorage designated in your order of the 5th instant. . . . We reached here on the 13th and found at anchor the *Pawnee*, *Harriet Lane*, and *Baltic*." [32]

He found them at anchor. The battle was then in its second day. And there, so close to the scene of action that from the fleet the smoke and shells from the batteries

---

[27] *O. R. A.*, Ser. 1, Vol. I, p. 306.

[28] *The Genesis of the Civil War*, p. 418. See also *ibid.*, p. 432.

[29] *B. & L.*, I, 47; Crawford, *The Genesis of the Civil War*, pp. 434, 437.

[30] *B. & L.*, I, 68.   [31] *O. R. N.*, Ser. 1, Vol. IV, p. 249.

[32] *O. R. N.*, Ser. 1, Vol. IV, p. 243.

and the flashes of Anderson's guns were distinctly visible, and from the fort the flags of the men-of-war could be seen, a United States naval squadron rode at anchor in perfect safety, privileged spectators of a thrilling drama, the bombardment of a fort flying the flag of the United States.

A SPECTACLE FOR THE GODS

It is not recorded whether the fifteenth of April, 1861, was a busy day on Olympus but it is certain that, if the gods chanced to be looking in the direction of Charleston harbor, they witnessed a scene which must have thrilled the most phlegmatic of the group. The bombardment of Sumter, begun at four-thirty on the morning of the twelfth, had continued for about thirty hours. Cooped up inside the walls of the fortress, Anderson and his command had confronted the alternative, either to surrender, or to hold out till the bitter end, giving the best possible account of themselves. They had chosen the latter course. Through the hell of shot and fire and possible disaster, the garrison had doggedly stood by its guns. So moving had been the spectacle that, in the words of the official report of Beauregard, "Our brave troops, carried away by their naturally generous impulses, mounted the different batteries, and at every discharge from the fort cheered the garrison for its pluck and gallantry, and hooted the fleet lying inactive just outside the bar." [33]

In the early evening of the thirteenth the firing had ceased. The garrison's resistance had collapsed. The Confederates had not held Anderson and his men prisoners. Beauregard reported, "The arrangements being completed Major Anderson embarked with his command on the transport prepared to convey him to the United

[33] *O. R. A.,* Ser. 1, Vol. I, p. 32.

States fleet lying outside the bar." [34] "With banners flying," wrote one of Anderson's comrades, "and with drums beating 'Yankee Doodle,' we marched on board the transport that was to take us to the steamship *Baltic*, which . . . was anchored outside." [35]

On the fifteenth all was in readiness for the trip to the fleet.[36] For the purpose Beauregard had provided a steamer, the *Isabel*. With Anderson and his men on board, she slowly made her way down the channel past the Confederate batteries. A sorrowful journey it was for the little band who had just seen their flag hauled down in defeat. Soon, however, it developed that the occasion of their departure was not to be uneventful. From the batteries along the shore streamed the soldiers of the South who, but a few hours before, had manned the guns which had made wreckage of Sumter. Beauregard's official report tells the story:

> ". . . when, on the 15th instant he left the harbor on the steamer Isabel the soldiers of the batteries on Cummings Point lined the beach, silent, and with heads uncovered, while Anderson and his command passed before them, and expressions of scorn at the apparent cowardice of the fleet in not even attempting to rescue so gallant an officer and his command were upon the lips of all." [37]

What mattered it to these soldiers that, only two days before, they were pouring a deadly rain of shells on Anderson's garrison? What if this might prove the beginning of a ghastly war in which hundreds of thousands of young men were to die? Nothing counted that day save realization that the men now passing out to sea had

[34] *Ibid.*, p. 33.   [35] *B. & L.*, I, 48.
[36] *O. R. A.*, Ser. 1, Vol. I, p. 29.
[37] *Ibid.*, p. 28. See also Crawford, *The Genesis of the Civil War*, p. 447; Evans, *Confederate Military History*, V, 18.

fought a superb fight against hopeless odds, had remained at their posts when destruction seemed imminent. Pay tribute to the Yankees? To be sure they would—and did! With obvious satisfaction Beauregard reported this to the Confederate secretary of war. It was anything but war, but it was splendid, and the general was proud of his boys. Little wonder he thought, as he took occasion to write in his report, that, with material of this timbre, he could build an army which would prove invincible. Nor was this all. To their tribute of respect for the garrison, the soldiers added their contempt for the powerful naval squadron. Its inactivity may or may not have justified their feeling. Various apologists have offered varied explanations. Commander Gillis of the *Pocahontas* reported to the secretary of the navy on April sixteenth. He had arrived, he said, at the designated anchorage off Charleston on the thirteenth and had found there the *Pawnee*, the *Harriet Lane*, and the *Baltic*. From the *Pawnee's* commander he had secured a duly certified copy of the orders from the secretary of the navy. By way of explanation of the failure of the *Pocahontas* to participate in the Sumter engagement, he had this to say: "Had there been pilots for the channel on board, I would have proceeded up to the assistance of Sumter, or made the attempt to pass the long line of batteries, as the impulse was strong to render assistance to the gallant men in Sumter; but without pilots, the buoys and marks being removed, we would probably have grounded." [38]

There was no possible excuse for the presence of the squadron unless, as Fox understood, it was to be on hand for the express purpose of using its power should there be resistance to the relief of the fort. Moreover, the Federal navy department could hardly have failed to under-

[38] *O. R. N.*, Ser. 1, Vol. IV, p. 251.

stand that local pilots would not be available for a hostile expedition. The possibility of grounding was one of the unavoidable risks incident to any naval attempt to force a way into a closed harbor. The commander of the *Pocahontas* chose not to take the chance.

Later General Doubleday, noting that the fleet's inaction was the subject of severe criticism, remarked that the effort to go in would probably have resulted in the sinking of every vessel.[39] To be sure there would have been possibility of injury to the men-of-war, but, to say the least, there was also likelihood that their participation in the engagement would have lessened appreciably the ease with which the enemy accomplished the capture of the fort. A seasoned soldier here gives the impression that, in an emergency when Anderson sorely needed all possible assistance, the matter of the safety of the warships was sufficient excuse for the squadron merely to stand by. Still another theory appeared in an account in Appleton's *American Annual Cyclopædia* of 1861. Mentioning the arrival of the naval force prior to the commencement of the assault, it explains that a gale of wind prevented the ships from entering the harbor until after "the attack began." [40] There was a failure, however, to state whether or not the gale continued throughout the two full days the battle was in progress.

Commander Gillis would have thought twice before giving the excuse that his ship would probably have grounded had he known that, three months to the day before he wrote his report, J. S. Black, secretary of state of the United States, in a letter to the commanding general of the army, had discussed this very matter of forcing a passage into Charleston harbor. An enthusiastic cham-

39 Roman, *Military Operations of General Beauregard*, I, 45.
40 I, 669.

pion of the proposed reinforcement, the secretary had become impatient with objectors who were presenting what General Crawford characterized as "the comparatively trifling nature of the obstacles existing." [41] His letter, dated January 16, 1861, thoroughly covered the ground:

"I am persuaded that the difficulty of relieving Major Anderson has been very much magnified. . . . I am thoroughly satisfied that the battery on Morris Island can give no serious trouble. A vessel going in where the Star of the West went will not be within the reach of the battery's guns longer than from six to ten minutes. The number of shots that could be fired upon her in that time may be easily calculated, and I think the chances of her being seriously injured can be demonstrated by simple arithmetic to be very small. A very unlucky shot might cripple her, to be sure, and therefore the risk is something. But then it is a maxim, not less in war than in peace, that where nothing is ventured nothing can be gained. The removal of the buoys has undoubtedly made the navigation of the channel more difficult. But there are pilots outside of Charleston, and many of the officers of the Navy, who could steer a ship into the harbor by the natural land-marks with perfect safety. This, be it remembered, is not now a subject of speculation; the actual experiment has been tried. The Star of the West did pass the battery, and did overcome the difficulties of the navigation, meeting with no serious trouble from either cause. . . .

"I am convinced that a pirate, or a slaver, or a smuggler, who could be assured of making five hundred dollars by going into the harbor in the face of all the dangers which now threaten a vessel bearing the American flag, would laugh them to scorn, and

[41] *The Genesis of the Civil War,* pp. 238, 239.

to one of our naval officers who has the average of daring, 'the danger's self were lure alone.' " [42]

On this subject others than Mr. Black were on record. Fox himself had enjoyed the distinction of being escorted by a member of the cabinet to discuss the question in the office of President Lincoln. General Scott was one of those present but the captain held the center of the stage. Scott was protesting with vehemence that the experiment would be a blunder and his opposition was embarrassing Lincoln. With the scheme's originator and its most influential opponent facing each other across the conference table, the president felt that all phases of the expedition plan could be threshed out. Despite the personal character and the official prestige of the commanding general of the army, the former naval captain experienced little difficulty. It is not hard to win the game when the umpire is anxious to assist. So, to Lincoln's satisfaction, Fox refuted Scott's insistence that the then-established batteries would render extremely hazardous an attempted entrance. His argument was that a steam naval force "could pass any number of guns there, and for the reason that the course was at right angles to the line of fire, and the distance, 1,300 yards, too great for accurate firing at night." [43]

In a request which on April fifteenth General Beauregard received from Lieutenant Huger of the Confederate States navy, there comes out a sequel to the story of the attitude of the commander of the *Pocahontas*. Resenting the presence of the United States squadron and observing that its attitude was one of great disrespect, the lieutenant had a proposition to make:

[42] *O. R. A.*, Ser. 1, Vol. I, pp. 141, 142; Crawford, *The Genesis of the Civil War*, p. 238.   [43] *Ibid.*, p. 347.

". . . I would like to have the pleasure of driving them off from our port; and, if we cannot succeed in that, at least make them keep at a respectful distance. I volunteer for the service. If you will allow me to put the rifled cannon on board the Lady Davis, under my command, I can go out, and, at long range, try the effect of the shot on them. I think in this way I may be able to annoy, if not to drive them off." [44]

In the face of all the record shows, there are those who present a novel theory; namely, that inasmuch as there was nothing to prevent the squadron's going to the relief of Anderson, its remaining outside is proof that, because he did not care to start a war, Lincoln withheld from the warships the privilege of proceeding to the rescue. This is highly impressive, if true. So far as appears, however, the theory is without support from any word from Lincoln, any known authority, any established fact. Upon its sponsors, therefore, devolves responsibility for harmonizing such speculation with the plain recitals of the record.

The undisputed facts point the other way. After the president had spent weeks planning for and preparing his expedition, assembling supplies, arms, ammunition, troops, and warships, what ground is there for belief that he was responsible for secret instructions which kept his war vessels at anchor while an enemy was battering to pieces a United States fort? Long before plans for the expedition matured, Fox had talked of one consisting of three tugs, using the words, "the first tug to lead in empty, to open their fire." [45] Upon his return from his trip to Sumter, a visit which Lincoln inspired, Fox had reported that Major Anderson seemed to think that

[44] *O. R. A.,* Ser. 1, Vol. I, p. 315.
[45] *O. R. N.,* Ser. 1, Vol. IV, p. 225.

relief of the fort would necessitate landing an army on Morris Island.[46] In the interview at Sumter, Anderson had impressed on Fox that the sending of reinforcements would open civil war.[47] Disregarding repeated warnings, one from his secretary of war, one from the chief of engineers, a third from the commanding general of the army, all notifying him that he was heading the ship of state into a storm, the president had steered straight ahead.[48] Assigned to command the expedition, Fox had received on April fourth orders that, in the event he encountered opposition, he was to report the fact to the senior naval officer of the harbor who would hold instructions from the secretary of the navy to use his entire force to open a passage.[49] Immediately upon learning of the coming of the expedition, Major Anderson had written Washington that his heart was not in the war about to be commenced.[50] In Fox's report of April 19, 1861, voicing his disappointment over the failure of the *Powhatan* to join the squadron at Charleston, he had said: "I only felt anxious to get in a few day's provisions to last the fort *until the Powhatan's arrival.* The Pawnee and Lane were both short of men, and were only intended to afford a base of operations whilst the tugs and three hundred sailors *fought their way in. . . .* with the Powhatan a re-enforcement would have been easy." [51]

When on April thirteenth Captain Gillis arrived off Charleston on the *Pocahontas,* he secured from the captain of the *Pawnee* a certified copy of his orders from the secretary of the navy; yet, reporting three days later to that same secretary, he wrote that, had he been able to secure a pilot, he would have taken his ship into

[46] *Ibid.,* p. 247.
[47] Crawford, *The Genesis of the Civil War,* p. 371.
[48] *O. R. A.,* Ser. 1, Vol. I, pp. 198, 200.
[49] *Ibid.,* p. 236.   [50] *Ibid.,* p. 294.   [51] *Ibid.,* p. 11. Italics supplied.

the thick of the battle.[52] It may reasonably be inferred that a naval captain would hardly have given to the secretary of the navy such an explanation if, at the crucial moment he was describing, he had known of orders directing the warships, whatever the provocation, to remain outside. Furthermore, along with the rest of the Sumter command, General Doubleday sailed from Charleston to New York on the *Baltic*, Fox's own ship, and so had ample opportunity to learn the facts; yet his account attributes the squadron's failure to assist, not to any order, but to the fact that such a course would probably have meant the loss of every vessel. Again, better probably than any other man, Nicolay knew the mind of the president. What of his reference, not only to the presence of warships with the expedition, but to their orders to use their guns in case of resistance? [53]

Speculation as to motives and undisclosed intentions is futile. Assume, however, that it was not part of Lincoln's plan for the warships to participate; is not this clearly beside the main point? The fact is, the naval vessels went to Charleston. It is undisputed that Lincoln gave the necessary orders. Their presence was unnecessary if, regardless of what was to happen, the expedition was to restrict its activities to a peaceable effort to deliver supplies. The real point is that the president surely was aware that, when the warships put in an appearance, the Confederates would conclude that the squadron was there to supplement the power of Sumter. He knew that they would regard this as a hostile movement. He knew that they would resist any effort to relieve the fort. Did not he, therefore, have every reason to expect that there would happen precisely what did happen?

[52] *O. R. N.*, Ser. 1, Vol. IV, p. 251.   [53] *Lincoln*, IV, 45.

CHAPTER XV

LINCOLN GOT WHAT HE WANTED

INTERPRETATIONS OF THE SENDING OF THE EXPEDITION

In the light of the record's disclosures, why did Lincoln adopt a course which he had every reason to believe would result in war?

As matters stood at the date of the inauguration, it was obvious that the administration was not ready for a showdown. There were trouble-promising hurdles to clear before the track was open. For one thing, there were many in the North who openly sympathized with the Southern position;[1] more who quailed at the suggestion of coercion of those who, rightly or wrongly believing it to be their constitutional right, were merely withdrawing from the Union. This sentiment became articulate in the outspoken proposal to let the erring sister states go out in peace. Another restraining factor loomed large; the emergency called for wide-awake handling of the border states, states with slaves, and, besides, with sharply divided loyalty. Should these cast in their lot with the seceders, there would be a decided change for the worse, but if Lincoln could devise an effective method to insure their continued allegiance, this would lessen decidedly the Southern Confederacy's prospect of success. If he could cleverly play the Southerners into committing the first overt act of hostility, he could go to the country with a far stronger appeal. Such apparently uncalled-

[1] *Diary of Gideon Welles*, I, 10, 55.

for defiance of constituted authority would fan into flame the indignation of those not yet estranged. Then the stage would be set.

Jefferson Davis saw through the plan. He knew the shrewdness of his opponent and watched the moves by which a clever trap was being laid. Knowing full well that it was likely only a matter of days when the formidable jaws would snap to, no course was open but patiently to sit and wait. Upon Anderson's final refusal to surrender, a Confederate cabinet meeting ended in spirited disagreement as to future procedure. The ultimate responsibility was Davis' and he shouldered it:

> "The order for the sending of the fleet was a declaration of war. The responsibility is on their shoulders, not on ours. The juggle for position as to who shall fire the first gun in such an hour is unworthy of a great people and their cause. A deadly weapon has been aimed at our heart. Only a fool would wait until the first shot has been fired. The assault has been made. It is of no importance who shall strike the first blow or fire the first gun." [2]

Partisan writers have rung the changes with a supposedly damning indictment: "The South fired the first shot." The Confederate president was not without a presentiment as to the reverberations which would follow exploitation of this fact. This he was powerless to prevent but at least he would make the Southern position clear. In the case of nations, as of individuals, he was aware, actions were to be weighed judicially only in light of antecedent aggravation. He knew that in courts of law the case of a reckless swaggerer, driven by unreasoning passion to fire first, differed materially from that of a man who luckily discovered an enemy creeping up

[2] McElroy, *Jefferson Davis,* I, 289-290.

on him with a gun. Long before, Henry Hallam had
written, "The aggressor in a war (that is, he who begins
it), is not the *first* who *uses force,* but the first who
renders force *necessary.*" [3] Something akin to this the
Confederate leader clearly had in mind when, later, he
appealed the case to the discriminating judgment of the
future:

> "The dangerous rant of demagogues about 'firing
> on the flag' might serve to rouse the passions of
> insensate mobs in times of general excitement, but
> will be impotent in impartial history to relieve the
> Federal government from the responsibility of the
> assault made by sending a hostile fleet against the
> harbor of Charleston, to cooperate with the menac-
> ing garrison of Fort Sumter." [4]

Davis' views, however, were those of a partisan. What
thought some of Lincoln's friends and contemporaries?
Already familiar are the solemn warnings of Cameron,
his secretary of war, Scott, commander in chief of the
army, and Totten, the army's chief of engineers, that
the course upon which he had set his heart would end in
tragedy. The New York *Herald* of May 11, 1861, said,
"The demonstration which precipitated the attack on
Fort Sumter was resolved upon to prove to the country
and the world the true character and nature of the rebellion." Quoting this, George Lunt, the Massachusetts
historian, added his own comment; namely, that the purpose of the expedition was to draw the fire of the Confederates; "a *silent* aggression," he characterized it,
"with the object of producing an *active* aggression from

---

[3] *The Constitutional History of England* (2 vols. New York, 1897),
II, 219, quoted Stephens, *Constitutional View of the War between the
States,* II, 35.

[4] McElroy, *Jefferson Davis,* I, 287.

the other side." [5] Lincoln's secretary of the navy quoted the secretary of state as observing that the attempt to hold Sumter "would be a waste of effort and energy and life, would extinguish all hope of peace, and compel the Government to take the initiative in hostile demonstrations." [6]

What of the views of Northern writers who have made intensive study of the events of the period? John T. Morse, Jr., a biographer of Lincoln, wrote that the president "finally gained his point in forcing the Confederacy into the position of assailant, and there is every reason to believe that he bought that point cheaply at the price of the fortress." [7] The writer of a life of Seward made this comment, "The Sumter expedition failed of its ostensible object, but it brought about the Southern attack on that fort. The first gun fired there effectively cleared the air . . . and placed Lincoln at the head of a united people." [8]

Nicolay lived in the White House and was Lincoln's intimate and confidant. It was his view that the Sumter expedition placed the Confederacy in a dilemma. If they fired on it they would thereby alienate their Northern sympathizers; if, after the determined stand they had taken, they backed down when the time arrived for action, such a surrender of principle would chill the enthusiasm of the South. He knew that Lincoln was under no illusion as to the consequences of his course. He tells much in a single sentence: "The presence of armed ships with the expedition and their instructions to fight their way to the fort in case of opposition, show

[5] *Origin of the Late War,* pp. 447, 448.
[6] *Diary of Gideon Welles,* I, 14.
[7] Morse, *Lincoln,* I, 250.
[8] Thornton K. Lothrop, *William Henry Seward* (Boston, [c1896]), p. 257.

that he believed the arbitrament of the sword to be at
hand." [9] As well as his chief, Nicolay knew the wisdom
of a course the ultimate result of which would be a more
widespread conviction that the Southerners were in the
wrong. Observing that Fox reminded the president that
but nine days remained for him to reach Charleston from
New York, and that this limitation of time might jeopardize his chance of success, he wrote: "But the President,
who had calculated all the probabilities of failure, and
who with more comprehensive statesmanship was looking
through and beyond the Sumter expedition to the now
inevitable rebel attack and the response of an awakened
and united North, calmly assured him that he should best
fulfil his duty by making the attempt." [10]

Fortunately, for the sake of historical truth, the evidence is not restricted to views of Southerners, nor to
opinions of biographers, nor to speculations of outsiders.
There is a final, a more authoritative source to which
resort may be made. On April fifteenth Lincoln issued
his proclamation calling for troops to suppress resistance
to the laws of the United States. Fifteen days later, he
wrote Fox the following letter:

"WASHINGTON, D. C., May 1, 1861
"CAPTAIN G. V. Fox. *My Dear Sir:* I sincerely
regret that the failure of the late attempt to provision Fort Sumter should be the source of annoyance to you. The practicability of your plan was
not, in fact, brought to a test.

"By reason of a gale, well known in advance to be
possible, and not improbable, the tugs, an essential
part of the plan, never reached the ground, while
by an accident, for which you were in nowise respon-

[9] Nicolay and Hay, *Lincoln,* IV, 44, 45.
[10] *Ibid.,* p. 28. See also *ibid.,* pp. 33, 44, 45, 62; *O. R. N.,* Ser. 1,
Vol. IV, p. 248.

sible, and possibly I to some extent was, you were deprived of a war vessel, with her men, which you deemed of great importance to the enterprise. I most cheerfully and truly declare that the failure of the undertaking has not lowered you a particle, while the qualities you developed in the effort have greatly heightened you, in my estimation. For a daring and dangerous enterprise of a similar character you would to-day be the man of all my acquaintances whom I would select. You and I both anticipated that the cause of the country would be advanced by making the attempt to provision Fort Sumter, *even if it should fail;* and it is no small consolation now to feel that our *anticipation is justified by the result.*

"Very truly, your friend,

"A. LINCOLN" [11]

[11] *Ibid.,* p. 251. See also Nicolay and Hay, *Lincoln,* IV, 56; Crawford, *The Genesis of the Civil War,* p. 420. Italics supplied.

III. THE SOUTH'S DESIRE FOR PEACEABLE SEPARATION

The effort to adjust the differences between the sections began in February, 1861, with the adoption of the Constitution for the Provisional Government of the Confederate States. To that period, therefore, the story returns.

CHAPTER XVI

THE CONFEDERATE GOVERNMENT
MOVES FOR PEACE

Shortly after Lincoln's election, the legislature of South Carolina called a state convention. This body assembled in Charleston. On December 20, 1860, by unanimous vote, it enacted the ordinance of secession. By the first of February the list of seceding states had reached the number of seven, South Carolina, Mississippi, Florida, Alabama, Georgia, Louisiana, and Texas. Three days later a group of the foremost men of the South gathered in Montgomery as delegates to a convention on which devolved responsibility for the organization of a new government. The initial undertaking was the writing of a constitution. Four days after the opening session, they adopted a "Constitution for the Provisional Government of the Confederate States of America." Appraising the epochal movement, Gladstone observed that they had created a nation.

A constitution is a formal statement of fundamental principles of government. Immune from attack by mere legislative action, its tenets can be changed only by the people and by them only in accordance with procedure outlined in the instrument itself. The incorporation into a constitution of any provision attests its importance in the eyes of the framers. In this light, Section 2, Article VI, of the Confederate Constitution assumes a largely unappreciated significance:

"The Government hereby instituted shall take immediate steps for the settlement of all matters be-

tween the States forming it, and their other late
confederates of the United States, in relation to the
public property and public debt at the time of their
withdrawal from them; these States hereby declaring it to be their wish and earnest desire to adjust
everything pertaining to the common property, common liability, and common obligations of that Union
upon the principles of right, justice, equity, and
good faith." [1]

It was a notable pronouncement, one not lightly to be
discounted. In line with the observation that it is a serious
matter to indict a whole people, it similarly verges on
presumption to undertake to discredit the sincerity of a
constitutional convention. With all the formality at their
command, the seceding states were, by this article in their
constitution, notifying the world of their hope for peaceable separation.

Nor did they stop with this. One week later, they
proceeded to put into action what they had expressed
in words. To Jefferson Davis, the president-elect, the
convention sent a formal resolution. This carried the
recommendation that, as early as convenient after his
inauguration, he should appoint commissioners charged
with the duty to negotiate with the government of the
United States to the end that all questions of disagreement should be adjusted and an amicable future assured. [2]
A circumstance indicating the gravity of the step, as
the membership of the convention viewed it, is that the
adoption of the resolution preceded the inauguration of
the president of the Confederate States.

[1] Jefferson Davis, *The Rise and Fall of the Confederate Government*
(2 vols. New York, 1881), I, 647.
[2] Statutes; Davis, *The Rise and Fall of the Confederate Government*,
I, 244.

On February twenty-fifth, Jefferson Davis appointed as commissioners A. B. Roman, of Louisiana, Martin J. Crawford, of Georgia, and John Forsyth, of Alabama. In a contemporary newspaper account, the Montgomery *Weekly Advertiser* evaluated its personnel:

"Mr. Roman has been governor of Louisiana, and was formerly of Opposition politics, having been a supporter of Mr. Bell in the recent contest for President of the United States, and subsequently a Co-operationist.

"Mr. Crawford is familiar to the public as a representative from the neighboring state of Georgia to the congress of the United States. His politics have been States Rights. Mr. Forsyth was a secessionist in 1851—was Minister to Mexico under Mr. Buchanan's administration of the old government— and was a leading advocate of Douglas through his paper, the Mobile Register, in the later race for President of the United States. These appointments represent all shades of political and partisan opinion, and the gentlemen being well qualified for the duties of their mission, we doubt not the selection is a good one." [3]

The next move was a communication of February twenty-seventh addressed to President Buchanan, introducing Martin J. Crawford as a special commissioner. The opening words were, "Being animated by an earnest desire to unite and bind together our respective countries by friendly ties." The name signed was not unfamiliar. It was that of Jefferson Davis, who had served in the war with Mexico, had later become a member of the senate of the United States, and had, from 1853 to

[3] Issue of March 6, 1861.

1857, held the office of secretary of war under President Pierce.

Within a few days after Lincoln succeeded Buchanan the peace commissioners were in Washington. Through Senator Hunter, of Virginia, they endeavored to secure an interview with Lincoln's secretary of state, but Seward replied that before consenting he would have to consult the president.[4] The following day he declined to receive them. This rebuff was an intimation that the activities of the newcomers would likely conclude precisely where they had begun. A complete breakdown seemed inevitable but there occurred a bit of rare good fortune. The appearance in the capital of accredited representatives of the Confederate government on what purported to be a mission of pacification stirred the interest of two justices of the Supreme Court of the United States. The happy circumstance that one of the justices was from the North, the other from the South was a guarantee that their advice would not be colored by sectional leaning. Nor was this all. Justice Campbell, from Alabama, had vigorously opposed the secession movement in his home state. Justice Nelson, from New York, a personal friend of Secretary Seward, after a recent study of the respective war powers of president and congress, had arrived at the conclusion that the chief executive could not use coercion without very serious violation of both constitution and statute.[5] Thus the Southern justice shared the Northern view of secession, while the Northern justice questioned the right of the Federal government to resort to extreme measures in its dealing with the

[4] Rhodes, *A History of the United States,* III, 329; Crawford, *The Genesis of the Civil War,* p. 324; Nicolay and Hay, *Lincoln,* III, 402.

[5] Davis, *The Rise and Fall of the Confederate Government,* I, 267; Crawford, *The Genesis of the Civil War,* pp. 325, 326; Rhodes, *A History of the United States,* III, 330.

seceders. All in all, it was an advisory combination which promised much.

Inspired by confidence in the sincerity of the Southerners, genuinely concerned for the success of this mission of peace, Nelson and Campbell temporarily laid aside their judicial robes and threw themselves into the breach. Denial to the distinguished visitors of even the courtesy of a hearing they knew would be a stupid blunder on the part of official Washington; it would never do to shut the door in the face of those who came voicing the message of the people of seven states, offering friendship and asking peace. With this in mind, the justices pressed Seward to consider, in the same spirit manifested in the document, the communication from the commissioners. This would have insured for the negotiations an atmosphere of cordiality, for the paper in question opened with a sentiment which defied misunderstanding:

> "With a view to the speedy adjustment of all questions growing out of this political separation, upon such terms of amity and good-will as the respective interests, geographical contiguity, and future welfare of the two nations may render necessary, the undersigned are instructed to make to the Government of the United States overtures for the opening of negotiations, assuring the Government of the United States, that the President, Congress, and people of the Confederate States earnestly desire a peaceful solution of these great questions; that it is neither their interest nor their wish to make any demand which is not founded in strictest justice, or to do any act to injure their late confederates." [6]

Carried forward into this announcement was the spirit which led the authors of the Confederate constitution to

[6] Davis, *The Rise and Fall of the Confederate Government*, I, 676. See also McElroy, *Jefferson Davis*, I, 278.

write Section 2, Article VI, and later inspired the Confederate congress to adopt its resolution. Conscious that they were treading on thin ice in presenting an issue which would call for the utmost tact and tolerance from all quarters, the commissioners came with outstretched hands and reiterated assurances of respect and good will. They felt, however, that their position was not unreasonable. Now that the two sections had reached a point where it appeared to one that diversity of interests required them to separate, was there aught to justify the other in saying that it should not go its own way in peace?

At this juncture, others than the commissioners were of the opinion that, with statesmanlike approach and sympathetic handling, the threatening crisis could yet be sidetracked. As sturdy an opponent of disunion as Welles of the Lincoln cabinet confided to his *Diary* his impression of a widespread belief in the likelihood of an adjustment.[7] Later Channing had the view that a majority of the advocates of secession had no expectation of permanent separation, but were of the opinion that so bringing matters to a head would open the way more easily to secure desired concessions.[8] The theory advanced by these stalwarts of the North finds an echo in the reference by the leading biographer of Jefferson Davis to the desire of the Southern leader to avoid conflict. It further coincides with the belief of this biographer that most of the colleagues of the Confederate president expected that, ultimately, secession would lead to a better understanding, and so be conducive to peace. It is also in line with what the same author records as the settled conviction of Alexander H. Stephens; namely, that as a last resort

[7] I, 10.
[8] *A Students' History of the United States,* pp. 475, 476.

Lincoln would accede to the demand that all United States forces be withdrawn from the South.[9]

Seward's reply to the proposal of the commissioners took the form of a memorandum which he filed in the department of state. Declining to concede that the Confederate States constituted an independent nation, it referred the commissioners to the president's inaugural address. The secretary, it noted, was not at liberty to enter into correspondence with them. It revealed something more; its views were not those of the secretary alone:

> "Finally, the Secretary of State would observe that, although he has supposed that he might safely and with propriety have adopted these conclusions, without making any reference of the subject to the Executive, yet, so strong has been his desire to practice entire directness, and to act in a spirit of perfect respect and candor toward Messrs. Forsyth and Crawford, and that portion of the people of the Union in whose name they present themselves before him, that he has cheerfully *submitted this paper to the President, who coincides generally in the views it expresses,* and sanctions the Secretary's decision declining official intercourse with Messrs. Forsyth and Crawford." [10]

Seward, Crawford, and Forsyth held the stage and were speaking the lines, but in the background loomed the figures of Lincoln and Davis. Seward was guarding his steps. Occupying a position which clothed him with prestige second only to that of the president, he never-

[9] McElroy, *Jefferson Davis,* I, 272, 282, 283.
[10] Davis, *The Rise and Fall of the Confederate Government,* I, 678. Italics supplied.

theless was sidestepping the assumption of sole responsibility in these negotiations. At the very outset, when
Senator Hunter requested an audience for the Southerners, before giving an answer he had consulted Lincoln.
Here he was pursuing the same course.

Despite his refusal to deal directly with the Confederate envoys, it was altogether a different matter to
ignore two members of the nation's highest court. In
response to the urging of Justices Nelson and Campbell,
Seward remarked that, had Jefferson Davis known the
state of affairs in Washington, he would not have sent
the commission. In this connection, he volunteered the
further observation, "The evacuation of Sumter is as
much as the Administration can bear." [11] This plain intimation that there was under advisement such a course,
one which to a great extent would have cleared the atmosphere of the mist of suspicion, emboldened Campbell to
resort to the directness and candor which Seward had
invoked in his memorandum. It occurred to the justice
that it might be advisable to write Jefferson Davis. He
inquired of Seward what he should say to the Confederate
president regarding Forts Sumter and Pickens. The secretary authorized him to write that within less than ten
days, *even* before a letter could go from Washington to
Montgomery, Davis would learn by telegraph of the issuance of an order for the evacuation of Sumter.[12] While
this seemed altogether too good to be true, Campbell
noted that the answer was silent as to Fort Pickens. In
view of the fact that this fort also had a Federal garrison,
he had another question: What of the government's

[11] *Ibid.*, p. 268. See also Rhodes, *A History of the United States*, III,
330.

[12] Davis, *The Rise and Fall of the Confederate Government*, I, 268;
Stephens, *A Constitutional View of the War between the States*, II,
348; Rhodes, *A History of the United States*, III, 331.

intentions as to Pickens? Seward's reply was that conditions there were satisfactory and that there would be no change.[13]

This was March fifteenth. With the unqualified pledge of early evacuation of Fort Sumter, assuredly they were making progress. Campbell at once sent to Commissioner Crawford the cheering tidings. He added, moreover, that he had perfect confidence that the secretary of state was sincere in the assurances he was giving. Telling Seward what he had reported to Crawford,[14] he took occasion to advise the commissioners to wait ten days before insisting on a reply from Seward. Five days passed. The garrison remained in Sumter. On March twenty-first, at the instance of the commissioners, Nelson and Campbell again went to the secretary and, when the conference was over, Campbell reassured the commissioners of his entire faith in the promise to give up the fort.[15] The next day Campbell gave to the commissioners a written report of a later conversation with Seward. In this he restated his confidence that all would be well and declared that the delay had not left him with either apprehension or distrust.[16] At about this time, the progress they had made so satisfied Justice Nelson that, in the belief that further participation on his part was unnecessary, he felt free to take his departure from the capital, leaving Campbell in charge of negotiations, counseling him, however, to continue his activities until the removal of the garrison.[17]

[13] Davis, *The Rise and Fall of the Confederate Government,* I, 268; Rhodes, *A History of the United States,* III, 331.

[14] Stephens, *A Constitutional View of the War between the States,* II, 348; Rhodes, *A History of the United States,* III, 331.

[15] *Ibid.,* p. 332; Stephens, *A Constitutional View of the War between the States,* II, 349.

[16] Davis, *The Rise and Fall of the Confederate Government,* I, 270; Rhodes, *A History of the United States,* III, 332.

[17] Crawford, *The Genesis of the Civil War,* p. 333.

That Mr. Lamon, regarded in Charleston as a confidential agent of the president, told both Governor Pickens, of South Carolina, and Major Anderson that the government was preparing to withdraw the Sumter command seems well established. Nor was Lamon alone in this belief; it was common talk in the capital.[18] Nevertheless, contrary to general opinion, the government's procedure was still an open question. At a cabinet meeting on March twenty-ninth the situation at the fort provoked spirited discussion. Of those present only Seward and Smith were in favor of evacuation. At the close of the session Lincoln instructed the secretary of war and the secretary of the navy to prepare an expedition to be ready to sail as early as the sixth of April.[19] On April first Campbell saw Seward twice, and again the secretary went to Lincoln. Following the conference with the president, Seward informed Campbell that he was satisfied the government would not undertake "to supply Fort Sumter without giving notice to Governor Pickens." Detecting the new note, Campbell immediately put the question, "Does the President design to attempt to supply Fort Sumter?" Seward replied, "No, I think not. It is a very irksome thing to him to surrender it. His ears are open to every one, and they fill his head with schemes for its supply. I do not think that he will adopt any of them. There is no design to reinforce it." [20]

In Seward's conversation, it will be noted, there cropped out a new word, "reinforce." Clearly here is ground for inference that he regarded "supply" and "provision" as interchangeable with "reinforce." For that matter, it was the judgment of careful observers in both sections that talk of supplying and provisioning was

18 Rhodes, *A History of the United States,* III, 332, 333.
19 *Ibid.,* p. 335.   20 *Ibid.,* p. 336.

mere verbiage. To the informed it was no secret that the administration was planning reinforcement. Gideon Welles was in a position to know; what he had to say of the conduct of his fellow cabinet member Seward removes all doubt as to the nature of his view:

> "The Secretary of State writes the Rebel commission he is satisfied the Government will not undertake to *supply* Fort Sumter without giving notice to Governor P., when at that very moment he knew that the whole energies of the War and Navy Departments were engaged by order of the President in preparations to forward supplies and *reinforcements* to Sumter." [21]

Rumors of the preparations reached the ear of Campbell, and on April seventh he wrote Seward asking if the report was "well or ill founded." The secretary answered, "Faith as to Sumter fully kept—wait and see." [22] Still there was no evidence of insincerity in his attitude and Campbell placed full trust in his statement. It was perfectly natural that a justice of the Supreme Court of the United States, conferring with the secretary of state relative to a matter of most serious moment, should take for granted that the secretary's words might be accepted at face value.

Neither Campbell nor the commissioners had any inkling of what had taken place in the March twenty-ninth cabinet meeting. But Secretary Welles knew. And Welles knew that Seward knew. After sitting through that session, at the close of which Lincoln directed the making up of the expedition, Seward could hardly have failed to grasp the import of one outstanding feature: Lincoln

[21] *Diary of Gideon Welles*, I, 27. Italics supplied.
[22] Stephens, *A Constitutional View of the War between the States*, II, 349. See also Rhodes, *A History of the United States*, III, 337.

saw fit to commit his project, persistently camouflaged as one to carry "supplies" or "provisions," to the departments of war and navy. And yet, on April seventh, just ten days later, when the two departments were concentrating their energies to meet the president's requirements, the secretary of state was reiterating to Campbell his assurance that he could rely on the good faith of the promise of the abandonment of the fort. Welles further clarified the matter: "I make no comments on these proceedings, by which I, and the President, and others, as well as the Rebel commissioners, were deceived"; and again, "It was a misfortune of Mr. Seward, and one of his characteristics, that he delighted in oblique and indirect movements." [23]

Some writers have implied that the Confederate representatives were in Washington playing for time, hoping to drag out negotiations until their government was ready for conflict. It is, however, not to be overlooked that, had the Southern leaders cared to resort to deception, there was available a much simpler, a far more effective method. A dozen men could have met in Montgomery and formulated a program to throw the North off its guard; a simple agreement secretly to impress upon their respective states the expediency of deferring secession to a date sufficiently far in the future to afford ample opportunity for adequate preparation.

LINCOLN'S CONSULTATIONS WITH THE SECRETARY
OF STATE

It was on March twenty-ninth that Lincoln directed to be assembled a fleet of warships, transports, and tugs to carry supplies, arms, ammunition, and troops. Decid-

[23] *Diary of Gideon Welles,* I, 28, 39.

ing on April fourth to order this expedition to Sumter, two days later he dispatched a messenger to notify Governor Pickens of the proposed relief program. From March fifteenth until April eighth, with the assistance of Nelson and Campell, the commissioners had carried on negotiations with Secretary Seward during the course of which Seward had consulted Lincoln on no fewer than three occasions. Besides, the secretary and the president were together in the cabinet session at the close of which Lincoln gave orders for the expedition.[24] Rhodes was evidently of the opinion that the situation called for comment:

> ". . . Justice Campbell, whose sincerity and straightforwardness cannot be questioned, averred that 'the equivocating conduct of the administration' was the 'proximate cause' of the commencement of the war in Charleston harbor. If, as these gentlemen more or less directly assume, the President consented to this negotiation, and knew of the assurances which Seward gave, his course cannot successfully be defended. Nicolay and Hay do not tell us in set terms how far he was privy to the quasi-promises of his secretary, but from their narrative it is a reasonable inference that he knew little or nothing about them. . . . Considering Lincoln's character and manner of action, nothing but the most positive evidence should convince us that he was in any way a party to this negotiation, and of this there is none. . . . The truth is that the assurances to Campbell were simply those of an officious Secretary of State whose vanity had grown by what it fed on, until now he deluded himself with the idea that he and not another was the executive of the nation." [25]

Curiosity is aroused when a historian of the caliber of Rhodes resorts to such an intemperate outburst. Rarely

[24] Rhodes, *A History of the United States,* III, 335.
[25] *Ibid.,* pp. 338-339.

has there come to the public eye as acrid a criticism of one holding such a high position. Neither before nor after his inauguration did Lincoln share this low estimate of his secretary. There is difficulty also in reconciling the quoted Rhodes paragraph with the well-established fact that repeatedly, during his conferences with Campbell, Seward went to consult with the president. And what is the meaning of the strangely worded reference to Nicolay and Hay; namely, that they fail to tell "in set terms" to what extent Lincoln was party to the "quasi-promises" of Seward, but that from their account there follows the "reasonable inference" that the president knew "little or nothing" about them? Private secretary as well as personal intimate of Lincoln, Nicolay was of course in a position to secure information as to the actions of his chief. How much simpler for Nicolay to write, if it were true, that Lincoln neither participated in nor had knowledge of the negotiations. In her biography of Lincoln, Miss Ida Tarbell felt impelled to take up the same theme:

"During the period when the President was waiting to hear from Fort Pickens, commissioners from the Southern Confederacy had been in Washington. Mr. Seward had not received them but through a trusted agent he had assured them that Sumter would be evacuated. There is no proof, so far as I know, that Mr. Lincoln knew of the quasi-promise of his secretary of state. As we have seen, he did not decide to order an expedition prepared to relieve the fort until March 29. From what we know of the character of the man, it is inconceivable that he should authorize Mr. Seward to promise to do a thing which he had not yet decided to do. The secretary assumed that, because he believed in evacuation, it would follow, and he assured the Southern commissioners to that effect." [26]

[26] *The Life of Abraham Lincoln,* III, 28.

The language is strained. The author speaks of a "quasi-promise" of the secretary of state, apparently forgetful of having written in the immediately preceding sentence that Seward "had assured" the Southern representatives that the fort would be evacuated. As to the president's connection with the promise, she writes that there is no proof "so far as I know." Nicolay knew. Seward knew, and Seward was on record regarding his consultations with Lincoln. Why retreat to theorizing concerning the inconceivableness of Lincoln's authorization of Seward's action when, if only it was the fact, it would have been so much more convincing to say in so many words that he did not authorize it?

Channing writes that Seward and Chase were the most prominent members of the party,[27] and Miss Tarbell says that for years Seward had been the leader of the Republican group.[28] In the Republican convention of 1860 Seward was leading candidate for the presidential nomination and, on the first ballot, his name led the field. Referring to Seward and Chase, Lincoln himself said, "The very first thing that I settled in my mind was that these two great leaders of the party should occupy the two first places in my cabinet." [29] There is one other circumstance, inclusion of which would have complicated the explanations of Rhodes and Tarbell. After all this, Seward remained secretary of state under Lincoln throughout the latter's entire term. Furthermore, Nicolay tells that, to the end of their association, the president gave to his secretary his "generous and unwavering trust." [30]

[27] *A Students' History of the United States,* p. 469.
[28] *The Life of Abraham Lincoln,* III, 26.
[29] Hart, *Salmon Porter Chase,* p. 197.
[30] *Lincoln,* III, 449.

CAMPBELL ASKS SEWARD TO EXPLAIN

John A. Campbell must have possessed a powerful personality. For good or ill, he strongly impressed those who came into contact with him. In the eyes of Nicolay he was the leading conspirator, the messenger of rebellion. "Owing to his station and professions," this author observes, "Seward gave him undue intimacy and confidence, enabling Campbell, under guise of promoting peace, to give aid and comfort to the enemies of the United States in violation of his oath and duty." [31] In sharp contrast with this vicious accusation, Rhodes characterized Campbell as one whose sincerity and straightforwardness were beyond question.[32] General Crawford shared this estimate, saying, "Thus ended the 'voluntary interposition' of an official high in position, and whose sole object was to prevent a collision which would inaugurate war between the States." [33]

Justice Campbell wrote Chief Justice Taney of the supreme court on April 29, 1861, that he had forwarded to the president his resignation as associate justice. Retiring to private life, he engaged in the practice of his profession. When his death occurred in 1889, twenty-eight years had elapsed since the Seward incident, an interval affording ample time for reflection on the part of those who knew him and were conversant with the negotiations of 1861. Appropriate resolutions were presented to the Supreme Court of the United States and, on accepting them and ordering their incorporation into the records of the court, Chief Justice Fuller said:

"The Court recognizes in the decease of Mr. Justice Campbell the departure of an eminent citizen,

[31] *Lincoln,* III, 405.
[32] Rhodes, *A History of the United States,* III, 338.
[33] *The Genesis of the Civil War,* p. 344.

who through his power of intellect, profound learning, and unremitting diligence, coupled with integrity of mind and sincere love of justice, deservedly
achieved high reputation as a jurist and reflected
corresponding credit upon this Bench during the
years he adorned it. His accession here had been preceded, as his regretted retirement was followed, by
distinguished service in the legal profession." [34]

With this insight into the character of the man, more
significance attaches to the aftermath of the negotiations.
On April thirteenth, during the bombardment of Sumter,
Campbell wrote Seward. He reviewed the details of their
conversations, the unqualified pledges received and transmitted to the commissioners. A fact which he impressed
was that, on the day after Seward's "faith as to Sumter
fully kept" message, the papers had carried not only the
story of the president's notice to Governor Pickens, but
that of the deception practiced by Captain Fox whom the
governor permitted to visit Major Anderson on the
pledge that his purpose was pacific. He explained his
own entry into the negotiations:

"My connection with the commissioners and yourself was superinduced by a conversation with Justice
Nelson. He informed me of your strong disposition
in favor of peace. . . . I told him I might, perhaps, be
of some service in arranging the difficulty. I came to
your office entirely at his request and without the
knowledge of either of the commissioners. I was
gratified at the character of the counsels you were
desirous of pursuing, and much impressed with your
observation that a civil war might be prevented by
the success of my mediation." [35]

[34] Henry G. Connor, *John A. Campbell* (Boston and New York,
1920), p. 285-286.
[35] Stephens, *A Comprehensive and Popular History of the United
States*, p. 989.

If it was true that Nelson, not Campbell, had taken the initiative in the approach to Seward, the door is wide open for speculation as to why Nicolay did not include Nelson in his bitter denunciation of Campbell. In view of subsequent occurrences, Campbell's letter to Seward continued, the commissioners felt they had been trifled with, and only his strong remonstrance had prevented them from "arraigning you before the country in connection with the President." He wrote of the anomalous position in which he had found himself, of his fear that the Southerners might even suspect him of complicity in the deception. With incisive directness, he placed the blame for the tragedy in progress at the moment in Charleston: "I think no candid man who will read what I have written and consider for a moment what is going on at Sumter but will agree that the equivocating conduct of the Administration, as measured and interpreted in connection with these promises, is the proximate cause of the great calamity." [36]

The message ended with a demand for an explanation. To say nothing of the respect to which a justice of the highest court of the nation is entitled, courtesy required a reply. There was no reply. With the passing of a week, Campbell wrote a second time, earnestly reasserting his right to an explanation of matters which were confusing and embarrassing him:

"I have not adopted any opinion in reference to them which may not be modified by explanation. Nor have I affirmed, nor do I in this, any conclusion of my own unfavorable to your integrity in the whole transaction. All that I have said and mean to say is, that an explanation is due from you to myself. I will not say what I shall do in case this request is

36 Connor, *John A. Campbell*, pp. 134-137; Stephens, *A History of the United States*, p. 989.

not complied with, but I am justified in saying that I shall feel at liberty to place these letters before any person who is entitled to ask an explanation of them." [37]

With rare exceptions, only men of the highest ability and integrity have sat on the bench of the Supreme Court of the United States. Long judicial training has inculcated in its members the habit of deliberation, repression of feeling, restraint of expression. This circumstance accentuates the significance of the plainness of speech in which Justice Campbell indulged. His forthrightness must have provided the secretary of state with some extremely uncomfortable moments. At the time of his receipt of Campbell's last communication, Seward had not answered the first. Nor did he answer the last.

[37] Connor, *John A. Campbell,* p. 137; *A Compilation of the Messages and Papers of the Confederacy, including the Diplomatic Correspondence, 1861-1865* (Vol. I, Nashville, 1905-   ), I, 96.

AFTERWORD

"In stating a simple condition of peace, I mean simply to say that the war will cease on the part of the Government whenever it shall have ceased on the part of those who began it."—President Lincoln's December 6, 1864, message to congress. *A Compilation of the Messages and Papers of the Presidents,* VI, 255.

APPENDICES

APPENDIX I

SCHOOL HISTORIES AND THE FIRING ON FORT SUMTER

In the light of the story as told by the *Official Records,* accounts in school histories invite scrutiny. As illustrative of what is being taught today, even in schools in the South, it may be worth while to consider a few typical excerpts from texts in use in high schools in certain of the Southern state capitals.

In Atlanta, Georgia, and Jackson, Mississippi, one text is *Our Nation's Development* (1934), by E. C. Barker, William E. Dodd, and H. S. Commager. Its account of the firing on Fort Sumter is as follows:

"Since December 20, the status of Fort Sumter, in the middle of the harbor of Charleston, had been a matter of intense anxiety. The state-rights men, North and South, thought it belonged as of right to South Carolina. The strict nationalists of the North regarded it as peculiarly the property of the United States. President Buchanan maintained *Colonel* Robert Anderson and a few score soldiers in the disputed fort till his successor came into office. Colonel Anderson *was at the mercy* of the South Carolinians. But when South Carolina became a member of the Confederacy, Jefferson Davis and his cabinet were determined to avoid a conflict until they could negotiate with Lincoln's government for the peaceful surrender of the fort.

"Charleston and the devoted garrison in Fort Sumter were thus from December 20 to April 12 the objects of keen anxiety all over the doubting North, and a subject of bitter debate throughout the South. After long hesitation President Lincoln started re-enforcements by sea, and gave *unofficial notice* of the fact to Governor *Andrew* Pickens of South Carolina. General Beauregard, in command of Confederate forces at Charleston, asked instructions from

293

Davis. The Confederate President refused to authorize an attack.

"Charleston was in an uproar. On the night of April 12, 1861, Roger Pryor, an ardent secessionist from Virginia, led *a group of four impatient secessionists* to demand *immediate surrender* of Colonel Anderson. He replied that he must, under existing circumstances, surrender in twenty-four hours for want of food. *Without reporting to Beauregard,* and thus without the consent of Jefferson Davis, *Pryor decided* that the answer was not satisfactory and *gave the signal for attack.* The batteries along the shore began *at once* the long expected bombardment. *Neither Davis nor Lincoln* had ordered it. It was war." [1]

The Union commander of Fort Sumter is here Colonel Robert Anderson, but he signed his official reports "Robert Anderson, Major." Governor Francis W. Pickens, of South Carolina, here appears as "Governor Andrew Pickens." We learn that Lincoln gave "unofficial notice" to the governor of the sending of reinforcements. It so happens that Captain Talbot went to Charleston with the formal notification, a document prepared by Lincoln himself, the opening words of which were, "I am directed by the President of the United States to notify you." Mention is made that Anderson was at the mercy of the South Carolinians; this would have been an appropriate place to refer to the supplies of food, as well as other courtesies for which Anderson from time to time expressed appreciation. Here again is a story of how Roger Pryor and his associate "impatient secessionists" demanded immediate surrender of the fort, and how, "without reporting to Beauregard," who was in command of the Confederate forces at Charleston, and "without the consent of Jefferson Davis," Pryor assumed all responsibility, usurped all authority, and "gave the signal for attack."

Strongly at variance with this account are the facts set out in the Official Records. On April tenth, Confederate Secretary of War Walker telegraphed Beauregard that, if he considered as authoritative the notice of Lincoln's "intention to supply Fort

[1] Pp. 311, 312. Italics supplied. Quoted by permission of Row, Peterson and Company, Evanston, Ill., and New York.

Sumter by force," he should at once "demand its evacuation," and, in the event of a refusal, "proceed to reduce it." Declining to surrender, Anderson remarked upon the hopelessness of his position; thereupon, by direction of Secretary Walker, Beauregard withdrew his demand and proposed to Anderson that he should set the date on which he would give up the fortress. The new proposal came to naught and at 3:20 A.M., April 12, 1861, Beauregard's aides, James Chesnut and Stephen D. Lee, personally delivered to Anderson the final message: "By the authority of Brigadier-General Beauregard . . . we have the honor to notify you that he will open the fire of his batteries on Fort Sumter within one hour from this time."

The quoted excerpt closes with the arresting statement that "neither Davis nor Lincoln" ordered the bombardment which the Confederate shore batteries began.

Another text, in use in the Atlanta high schools, is *The History of the American People* (1938), by J. H. Latané. It tells this story:

> "All eyes were now turned on Fort Sumter. South Carolina at once collected troops and stationed batteries so as to bear on the fort in case any attempt should be made to re-enforce it. On January 9, 1861, The Star of the West, a merchant vessel, which had been dispatched from New York with men and provisions for Fort Sumter, approached the entrance to Charleston harbor and was fired on by the South Carolinians. The ship withdrew and returned to New York.
> "The War Department informed Lincoln *as soon as he was inaugurated* that Major Anderson was *running short of provisions,* and Lincoln was much perplexed as to what policy he should pursue. Each side wished if possible to avoid the odium of firing the first shot. Lincoln's cabinet was divided upon the subject. Some of them advised holding and strengthening the fort, while others advised the withdrawal of the garrison in order to avoid war. Major Anderson himself favored evacuating the fort, and General Scott held the same view. Meanwhile, there were in Washington three agents of the newly organized Confederate government, who were carrying on unofficial negotiations

with Secretary Seward. Seward favored the withdrawal of the garrison from Fort Sumter, and he assured the commissioners that no effort would be made to send any reenforcements.

"The Navy Department in the meantime was making preparations to send *an expedition to relieve the fort.* When rumors of this expedition reached the commissioners, they demanded an explanation of Seward. He replied through a confidential agent: 'Faith as to Sumter fully kept. Wait and see.' On the following day, April 8, the relief expedition sailed from New York. On the same day Lincoln officially announced to Governor Pickens of South Carolina that he intended to supply the fort *with provisions.* Southern writers have generally charged Lincoln with bad faith, but the evidence does not justify this charge. Seward's negotiations with the commissioners were *in no way* sanctioned by Lincoln. Seward himself was strongly opposed to sending the relief expedition, and up to the last moment he sincerely believed that his influence would be sufficient to prevent it.

"The *decision to maintain the fort* crystallized the attitude of South Carolina. On April 11 General Beauregard formally demanded the surrender of Fort Sumter. Anderson refused, saying, however, that he would soon be starved out. On April 12 at 4:30 a.m., the Confederate batteries opened fire on the fort, and on the thirteenth Anderson surrendered." [2]

Here is a reference to the *Star of the West,* with no mention of orders to the warship *Brooklyn* to convoy her, no information that she was carrying two hundred seasoned troops and ample ammunition, no suggestion of the order to the officer in charge of the troops which read in part: "It is important that all your movements be kept as secret as possible. On approaching the Charleston bar, you will place below decks your entire force, in order that only the ordinary crew may be seen by persons from the shore or on boarding the vessel." The account omits the detail that a member of Buchanan's cabinet denounced the attempt as "a concealed trick." There is no statement of the

[2] Pp. 418-420. Italics supplied. Quoted by permission of Allyn and Bacon, Publishers, Boston.

fact that the Carolina officials warned the ship not to attempt
to enter the harbor.

The "starving garrison" theory is hinted at. We learn that
the war department informed Lincoln "as soon as he was inaugurated" that Anderson was "running short of provisions." No
explanation is offered of the fact that on January 19, 1861,
in answer to the offer of Governor Pickens to send daily to
Sumter supplies of fresh meat and vegetables, Anderson wrote,
"I have not represented in any quarter that we were in need
of such supplies"; or, of the further fact that after the governor's
plan for the supplies was in effect for some time, Anderson wrote
on March 17, 1861, "I am satisfied with the existing arrangement."

The account tells of an "expedition to relieve" the fort,
gives the date on which the "relief expedition sailed," and states
that Lincoln notified Governor Pickens that "he intended to
supply the fort with provisions"; there is omitted that portion
of the notice which suggests his intended course should the
Confederates oppose his plan. The Atlanta students would likely
have read with wide eyes that the president was sending his
provisions under the chaperonage of two warships and an armed
cutter. Again, assurance is given that Lincoln "in no way"
sanctioned Seward's negotiations with the Confederate peace
commissioners; strictly construing the word "sanction," this may
be true, but the force of the statement would have been weak-
ened by recital of the fact that during the negotiations Seward
repeatedly consulted the president. And, again, there is no hint
of the presence of a squadron of Federal warships off Charleston
bar during the bombardment of Sumter; no mention of the
humanitarian proposal made by Secretary Walker and General
Beauregard when Major Anderson admitted the certainty of
his fate.

In Richmond, Virginia, the John Marshall High School uses
The Development of America (1938), by Fremont P. Wirth. Its
recital of the events leading up to the Sumter incident appears
as follows:

"The states which had withdrawn from the Union promptly seized the Federal forts and arsenals within their bounds, that could be taken without violence, and sent commissioners to Washington to arrange compensation. They hesitated to take any action which might precipitate bloodshed, and consequently permitted Fort Sumter, in Charleston harbor, and three other forts, to remain in the hands of the Federal government. It was evident that if the Southern states established their independence, these forts would eventually fall into their hands. What should be the policy of the Union government with regard to this delicate question? Although Lincoln had been elected in November, his term of office would not begin until March 4, and in the meantime President Buchanan had to deal with the problem. He did not believe in secession, yet he believed that the United States constitution did not give the right to employ force to prevent secession. When the commissioners from the *seceded states* came to Washington to negotiate on the question of the forts, Buchanan refused to treat with them.

"Fort Sumter was held by a small force under the command of Major Anderson. *The supplies soon became exhausted,* and Major Anderson appealed to the President for provisions and reinforcements. *Early in January,* Buchanan sent the merchant vessel Star of the West to the *relief of the fort,* but it was fired upon by the batteries located on Morris Island, and returned to New York without accomplishing its mission.

"The Die is cast. When Lincoln took office on March 4, 1861, he faced a critical situation. Seven Southern states had already seceded from the Union and had set up a separate government. Whether these states should be allowed to depart in peace, or whether the Union should be preserved at the cost of a terrific fratricidal war, depended upon the fateful decision of Lincoln. The entire country anxiously awaited the decision of the new President. In his inaugural address, Lincoln left no room for doubt as to the policy he had determined upon. While he expressed a kindly feeling for the South, he also denied the right of secession, and declared that his oath of office required that he should 'preserve, protect and defend' the Union. He also announced that he would 'hold, occupy and possess the property and places belonging to the government, and collect the duties on imports.' *A month later he notified the Governor of South Carolina that he would attempt to send a supply of provisions to Fort Sumter. The Confederate government at Montgomery regarded this announcement of Lincoln's policy as equivalent to a declaration of war, and President Davis ordered General Beauregard, who commanded a force of about seven thousand troops, to demand the immediate surrender of the fort.*

"The Appeal to arms. Major Anderson and his little band of less than a hundred men courageously refused the demand to surrender, and made preparations for a stubborn defense of Fort Sumter. It was before dawn, April 12, 1861, that the thunder of a cannon at Fort Johnson announced that war had begun." [3]

We read that when the commissioners from "the seceded states" came to Washington, Buchanan refused to treat with them. The commissioners appointed by the South Carolina convention reached the capital on December 26, 1860, at which time only their own state had seceded, and it only six days before. Buchanan did refuse to receive the South Carolina commissioners in their official character, but he had a spirited correspondence with them which the *Official Records* set out. It was not until February 25, 1861, that President Davis appointed the Confederate commissioners; they did not reach Washington in time to confer with Buchanan.

The account relates that Anderson's supplies "soon became exhausted," that he appealed to President Buchanan for "provisions," and that early in January the president sent the *Star of the West* with relief. This is in striking contrast with what Major Anderson wrote his friend, Mr. Robert N. Gourdin, of Charleston, on December 29, 1860, eleven days before the Carolina batteries stopped the *Star of the West:* "I have supplies of provisions of all kinds to last my command about five months." There is, further, no reference to the secrecy of the mission of the vessel, the concealed troops, the warning not to enter the harbor.

At what conclusion do the Richmond students arrive as to

[3] Pp. 376-381. Italics supplied. Quoted by permission of the American Book Company, Publisher, Chicago and New York.

the immediate cause of the firing on Fort Sumter? The answer is here made quite simple. A month after his inaugural, Lincoln notified Pickens "that he would attempt to send a supply of provisions to Fort Sumter," whereupon, with no provocation other than this announcement of "Lincoln's policy," Jefferson Davis ordered Beauregard to demand "the immediate surrender of the fort." Major Anderson refused to surrender, and the bombardment followed.

The account tells of an expedition to carry provisions but gives no intimation of the real make-up of the expedition. There is no explanation of the confident expectation of its commander, Fox, that it would "open the fire of the Carolina batteries." It says nothing of the circumstance that General Scott, commander-in-chief of the army, General Totten, chief-of-engineers, and Simon Cameron, secretary of war, all warned Lincoln that to send the expedition meant to bring on war. No hint appears of the significance of what Beauregard said in his official report of the incident of Sumter:

> "As, in consequence of a communication from the President of the United States to the Governor of South Carolina, we were in momentary expectation of an attempt to reinforce Fort Sumter, or of a descent upon our coast to that end from the United States fleet then lying at the entrance of the harbor, it was manifestly imperative to reduce the fort as speedily as possible, and not to wait until the ships and the fort should unite in a combined attack upon us."

In Austin, Texas, the high school's most advanced text on American history is *The Record of America* (1938), by James Truslow Adams and Charles G. Vannest, in which appears the following account:

> "The Confederates fire on Fort Sumter. Secretary Seward, apparently on his own responsibility, had also been negotiating with three agents of the Confederate government. He promised them that no effort would be made to relieve Sumter when, in fact, Lincoln had already *ordered* the *vessels* from New York. This fact having been dis-

covered by the Southern agents, the Confederate cabinet
decided, after much hesitation, to capture the position before *relief* arrived. On April 12 the bombardment from
the shore batteries began against Fort Sumter." [4]

Here are no wasted words. The student learns that when
the Confederates discovered that Lincoln had "ordered the vessels," they decided to act before relief arrived and so proceeded
to begin the war. Would the most imaginative of the Texas
youths suspect that among these "vessels" were the warships
Pawnee and *Pocahontas,* and the armed cutter *Harriet Lane?*
Would not they be mystified to learn that when Washington
notified Major Anderson of the coming of the expedition, he
said in his reply, "I frankly say that my heart is not in the
war which I see is to be thus commenced"? Would not it come
as a revelation that, during the bombardment, the United States
warships were so near that the flashes of Anderson's guns could
be distinctly seen from the Federal squadron? Would it enter
their minds that the secret purpose of the expedition was to
drive the Confederates to the desperation of firing the first
gun? What would they think of Nicolay's admission that it
was not without significance that the expedition was proceeding
under convoy of warships whose commanders carried orders to
use their guns to crush resistance?

The Hugh Morson High School of Raleigh, North Carolina,
uses the *History of the United States,* by Charles A. and Mary
R. Beard (1932). The following story of the Sumter bombardment is given:

"Reviewing the same facts, Republican leaders were
themselves uncertain as to the outcome of a civil war and
they made many efforts to avoid it. Thurlow Weed, an
Albany politician who had helped to carry New York for
Lincoln, proposed to extend the Missouri Compromise to
the Pacific—with freedom on one side and slavery on the
other. Jefferson Davis, warning his followers that a war

[4] P. 316. Italics supplied. Quoted by permission of Charles Scribner's
Sons, Publishers, New York and Chicago.

if it broke out would be terrible, was willing to accept the offer; but Lincoln, who had pledged himself to the abolition of slavery in all the territories, stood like a rock against it. His followers in congress took the same position with regard to a similar plan made by Senator Crittenden of Kentucky.

"Though he adhered to his promise to oppose slavery in the territories, Lincoln gave his word to Southern leaders that he would not meddle in any way with slavery in the states. Anxious to reassure the South on this point, the Republicans in congress agreed that the constitution should be so amended as to forbid forever the abolition of slavery or any interference with it in any state. Indeed a resolution to this effect, duly passed, was sent forth on March 4, 1861, with the approval of Lincoln, and it was actually ratified by three states before the storm of war destroyed it. By the irony of fate, the thirteenth amendment was to abolish, not guarantee, slavery.

"The bombardment of Fort Sumter by Confederate forces on April 12-14, 1861, led President Lincoln and congress to turn from negotiations to problems of warfare. Lincoln's first call for volunteers, issued on April 15, 1861, limited the number to 75,000 and put their term of service at three months. A rude awakening swiftly followed. A terrible defeat of the Federals at Bull Run on July 21 revealed the grave character of the work before them; and by a series of measures congress put the entire man power of the country at the President's command." [5]

This is very interesting but, after reading it, what do the North Carolina boys and girls know of the real happenings which immediately preceded and caused the attack on Fort Sumter? Insofar as explanation of the bombardment is concerned, is not this a clear instance of *parvum in multo,* a veritable avalanche of omission?

In Tallahassee, Florida, the Leon High School uses as an advanced American historical text, *America, Its History and People* (1934), by Harold U. Faulkner and Tyler Kepner, in which appears its explanation of the attack on Fort Sumter:

[5] P. 392. Quoted by permission of The Macmillan Company, Publisher, New York.

"Fort Sumter. Pursuing his announced policy, Lincoln notified South Carolina early in April that he intended to *provision* Fort Sumter, the one fort in Charleston harbor still under Federal control. *Fearing that reinforcements would also be sent,* the Confederate government instructed General Beauregard to demand the fort's surrender; if this was refused, he was to destroy it. Major Anderson, in command of Sumter, refused to evacuate; and at daybreak on April 12, 1861, the Confederate forces, after giving notice, began bombardment. Anderson's 128 men held out courageously for 34 hours against more than 5,000 Confederates. But with provisions nearly exhausted, fort aflame and magazines exploding, the Federal forces surrendered and retired with colors flying. The 'Brothers' War' had begun." [6]

This tells the story in a few words. The president gave notice of his intention to send food to Sumter. The Confederates feared that he would also send reinforcements. They, therefore, destroyed the fort. That is all. How much more interesting to the students a few facts would have made the narrative! What if the account had explained how fully justified were the Confederates in their apprehension of a plan to throw in reinforcements? In strict keeping with the record, it might have added, not only that ships carrying troops, arms, and ammunition, were headed for Fort Sumter, but that a portion of the United States squadron of warships was lying off Charleston harbor while the bombardment was in progress. There could have been no harm in relating that, moved by sympathy for Anderson and his men, the Confederates withdrew their first demand for surrender and proposed that the Sumter commander himself should name his own date for the abandonment of the fort.

In Montgomery, Alabama, and in Baton Rouge, Louisiana, the text used is David S. Muzzey's *History of the American People* (1934). Its account of the Sumter incident follows:

"A few days after his inauguration, President Lincoln called the members of his cabinet together and laid before

[6] Pp. 249-250. Quoted by permission of Harper and Brothers, Publishers, New York and London.

them the critical situation in Charleston harbor. Buchanan
had sent the merchant vessel Star of the West, flying the
American flag at masthead, *with provisions* for Major Anderson's garrison in Fort Sumter. The ship had been forced
to turn back by the fire from the guns on Morris Island
and the South Carolinians had strengthened the harbor
batteries that bore on Fort Sumter until Anderson reported
that reinforcements of twenty thousand men would be
necessary for him to maintain his position. Lincoln was
determined that Anderson should not *be starved out.*

"Therefore, with the approval of all but two members
of his cabinet, he notified the Governor of South Carolina
on April 8 that an attempt would be made to supply Fort
Sumter *with provisions.* The Confederate government at
Montgomery was convinced that Lincoln intended to send
reinforcements as well as food to Fort Sumter. Therefore,
President Davis ordered General Beauregard, who was in
command of some seven thousand troops at Charleston, to
demand the immediate surrender of the fort. Major Anderson refused to abandon his post and Beauregard prepared
to reduce Fort Sumter by cannon. Before dawn, on the
twelfth of April, 1861, a shell rose from the mortars of
Fort Johnson and, screaming over the harbor, burst just
above the fort. It was the signal for a general bombardment. In a few minutes, from the batteries of Sullivan's,
Morris, and James Islands, east and south and west, fifty
cannons were pouring shot and shell upon Fort Sumter.
Anderson stood the terrific bombardment for two whole
days, while Northern *steamers* lay rolling in the heavy
weather outside the bar, unable to come to his relief." [7]

In the face of the revelations of the record, here is repeated
the intimation of distressing conditions at the fort at or about
the date of Lincoln's inauguration. Coupled with this is the suggestion that the sending of the expedition was due to the president's determination that the garrison should not be "starved
out." Again, a reference to the *Star of the West's* going "with
provisions" for Anderson; and again significant omission of mention of the other portion of her cargo, the troops who were to
be hidden below decks upon the approach to Charleston. The
cause of the attack on Sumter appears as a conviction of the
Confederates that Lincoln "intended" to send reinforcements;

[7] Pp. 356, 357. Italics supplied. Quoted by permission of Ginn and
Company, Publishers, Boston and New York.

there is a failure to note the presence of the warships off Charleston during the bombardment. On this point the student learns only that Northern "steamers" were outside the bar; there is what appears to be studied avoidance of any gratification of curiosity as to just what these vessels were.

APPENDIX II

THE MYSTERIOUS ANDERSON LETTER

Others than Welles, Morse, and Tarbell made use of the purported Anderson communication, referred to on p. 182, *supra*. Thornton K. Lothrop, biographer of Seward, speaking of the morning following the inauguration, declares that Sumter's provisions "were nearly exhausted." [1]

Nicolay also supplies depressing details:

"A subtler and more unfailing enemy than the rebels—starvation—was rapidly forcing the little garrison to surrender. On the morning after inauguration, letters were put into the President's hands showing that the fort contained provisions for only a little more than a month longer and adding that a well appointed fleet and an army of twenty thousand men would be necessary to raise the siege." [2]

Rhodes' account is:

"On going to his office the morning of March 5 he found that the Sumter question was more perplexing than he had imagined. A letter from Holt, still acting as Secretary of War, gave the information that Anderson had written that his provisions would last only a few weeks longer, and that to reinforce the fort successfully with a view to holding it would require an army of 20,000 disciplined men." [3]

Nicolay and Hay make a contribution:

"This pacific purpose was now, however, destined to receive a rude shock. When on the morning of the 5th of March Lincoln went to his office . . . he found a letter from Mr. Holt, still acting as Secretary of War, giving him news of vital importance received on the morning of

[1] *William Henry Seward*, pp. 252, 269.
[2] *The Outbreak of the Rebellion*, p. 50.
[3] *A History of the United States*, III, 325.

306

his inauguration—namely, that Fort Sumter must, in the lapse of a few weeks at most, be strongly reënforced or summarily abandoned. Major Anderson had in the previous week made an examination of his provisions. There was bread for twenty-eight days; pork for a somewhat longer time; beans, rice, coffee, and sugar for different periods from eight to forty days." [4]

The accounts in school textbooks are in the same character. In *History of the American People,* by David Saville Muzzey, professor of history at Columbia University, we read of the crisis which Lincoln faced at his inauguration; that, among other troubles, Anderson, commanding a little garrison of eighty-three men, "was writing to the war department that his stores of flour and bacon were almost exhausted." [5]

The letter which the accounts say was brought to Lincoln's attention must have been a most remarkable document to admit of such variant interpretation. Hear them again—Muzzey: "The flour and bacon were almost exhausted"; Welles: "He could get no provisions in Charleston and destitution was only six weeks off"; Morse: "The food on hand was biscuit and pork and this would last about four weeks"; Nicolay: "The fort contained provisions for only a little more than a month"; Tarbell: "He had but a week's provisions"; Rhodes: "His provisions would last only a few weeks longer"; Nicolay and Hay: "In the lapse of a few weeks the fort must be reinforced or abandoned."

Inevitably, this stimulates speculation. Are these writers using the same letter as their source of information? If so, why such a variance of statement of its contents? There is ample justification for asking: Where is this letter? To whom was it written? Why not set it out verbatim and let it speak for itself? The effort to trace it is aided by only one clew. Rhodes indicates that light will be thrown on it by reference to "Lincoln: Nicolay and Hay, Vol. III, p. 376, and Official Records, Vol. I, pp. 197, 202." Turning to the volume cited, it appears that Nicolay and Hay do not set out the letter but in turn give as their reference, "Anderson to Cooper, Feb. 28, 1861. MS. Partly

[4] *Lincoln,* III, 376-377.   [5] P. 355.

printed in W. R. Vol. I, p. 197." Thus Nicolay and Hay agree
with Rhodes that "W. R. Vol. I, p. 197" will provide the desired
information. Turning to this last suggested source, which is
simply another name for the *Official Records,* attention at once
centers on the fact that this final reference unearths a letter
from Simon Cameron to Lincoln, a letter which Cameron did
not write until March 15, 1861. Lincoln did not read this letter
on March fourth or fifth. The Cameron letter, does, however,
contain the following passage:

> "Major Anderson, in his report of the 28th ultimo, says:
> " 'I confess that I would not be willing to risk my repu-
> tation on an attempt to throw re-enforcements into this har-
> bor within the time for our relief rendered necessary by
> the limited supply of our provisions, and with a view of
> holding possession of the same with a force of less than
> twenty thousand good and well-disciplined men.' " [6]

It is well to note that Nicolay and Hay gave as their reference "Anderson to Cooper, Feb. 28, 1861"; and that Cameron's
March fifteenth letter mentions the same date, "Major Anderson, in his report of the 28th ultimo." The brief excerpt, just
quoted, containing every word attributed to Anderson in the
Cameron letter, is clearly what Tarbell had in mind, for she
uses its very words, "20,000 good and well-disciplined men";
it is what Nicolay was referring to, for he mentions the force
of "twenty thousand men"; it is what Rhodes was thinking of,
for he too uses its expression, "20,000 disciplined men." There
is, however, no justification for the construction which Muzzey,
Morse, Tarbell, Nicolay, Welles, and Rhodes have placed on it.
If, as Nicolay and Hay say, the manuscript of the Anderson
letter is partly printed, the whole must have been available;
what became of the unprinted portion? To say the least, it is
unfortunate for authors of "starvation," "destitution," "supplies almost exhausted," "one week's provisions" theories that
the printed fragment fails to authenticate their accounts of the
garrison's privation.

[6] *O. R. A.,* Ser. 1, Vol. I, p. 197.

True, the excerpt quoted by Cameron from Anderson does refer to "an attempt to throw re-enforcements into this harbor within the time for our relief rendered necessary by the limited supply of our provisions." What does this mean? Later, in the same letter, Cameron quotes General Scott as saying that in order to reinforce the fort he would need a fleet which "could not be collected in less than four months," and an army of 5,000 regulars and 20,000 volunteers, the organization of which would "require from six to eight months." [7] Cameron's letter also set out this memorandum prepared by General Scott:

> "It seems from the opinions of the Army officers who have expressed themselves on the subject . . . that it is perhaps now impossible to succor that fort substantially, if at all, without capturing, by means of a large expedition of ships of war and troops, all the opposing batteries of South Carolina. *In the mean time—six or ten months—* Major Anderson would almost certainly have been obliged to surrender under assault or the approach of starvation." [8]

It is clear that the only reasonable interpretation of what Scott was saying in his statement quoted by Cameron and in his memorandum, also carried in the same Cameron letter, is as follows: He could not accomplish the relief of the fort without a naval force which he would not undertake to assemble in less than four months, and an army, the organization of which would require from six to eight months; "in the mean time— six or ten months," Anderson's provisions would of course be exhausted and, even if armed assault did not bring about his surrender, the approach of starvation would render it inevitable. The statement attributed to Anderson and that prepared by Scott tell in different words the same story; namely, that "the limited supply of provisions" could not possibly last during the period which the organization of the necessary relief force would require—a period estimated by Scott as "six to ten months."

In a further effort to run down the Anderson letter, the assistant librarian of the Montgomery Library Association made,

[7] *Ibid.*   [8] *Ibid.*, p. 200. Italics supplied.

on September 6, 1938, the following request of the Librarian of Congress:

"A patron of this library is engaged in historical research and at his request we are asking you to trace, if possible, a certain letter written by Major Robert Anderson, commander of Fort Sumter at the outbreak of the Civil War. This particular letter is not included in the Official Records of the War of the Rebellion, but has been referred to by several of the biographers and historians writing of that period. In this letter Major Anderson is supposed to have written, 'Supplies almost exhausted, could secure no provisions in Charleston.'

"The following writers use quotations from this letter:

Gideon Welles, Diary, Vol. I, p. 4.
Nicolay, The Outbreak of Rebellion, p. 50.
Morse, Abraham Lincoln, Vol. I, p. 244.
Tarbell, Life of Abraham Lincoln, Vol. III, p. 15.
Muzzey, The American People, p. 355.

"None of the writers, however, refer to any original source where the letter or a complete copy can be seen, and there are so many discrepancies in the various quotations that a doubt is raised as to whether the letter was written. If this letter has been printed in a book will you send it to us as soon as is conveniently possible? With deep appreciation for any aid you can give us,
"Very truly yours,
"BETTY ALDRIDGE,
"Ass't Librarian"

It will be noted that the letter inquired about was carefully identified by giving title, name of author, volume and page of no fewer than five references. The reply of the Librarian of Congress, signed by Louise G. Caton, secretary of the library, inclosed the following memorandum as supplying the desired information:

"Memorandum from the Acting Superintendent of the Reading Rooms. September 15, 1938
"To THE LIBRARIAN OF CONGRESS
"Referring to the letter from Mrs. Betty Aldridge, Assistant Librarian Montgomery Library Association, Car-

negie Building, Montgomery, Alabama, dated September 6, 1938.

"Acting under orders of General Beauregard Major Anderson's mail of April 8, 1861 was 'retained' by the South Carolina authorities. The contents of this 'official package' therefore do not appear in the regular sequence of Major Anderson's correspondence in the Official Records. They do appear with the Confederate correspondence and will be found in Ser. I, Vol. I, page 293. An enclosure by Capt. J. G. Foster addressed to the Chief Engineer says, 'Our supplies are entirely cut off from the city, and those on hand are very limited.' This same letter is printed on pages 385-6 of The History of the Fall of Fort Sumter by Sam'l W. Crawford.

"We also call attention to Major Anderson's letter No. 94, dated April 5, 1861, addressed to the adjutant-general and found in O.R. Ser. I, Vol. I, page 241, in which he says, 'Unless we receive supplies, I shall be compelled to stay here without food, or to abandon this post very early next week.'

"Respectfully submitted,
"DAVID C. MEARNS,
"*Acting Superintendent of the Reading Rooms*"

Purporting to give information relative to a communication from Major Anderson which Lincoln read not later than March fifth, the Librarian of Congress begins by mentioning an official package of Anderson's mail of April 8, 1861, which was "retained" by the South Carolina officials, the contents of which, including the enclosure by Captain Foster, appear in Ser. I, Vol. I, p. 293. Turning to this reference, it is discovered that on pages 292 and 293 appear two letters from Governor Pickens, the first to the president of the Confederate States, the second to the Confederate secretary of war, the latter enclosing the letter from Captain J. G. Foster to General Totten, chief engineer, U. S. army.[9]

So far, so good. But both of Governor Pickens' letters were written April 9, 1861, and the Foster letter was written April 8, 1861. That a letter, dated April eighth and sent by Pickens

[9] *Ibid.*, pp. 292, 293.

to Montgomery in a communication dated April ninth, could have been read by President Lincoln in Washington on March 5, 1861, renders the mystery more mysterious.

The Library of Congress memorandum gives as another citation a reference to a letter from Anderson, dated April 5, 1861, in which he wrote: "Unless we receive supplies I shall be compelled to stay here without food, or to abandon this post very early next week." But, assuredly, Lincoln did not read on March 5, 1861, a letter dated "Fort Sumter, S. C., April 5, 1861," which bears the indorsement, "Received A. G. O. [adjutant general's office] April 8." [10]

It is palpably absurd to suggest that any of these letters disclose any such conditions on March fourth or fifth as Muzzey and the other commentators pictured. What they do show is that, although the garrison's supplies from the city were entirely cut off on April eighth, even then they were not completely exhausted; that, according to Major Anderson's April fifth letter, they would be exhausted "very early next week."

That the Confederates should have delayed until April 7, 1861, the shutting off of the garrison's supplies from Charleston is, all circumstances considered, altogether remarkable. With their information as to what was going on in Washington, for them to continue to give material assistance to a hostile command would have been to pass beyond mere unwisdom to sheer stupidity. It was not the privation at Sumter which caused Lincoln to send his armed fleet to Charleston; it was the sending of the fleet which brought about the stopping of the supplies, thereby causing the privation.

10 *Ibid.,* p. 241.

INDEX

Abolitionists, unite with Republican party, xiv; efforts to liberate slaves, xiv; enmity to slave owners, xiv; Northern attacks on, xix; oppose compromise, xxii

Adams, Captain H. A., arrives at Pensacola, 30; discusses armistice, 30; ratifies armistice, 37; writes Welles of engagement of Mallory and Chase with U. S. government, 38; refuses Vogdes' request to land troops, 49, 50; "agreement entered into by U. S. government," 50; appeals for relief from embarrassment, 50, 51; states his position, 52; ordered to land troops, 53; Worden carries orders to, 55; troops landed by, 55; rebuked by Bragg, 57; armistice paves way for Worden, 59; writes DuPont of armistice, 62; reports reinforcement, 66; knew Confederates respected armistice, 68; Vogdes writes of Bragg's demand for explanation, 68; acted under orders, 69; Poor writes of armistice, 72

Adams, James H., of South Carolina peace commission, 116

Adams, James Truslow, history by, 300

Adams, John Quincy, advises secession, xiii

Advertiser. See Montgomery *Advertiser*

Albany *Evening Journal,* pacific attitude of, xix

Aldridge, Mrs. Betty, writes Librarian of Congress, 310

Alexander, General E. P., Memoirs, 110; blocking of Buchanan's order, 123, 124

America; Its History and People, by Faulkner and Kepner, used in Tallahassee, Florida, high school, 302; account of Sumter incident in, 303

Anderson, Major Robert, Dr. Crawford on staff of, xxxvi;

commands Sumter garrison, 98; record of, 98; his Union loyalty, 98, 109; warns against reinforcement, 99; knew Charleston sentiment, 100; moves to Sumter, 108; transfer arouses Washington, 109, 110; acted on own responsibility, 111; refuses to leave Sumter, 113; complains of Washington's silence, 113; Buchanan persuaded not to order back to Moultrie, 123, 124; *Star of the West* fired on by Charleston batteries, 133; tempted to return fire, 133; Holt declares attack on ship an act of war, 138; testimony of as to supplies, 140, 204; governor offers to send food daily, 141; supplies sent back by, 143, 144; satisfied with food arrangement, 146, 184; warns Washington not to send supplies, 147; relations of with Beauregard, 160, 161; fears conflict, 164; Fox visits, 176; army required to carry out Fox plan, 176, 177; warns Fox of war, 178; reputed report of privation at fort, 180; letter not located, 182, 306-12; sale of supplies, 185, 186; fears stopping of supplies, 186; knew why supplies cut off, 187; senate asks Lincoln for his correspondence, 189; Lamon announces evacuation imminent, 192; expects to leave fort, 195, 201, 212; reports "everything quiet," 200, 202; adjutant general fails to correct false impression, 202; notified of coming of expedition, 203, 204; looks for relief, 208; resents neglect by government, 211-13; food supplies stopped, 215, 216; advocates evacuation, 217; friendly to Beauregard, 218; significance of suggestion to hold out till April 11, 220; warns Washington of war, 223; says

313

bardment, 250; sends garrison out to fleet, 253; his troops cheer garrison for heroism, 253; Confederate tribute of respect for departing Sumter command, 254
Bell, John, vote for in 1860 presidential election, xvi
Belmont, August, for conciliation, xx; supports Crittenden Compromise, xx; message of to H. V. Johnson, xx
Benjamin, Judah P., favors conciliation, xxv
Black, J. S., secretary of state, makes estimate of Sumter food supplies, 140; says warships can enter Charleston harbor, 256-58
Blair, Montgomery, demands drastic action, 32; Fox outlines plan to, 158, 159; takes Fox to Lincoln, 166; threatens to resign, 167; favors reinforcement of Sumter, 173; denounces Scott to Lincoln, 199; Lincoln's decision to reinforce Sumter, 199; treason to abandon Sumter, 207
Bosquet, General Pierre, quoted, 235
Bragg, Braxton, Confederate General, commands at Pensacola, 35; seeks understanding with Slemmer, 35; pledges observance of armistice, 36; deceived by Worden, 55, 60; ordered to intercept Worden's dispatches, 56; causes shadowing of Worden, 56; orders Worden's arrest, 56; notifies Walker of reinforcement of Pickens, 57; says Adams violated agreement, 57; permits Worden to visit Adams, 60; demands explanation from Federal officers, 68, 69; Federals "obeyed orders," 68, 69; resentment of, 69; Colonel Brown threatens, 84; patience of with Brown, 85; Brown's chicanery, 86
Breckinridge, John C., vote for in 1860 presidential election, xvi-xvii
Brooklyn, warship, to carry reinforcements to Pickens, 13, 14; ordered to remain outside harbor, 23; to convoy *Star of the West,* 133

Brown, Colonel Harvey, in charge of reinforcement expedition, 40, 41; Lincoln orders "all officers" to assist, 41; stops Powhatan, 71, 74; Porter wonders at his authority, 76, 77; conflicting orders from Lincoln, 76, 77; threatens Bragg, 84; discovers "floating battery," 85; resorts to chicanery, 86; his pretended alarm, 86
Brown, John, Harpers Ferry raid, 33; glorified as saint, 33; Phillips and Garrison acclaim as a martyr, 33; Emerson compares gallows to cross of Jesus of Nazareth, 33; influence of, 33
Buchanan, President James, for conciliation, xx; Mallory warns against reinforcement at Pensacola, 16, 21; approves armistice order, 24; Davis informs of Anderson's removal to Sumter, 110; no order for Anderson's action, 114; peace commission's message to, 117; pledge not to reinforce Sumter, 118; commissioners insist garrison a menace, 118; audience with South Carolina congressmen, 121; to maintain status at Charleston, 121, 122; denies making pledge, 122; prevented from ordering Anderson back to Moultrie, 123, 124; Cass and Floyd resign from cabinet, 125, 126; his piety, 126; commissioners denounce, 127; declines to receive document, 127; transfer of garrison equivalent to reinforcement, 128; countermands order for *Star of the West* venture, 136; refuses offer of compensation for fort, 150; insists Sumter for protection of South Carolina, 151; Fox plan submitted to, 153
Buell, Major D. C., carries instructions to Anderson, 101

Cabot, George, on secession, xiii
Cameron, Simon, secretary of war, predicts reinforcement effort means war, 169, 171; orders Talbot to give notice to Governor Pickens, 213
Campbell, John A., justice of Su-

Benjamin, Sam Houston, B. H. Hill, xxvi; Lincoln against, xxiii; Richmond Whig endorses, xxviii; Savannah Republican's proposal, xxviii; Rhodes' confidence of popular approval, xxviii; Senate kills, xxviii-xxx

Conciliation. *See* Compromise, Crittenden

Confederate Government, organized, 271; assumes control at Charleston, 154; moves for peace, 271; constitution declares for equitable adjustment of differences, 271, 272; convention asks Davis to appoint peace commissioners, 272

Congress, United States, Lincoln's 1864 message to, 227, 290

Cooper, Samuel, Adjutant-General, Slemmer reports removal to, 5; Anderson reports to, 99, 112

Crawford, Martin J., Confederate commissioner, former congressman from Georgia, on vacillation of Washington, 219; tells Beauregard war policy prevails, 219; says diplomacy has failed, 230; Davis appoints on commission, 273; Davis introduces to Buchanan, 273

Crawford, General Samuel W., on Anderson's staff, xxxvi; *Genesis of the Civil War*, by, xxxvi; refers to armistice as "quasi truce," 26; comments on blanket authority to Porter, 43; on secrecy of procedure, 47; on Porter's concealment of identity, 69; writes of confusion prevailing, 78; says Lincoln's orders to Commander Foote contrary to all precedent, 79; gives estimate of Charleston secession convention, 102; refers to South Carolina legislature, 102, 117; relates interview of governor's aides with Anderson, 113; comments on "high state of health" of Sumter garrison, 147-48; quotes Seward on reinforcement of Sumter, 173; on Fox's conference with Anderson, 178; witnesses bombardment, 240; testifies to nearness of warships during Sumter engagement, 252; on the trifling nature of obstacles to warships' entering Charleston harbor, 257

Crittenden, Senator John J., speech of in senate, xxii. *See also* Compromise, Crittenden

Davis, Jefferson, for Crittenden Compromise, xxiii; attitude of toward secession, xxiv; endeavors to postpone withdrawal of states, xxiv; protests against assault on Fort Pickens, 17; informs Buchanan of Anderson's removal to Sumter, 110; "courage of the Yankees," 240; sends friendly remembrance to Anderson after surrender, 244; regards sending of fleet an act of war, 250, 263; difficult position of, 250; saw trap being laid by Lincoln, 263; took responsibility, 263; "South fired first shot," 263; convention asks to appoint peace commissioners, 272; appoints Crawford, Roman, Forsyth, 273

Davis, Varina Howell, on Jefferson Davis' attitude toward secession, xxiv

DeRussy, Colonel R. E., reports strength of Sumter, 104

Development of America, by Fremont P. Wirth, used in Richmond high school, 297-98

Dodd, William E., history by. *See* Histories of the United States

Doubleday, Captain Abner, overpowers laborers in Sumter, 108; counsels Anderson to return fire of batteries, 134; explains stopping of Sumter's supplies, 216, 217, 248; explanation of inactivity of fleet during bombardment, 256, 261

Douglas, Senator Stephen A., vote for in 1860 presidential election, xvi; argues for conciliation, xviii; Davis' attitude toward compromise, xxiii; danger in retention of Southern forts, 3; on right to hold Sumter, 190

Dred Scott decision, xxx

Dry dock at Pensacola, Brown calls "floating battery," 84, 86

"all officers" to assist Brown, 41;
confusion as to command of fort,
41, 42; secrecy of expedition, 42;
Lincoln places Porter on *Powhatan,* 42; Porter ordered to
Pensacola, 43; secrecy enjoined,
43; armistice provides quiet at,
44; no emergency at, 44; Lincoln removes Mercer from command of *Powhatan,* 45; "sealed
orders" for *Powhatan,* 46; reinforcement order reaches Vogdes,
48; Vogdes asks Adams for
boats, 49; conflicting orders con-
fuse Adams, 49; Adams refuses
to land troops and appeals for
instructions, 50; Adams' refusal
stuns Washington, 51; Welles orders troops landed, 53; Welles
ignores armistice, 54; Welles and
Lincoln make decision to reinforce, 55; Worden carries order
to Adams, 55; Worden deceives
Bragg, 55, 58, 59; Vogdes' company landed, 55; Worden arrested, 56; Bragg says Adams
violated agreement, 57; Worden's
story of his mission, 58; Worden
informed armistice would pave
way, 59; Bragg permits Worden
to visit Adams, 60; Adams
writes DuPont of armistice, 61,
62; Meigs writes "this is the beginning of the war," 63, 64;
Meigs' report to Seward, 63, 65;
Meigs tells of conferences in
Lincoln's office, 64; Adams reports reinforcement, 66; Confederates respected armistice, 67,
68; Federal officers participating
in reinforcement, 67; Bragg demands explanation of Federal
move, 68, 69; Porter conceals
identity, 70; takes command of
Powhatan, 70; reports to Seward
his failure to carry out order,
71; Meigs and Brown stop *Powhatan* flying English flag, 71, 74;
Porter protests interference, 75;
conflict of authority, 75, 82;
Porter amazed at Brown's authority, 76; Welles orders *Powhatan* to Charleston, 77, 78;
Porter, regarding Welles' message as bogus, telegraphs Se-

ward, 79; Seward orders Porter
to give up *Powhatan* to Mercer,
80; Porter disobeys Seward, 80;
Porter sails in *Powhatan,* 81;
steamer sent to "chase" *Powhatan,* 82; secretaries of state
and navy defied, 82, 83; Lincoln
returns Porter to navy department, 83; Brown threatens
Bragg, 84; orders to Porter and
Meigs missing from Washington
files, 88; "an executive act," 89;
Lincoln message refers to "quasi
armistice," 90; senate resolution
requests information regarding
armistice, 91; Welles' statement
to senate, 91, 92; Lincoln's
knowledge of **armistice, 93;**
senate learns nothing from Lincoln and Welles, 94
Fort Sumter, Channing's account
of assault on, xxxiii; naval
squadron en route to, xxxiv;
Montgomery's account of incident, xxxiv; Welles orders Porter to take *Powhatan* to Charleston, 77, 78; origin of name, 97;
Anderson commands Charleston
harbor, 98; Anderson warns
against reinforcement, 99; Anderson knew Charleston sentiment, 100; Carolinians demand
evacuation of forts, 100; government hesitates to increase garrison, 101; Crawford's estimate
of Charleston secession convention, 102; forts strengthened,
103, 104; activity in, puzzles
Charlestonians, 104, 105; Lincoln's secret message to General Scott, 105, 106; South Carolina secedes, 107; Anderson
transfers garrison to Sumter,
108; Anderson reports removal,
109; Anderson's act amazes both
Washington and Charleston, 109;
Floyd demands explanation, 109,
110; Buchanan exasperated, 110;
Anderson explains course, 110,
111; Anderson acted without orders, 111, 122, 123; Lincoln's letter to Scott, 105, 106, 112, 125,
137, 160; Governor Pickens demands Anderson's return to
Moultrie, 112; Anderson as-

army necessary to carry out
Fox plan, 176, 177; Fox reports
to Lincoln, 177; Anderson tells
Fox reinforcement will provoke
war, 178; Federal officers discuss
course upon evacuation of, 179;
Tarbell, Welles, Morse on privation of garrison, 180, 181; reputed letter from Anderson regarding privation, 182; Chisolm
on food supplies of, 185; Hall
on sale of food from, 186; fear
shutting off of supplies, 186;
Anderson knew why supplies
stopped, 187; Anderson's correspondence with department, 188-
91; Colonel Lamon visits, 192;
Anderson expects to leave, 193,
195, 201; Lincoln orders expedition made ready, 197, 198, 199;
Blair encourages reinforcement,
199; Welles orders out warships,
200; Marshall declines to aid
Fox, 200; Walker considers
stopping food supplies, 202;
Totten's ignorance of expedition
plans, 203; Lincoln notifies Anderson of coming expedition,
203, 204; Fox discloses furtiveness of plans, 205; messenger to
notify Governor Pickens, 205;
warships to assist expedition,
206; Scott bares scheme, 206,
207; departments concentrate on
preparation of expedition, 208;
Anderson expects to be relieved,
208, 212, 217; ruse of sending expedition to St. Domingo, 209;
Welles orders *Powhatan* to
Charleston, 209, 210; Welles
ignorant of Lincoln's orders,
210; squadron to reach Charleston April eleventh, 210; Governor Pickens informs Anderson
of report, 211; Anderson demands just treatment, 211, 212;
Anderson's confusion, 213; Talbot notifies Governor Pickens,
213, 220, 227; Welles describes
as "military expedition," 214,
221; Chase puzzled by talk of
"provisioning only," 214; Welles
opposes notification, 214; Lincoln disregards Welles, 214;
Beauregard stops supplies, 215,

216, 217; Doubleday on stopping
of supplies, 216; Anderson complains of Washington's neglect,
217; Scott orders out troops,
217; amenities at Charleston,
218; "extraordinary secrecy" of
war preparations, 218; Governor
Pickens inquires about squadron,
218; vacillation of administration, 219; Walker informed of
notice by Talbot, 220; Walker
orders stopping of provisions,
221; no reinforcement to be permitted, 221; Beauregard stops
Sumter mail service, 222; Anderson receives Lincoln's letter
announcing coming of expedition, 223; Anderson's reaction,
223-25; Nicolay censures Anderson, 226; Lincoln's 1864 message
to Congress, 227, 290; Talbot's
account of interview at Charleston, 227; Beauregard provides
escort for Talbot and Chew,
228; Confederates seize Anderson's mail, 228, 229; Governor
Pickens on deception by Fox,
229; Anderson's mail reveals
coming of expedition, 229; New
York *Tribune* story of expedition, 230; Confederate government orders Sumter taken, 231;
Beauregard demands evacuation,
231; Anderson refuses to surrender, 232; Anderson admits
position hopeless, 233; Beauregard tells Walker of Anderson's
remark, 233; Walker rescinds
attack order, 234, 235; date of
sailing of squadron, 234; Anderson asked to name date when he
will evacuate, 235; Anderson
names April 15, provided he receives no contrary orders nor
additional supplies, 236; warships arrive on April 12, 236;
Beauregard notifies Walker of
Anderson's reply, 237; Anderson notified of attack, 239; Anderson's friendly attitude, 239;
batteries fire on fort, 239; garrison in danger of annihilation,
239-40; Beauregard sends fire
engine and physicians to assist
Anderson, 241; Anderson thanks

ian, armistice order addressed to, 23

Gourdin, Robert N.,, Anderson writes of supplies, 141; writes that Governor Pickens permits Sumter garrison marketing privileges in Charleston, 146, 147

Greeley, Horace, favors conciliation, xx

Greever, Garland, ix

Hall, Lieutenant N. J., sale of Sumter food supplies to employes at fort, 186

Hallam, Henry, defines "aggressor," 264

Harriet Lane, armed cutter, in expedition to Fort Sumter, 197; sailed April 8, 234; armament of, 249; arrives at Charleston, 250; stands in to bar with Fox, 251; at anchor outside during bombardment, 252

Hart, Albert Bushnell, quotes Chase, 214

Hartstene, Captain H. J., takes Fox to Governor Pickens, 176, 178; assists Sumter garrison, 243

Hay, John, on Lincoln's self-confidence, 190

Hayne, I. W., attorney general of South Carolina, sent to offer compensation for relinquishment of Sumter, 149, 150

Herndon, William H., on Lincoln's stubbornness, 190

High School Histories. *See* Histories, Southern high school

Hill, Senator Benjamin H., urges appeal to South Carolina, xxvi

Histories of the United States, partiality of, xxxii-iv; in Southern high schools, accounts of Sumter incident, Atlanta, Georgia, 293, 295; Jackson, Mississippi, 293; Richmond, Virginia, 298; Austin, Texas, 300; Raleigh, North Carolina, 301; Tallahassee, Florida, 302, 303; Montgomery, Alabama, 303; Baton Rouge, Louisiana, 303. *See also* Appendix I

History of the American People, by J. H. Latané, used in the At-

lanta, Georgia, high school, 295

History of the American People, by D. S. Muzzey, used in Montgomery, Alabama, and Baton Rouge, Louisiana, high schools, 303

History of the United States, by Charles A. and Mary R. Beard, used in Raleigh, North Carolina, high school, 301

Holt, Joseph, secretary of war, signs armistice order, 23; Thompson denounces as co-schemer in "concealed trick," 136; writes Anderson regarding *Star of the West,* 137, 138; strange attitude relative to *Star of the West* incident, 139; on Sumter food supply, 144; Fox submits plan to, 153

Houston, Governor Sam, for preservation of Union, xxvi

Huger, Lieutenant T. B., asks permission to attack Federal fleet, 258-59

Hunter, Senator R. M. T., favorable to conciliation, xxvi; reports Anderson's removal to Sumter, 110; assists peace commission, 274

Isabel, steamer, carries Sumter garrison out to Federal fleet, 254

Jackson, General Thomas J. (Stonewall), opposes secession, xxvi

Jackson, Mississippi, high school history. *See* Histories of the United States

Johnson, Governor Herschel V., Belmont's message to, xx; opposed to secession, xx; urges Georgia convention to call southern convention, xxv

Kentucky legislature, for conciliation, xviii

Kepner, Tyler, history by, 302

Lamon, Colonel William H., visit to Sumter, 192; announces removal of garrison imminent, 192; convinces Anderson of coming order to leave, 224

celebration of Sumter surrender, 246

Senate, United States, asks Lincoln for information of "quasi armistice," 91; asks for Anderson's correspondence with department, 189; questions General Scott, 189; Douglas on retention of Sumter, 190

Senators, Southern, against assault on Fort Pickens, 17; report Republicans aiming at war, 18

Seward, William H., favors compromise, xx; his "higher law," 32; Meigs reports to, 63, 65; meddles in army and navy affairs, 63; Meigs writes "this is the beginning of the war," 63; orders Porter to give up *Powhatan*, 80; Porter defies, 80, 83; opposes reinforcement of Sumter, 173; Welles questions his good faith, 208, 281-82; assurances given when he knew of preparation of expedition, 208, 250; declines to receive Confederate peace commissioners, 274, 277; consults Lincoln during negotiations with commissioners, 274, 277, 283; Justices urge to receive Southern commissioners, 276; guards his steps, 277; concedes Sumter to be evacuated, 278; authorizes notice to be given Davis, 278; Campbell's faith in, 279; says Lincoln not to reinforce Sumter, 280; "faith as to Sumter fully kept" message, 250, 281; knew of Lincoln's ordering of expedition, 281; Lincoln's knowledge of his negotiations, 283; Rhodes denounces, 283; Tarbell on his assurances, 284; Lincoln's estimate of, 284-85; Lincoln retains throughout entire term, 285; Nicolay says Campbell deceived, 286; Campbell demands explanation from, 286; Campbell's entry into negotiations with, 287; commissioners threaten to denounce, 288; Campbell writes to a second time, 288; fails to answer Campbell, 289

Seymour, Horatio, Governor of New York, endorses Crittenden movement, xix

Seymour, Captain T., permitted to replenish store of ammunition, 147

Sickles, Congressman Daniel, his scheme to prevent Buchanan's ordering Anderson back to Moultrie, 123-24

Singleton, Congressman O. R., of Mississippi, on Davis' attitude toward secession, xxiv

Slaves, agitation for liberation of Southern, xiv; uprisings of, anticipated by Secretary Chase, 32; Gerrit Smith pictures terrors of insurrection of, 33

Slemmer, Lieutenant Adam J., see Fort Pickens; transfers garrison into Fort Pickens, 5; Floridians demand surrender of, 6; rejects Chase's plea to avoid bloodshed, 7-9; armistice order addressed to, 23; protests against Chase's erection of battery, 27; sends General Bragg copy of armistice papers, 36; reports "everything quiet" at Pensacola, 39; knew Confederates acted in good faith, 67; Bragg demands explanation of violation of armistice, 68; answers that he "obeyed orders" of government, 68

Smith, Secretary Caleb, opposes retention of Sumter, 173

Smith, Gerrit, pictures horrors of slave uprisings, 33

South, indictment against for "firing on flag," xxxiii, 263; conclusion of recklessness of, subject to question, xxxiii; reluctance to fire on Sumter, 235

South Carolina, revolutionary record of, 97, 106; names of Charleston forts, 97; independence of spirit of, 107; secession of, 107; peace commissioners go to Washington, 116; congressmen's pledge to Buchanan, 121; 128; Moultrie a memorial of gallantry of, 127; Sumter a testimonial to faith of, 127; offers compensation for relinquishment

53; his order ignores armistice, 55; he and Lincoln decide on reinforcement, 55; sends reinforcement order by Worden, 55; inspires violation of agreement at Pensacola, 57; gave Worden written dispatches, 58; told Worden armistice would open way for delivery of orders, 59, 60, 61; knew of armistice, 60; message to Adams preserved in official record, 60; criticism of Lincoln and Seward, 62; Adams reports armistice to, 66; effect of Lincoln's interference with *Powhatan,* 76; "the strange instructions" which Lincoln signed, 76; orders Mercer to take *Powhatan* to Charleston, 77, 78; orders Foote to delay sailing of *Powhatan,* 78; Porter regards order from as "bogus," 79; Porter prevents Foote from telegraphing to, 79; Foote notifies of *Powhatan's* sailing, 81; Porter defies his and Seward's orders, 81; Mercer disregards order from and obeys instructions from Lincoln, 82; Lincoln returns Porter to supervision of navy department, 83; Lincoln's orders kept secret from, 88; Lincoln requires him to answer senate inquiry concerning armistice, 91, 92; his report tells senate nothing, 91, 92, 94; scapegoat for Lincoln, 93; his "old Puritan conscience" not working, 93; Lincoln's message to congress puzzles, 93; knew Lincoln informed regarding armistice, 93; agreement to maintain status at Charleston, 118; attitude toward reinforcement of Sumter, 173; on privation at Sumter, 181, 183; "starving garrison" theory, 181; orders preparation of warship, 200; on Lincoln's early decision to reinforce Sumter, 207; says *Powhatan* "stolen away" from Charleston expedition, 208; impugns Seward's good faith, 208, 281, 282; "whole energies of departments" engaged in preparations to reinforce, 208, 281; war-

ship to use force if required, 210; ignorant of Lincoln's activities, 210; describes "military expedition," 214; his opposition to notification of Governor Pickens disregarded by Lincoln, 214; significance of his order to Mercer to be at Charleston on April eleventh, 220; his belief in possibility of adjustment of sectional differences, 276

Whiting, Major W. H. C., identifies warships off Charleston, 251

Wigfall, Colonel L. T., believes inaugural means war, 163; evacuation of Sumter considered iminent, 165; suspicious of Washington administration, 165; warns Beauregard of ruse, 165; interview with Anderson during bombardment, 242

Wilson, Woodrow, on Southern opposition to secession, xxvii

Wine and cigars, for Anderson's command, 185

Wirth, Fremont P., history by, 297

Wood, Captain R. C., aide of General Bragg, 35; carries Bragg's demand on Vogdes and Slemmer for explanation of violation of armistice, 68

Worden, Lieutenant John L., carries reinforcement order to Adams, 55; deceives Bragg, 55, 57; watched by Confederates, 56; arrested by Bragg, 56; release of, 58; Lincoln gives promotion to, 58; writes of Pensacola mission, 58; carried written dispatches, 58; statement to Confederate Secretary of War Walker, 59; told by Welles that armistice would pave way for reaching Adams, 59, 60; his "honor" as an officer and gentleman, 60; message carried to Adams preserved, 60; courtesies to by Confederates, 60; inconsistent statements by, 61

Wyandotte, Federal gunboat at Pensacola, 22, 30, 41; assists in landing Vogdes' company, 66; Meigs causes to be thrown across course of Porter and *Powhatan,* 71, 74, 77